Television
and the Preschool Child

A PSYCHOLOGICAL THEORY OF INSTRUCTION AND CURRICULUM DEVELOPMENT

EDUCATIONAL PSYCHOLOGY

Allen J. Edwards, Series Editor
Department of Psychology
Southwest Missouri State University
Springfield, Missouri

Phillip S. Strain, Thomas P. Cooke, and Tony Apolloni. Teaching Exceptional Children: Assessing and Modifying Social Behavior

Donald E. P. Smith and others. A Technology of Reading and Writing (in four volumes).

> *Vol. 1. Learning to Read and Write: A Task Analysis (by Donald E. P. Smith)*
>
> *Vol. 2. Criterion-Referenced Tests for Reading and Writing (by Judith M. Smith, Donald E. P. Smith, and James R. Brink)*
>
> *Vol. 3. The Adaptive Classroom (by Donald E. P. Smith)*

Joel R. Levin and Vernon L. Allen (eds.). Cognitive Learning in Children: Theories and Strategies

Vernon L. Allen (ed.). Children as Teachers: Theory and Research on Tutoring

Gilbert R. Austin. Early Childhood Education: An International Perspective

António Simões (ed.). The Bilingual Child: Research and Analysis of Existing Educational Themes

Erness Bright Brody and Nathan Brody. Intelligence: Nature, Determinants, and Consequences

Samuel Ball (ed.). Motivation in Education

J. Nina Lieberman. Playfulness: Its Relationship to Imagination and Creativity

Harry L. Hom, Jr. and Paul A. Robinson (eds.). Psychological Processes in Early Education

Donald J. Treffinger, J. Kent Davis, and Richard E. Ripple (eds.). Handbook on Teaching Educational Psychology

Harvey Lesser. Television and the Preschool Child: A Psychological Theory of Instruction and Curriculum Development

In preparation:

Donald E. P. Smith and others. A Technology of Reading and Writing (in four volumes).

> *Vol. 4. Preparing Instructional Tasks (by Judith M. Smith)*

Kay Pomerance Torshen. The Mastery Approach to Competency-Based Education

Television
and the Preschool Child

A PSYCHOLOGICAL THEORY OF INSTRUCTION
AND CURRICULUM DEVELOPMENT

HARVEY LESSER

Department of Psychology
Camden College of Arts and Sciences
Rutgers University
Camden, New Jersey

ACADEMIC PRESS   New York   San Francisco   London   1977

A Subsidiary of Harcourt Brace Jovanovich, Publishers

ACADEMIC PRESS, INC.
111 Fifth Avenue, New York, New York 10003

United Kingdom Edition published by
ACADEMIC PRESS, INC. (LONDON) LTD.
24/28 Oval Road, London NW1

Library of Congress Cataloging in Publication Data

Lesser, Harvey.
    Television and the preschool child.

    (Educational psychology series)
    Bibliography: p.
    1.   Television in education.   2.   Child psychology.
I.   Title.
LB1044.7.L37   791.45$'$01$'$3   76-50397
ISBN 0–12–444250–1

PRINTED IN THE UNITED STATES OF AMERICA

To the loving memory of my father,
Benjamin "Abe" Lesser

Contents

Preface

Since its invention television has been acclaimed as an efficient means of public education. Over the past few decades vast sums have been expended on television programs intended to educate, yet clear intellectual benefits, especially to the millions of faithful child viewers, have not been demonstrated. The lack of proof indicates either that television is not an effective educational tool or that the medium has not been properly used. This issue and the associated question of the limits of instructional television are explored in this book. Previous works on children's television have assumed that preschoolers can be educated through television and have concentrated on evaluating specific programs such as *Sesame Street*. This book provides, for the first time, a clear exposition of the problems involved in instructing young children through television and draws conclusions about the ways in which television can enhance preschoolers' learning. The book details specific qualities of young children's thought processes, provides a rich background of material from recent research in child development (surveying American, Soviet, and Swiss research), and applies this research, employing specific examples and rationales, to television presentations.

It has not been established that unaided television viewing can teach young children. This important fact is amply documented in this book. If instructional television for preschoolers is to be effective, it is necessary to combine a sound knowledge of recent developments in child psychology with the expertise found in television production studios. Since members of the two groups rarely interact, this book is designed to provide insights into children's thought processes that both groups would need in order to produce effective instructional children's programs.

This book is intended for those involved with or concerned about children's television. Child psychologists and specialists in early childhood education, educational media, and learning processes, who would benefit from a close examination of the problems involved in applying basic research to efforts to instruct through television; writers, producers, and technicians in the instructional television field, who will find this book useful both as a handbook and as an introduction to recent developments in the field of child development; students in advanced undergraduate and graduate courses involved in exploring the effects, actual and potential, that television can exert on young children; preschool, kindergarten, and elementary teachers; pediatricians and those associated with children's health care; child psychiatrists; and parents of young children—to all these this book is addressed.

Chapter 1 provides a general introduction to the history and economics of children's television and, in addition, examines broad social issues of violence, aggression, modeling, and censorship. Chapters 2 and 3 discuss the widely viewed *Sesame Street* as a prototypical instructional television program, its merits and weaknesses, as well as the general feasibility of teaching young children through the television medium. Chapters 4, 5, 6, and 7 review American, Soviet, and Swiss (Piagetian) research on children's cognition, language, perception, and memory, and include possible formats for television instruction that are in accordance with research findings. Chapter 8 concludes the book with a review of current technological advances in teaching methods and indicates directions for further research for instructional television.

The material in each chapter is dealt with in considerable detail, as this book is designed to be a desk-top companion to those working in the field of instructional children's television.

Care has been taken that the child is not automatically referred to as "he" or "him." Non-gender-specific pronouns have been employed throughout this book.

ACKNOWLEDGMENTS

Many thanks are owed to my wife, Rosemary, for constructive changes in the text. Virginia Cobey has also read various versions of my manuscript, and her valuable comments have led to several improvements. Two friends, Bob Maslow and Fred Rosenberg, have on numerous occasions given me sound advice. My friend and colleague in the Mathematics Department, James B. Rothschild, assisted me in the technical analysis of the ETS Report. Without his help several vital issues might have been neglected. Emily Willerman gave me encouragement to continue, especially when the work was hardest. My many thanks also go to the following people for their secretarial assistance: Eve Henry, Florence Biehler, Diane Bosch, Judy Sebastian, Carol Okeson, Bea Saler, and Nancy Freeman.

1

Television's Children:
An Overview

The central tenet of this book is that the educational potential of television for preschoolers is largely untapped. This chapter will review the evidence for and against the proposition that television exerts a considerable influence upon children's social perceptions of the world and consequently upon their reactions to it.

In recent years there has been an exponential growth in experimental studies exploring different aspects of television's influence on human behavior. For instance, a recent Rand Corporation annotated bibliography (Comstock, 1975) lists about 2300 references. Given the quantity of material available, the review in this chapter will restrict its focus to television's social effects on preschoolers. However, since this introductory chapter also has a broader historical focus, I will make occasional digressions to a consideration of research outside the preschool age range.

CHILDREN'S COMPREHENSION OF
TELEVISION CONTENT

Viewing Time

It seems advisable to ascertain the number of hours children spend in front of a television set before exploring their comprehension of television content. This is a fundamental indicator of influence.

Lyle and Hoffman (1972a, p. 132) estimate a total weekly viewing time of

1

22–24 hours for first-graders, 30–31 hours for sixth-graders, and 27–28 hours for tenth-graders. An estimate of total viewing time for preschoolers can be obtained from Lyle and Hoffman (1972b, p. 267). There is little indication of any substantial differences from estimates of first-graders' viewing habits. Lyle and Hoffman (1972b, p. 266) also found that about 50% of preschoolers indicated that they played games they saw on television; 67% indicated there were scary things on television, particularly monsters; 20–25% indicated they did not know "how kids get to be on your set" or "where do kids go when the TV is off." Interviews with mothers (Lyle & Hoffman, 1972b, p. 268) indicate that 74% of children sing commercial jingles, 62% at about 2 years and 31% at about 3 years. Overall, *The Flintstones* is more popular than *Sesame Street* (26.1% versus 16.3%), but *Sesame Street* is more popular with 3-year-olds (29.7% versus 10.8%). *Mister Rogers*, a prosocial television program for pre-schoolers, is listed by fewer than 2% as a favorite of 3- to 5-year-olds. Preschool-ers can also identify the pictures of major television characters (e.g., Fred Flintstone by 87.2%, 92.6%, and 97.1% and Big Bird by 74.4%, 76.5%, and 82.9% of 3-, 4-, and 5-year-olds, respectively).

A study by Murray (1972, pp. 345–366) provides an interesting contrast in that it explores viewing habits of 27 5- and 6-year-old black males from a sample of urban poor families. These children "overwhelmingly chose cartoons as their favor-ite form of television entertainment and regularly avoided all 'educational' pro-gramming [p. 363]." The few exceptions were usually the brighter children. Next preferred were situation comedies, and in the evenings prime-time situation comedies and action dramas were preferred. The boys averaged about 21 hours of viewing per week, heavy viewers ("addicted") watched as much as 42 hours per week. Intellectual ability did not predict addiction. The heavy viewer is described as "more interpersonally passive or shy, preferring solitary play to peer interaction." The casual viewer is described as "more likely to initiate interper-sonal contact" and as "task-oriented." Also, since these social behavior patterns were detected as early as 3 years of age, the speculation is that interpersonal passivity is not produced by heavy television use but that children who prefer a solitary environment turn to heavy television viewing.

Comprehension

Basic to an understanding of the influence of television on young children is a knowledge of exactly what they understand of the content of the television programs watched. Any effects television may have depend on the meaning of the program as interpreted by the child viewer. Unfortunately, this is a little-explored area of research. Most of the research that explores the possibility of television's influencing antisocial or prosocial behavior assumes a substantial level of understanding of content, even at the preschool level. However, the few studies available are in disagreement with this assumption.

One of the earliest and most informative studies in this area is the rarely cited international collaboration centered around the 1966 *Prix Jeunesse* films (Halloran, 1969). Five countries—France, Germany, England, Czechoslovakia, and the United States—evaluated the Swedish program *Patrik and Putrik* for younger children and the Czechoslovak film *Clown Ferdl* for older children. *Patrik and Putrik* is roughly 15 minutes in length and shows two puppets awakening, acting hungry, searching for a cookbook, mixing and baking cookies to eat, failing, and then attaching the round, hard cookies as wheels to a shoe, which they then ride. The mixture of situation and comedy was done at a level intended to be obvious to young children. No language was used, only musical accompaniment.

The English report (Noble, 1969) centers on the relation between the cognitive level of the children and their understanding. Noble cites previous research that reports that children of 6 years of age do not understand the interaction of film sequences and they they perceive films as a sequence of unrelated events (Flapan, 1965; Franck, 1955; Zazzo, 1956). Also, Gomberg (1961) suggests that under 5 years of age, children perceive everything on television as real and true. These observations support other research efforts, mainly Soviet and Piagetian, to be reported extensively in later chapters. The main conclusion is that in the early years (at least until age 7) the young child is passing through a cognitive revolution that profoundly restricts comprehension of filmed content. At 7 years a qualitative change occurs that leads the child to search for logical structure and order behind changes in appearances. It is the lack in cognitive ability in the early years that forms the basis for the similar observations of the various researchers from the five different nations involved.

Native English children and immigrant children (all English speaking) at 5, 6, 7, and 8 years of age were shown *Patrik and Putrik*. The English children averaged recall of 10.5 incidents, and the Indian children averaged 5.7 incidents, out of a total of 127 incidents. Five-year-old English children averaged recall of 6 incidents, and 8-year-olds averaged twice that number. In terms of recall of the seven basic sequences of the film, similar findings are reported. On a task requiring the children to "tell a story as it happened" 5-year-old English children recalled only 1.3 sequences in order as compared to 3.3 for 6-year-olds. Since verbal ability is not extensive at these ages, children may not be able to report verbally all they remember and understand about a film. Consequently, non-verbal tasks, photograph recognition, and sequencing tasks were used. Results show that 5- and 6-year-olds recognized significantly fewer photographs than older children and were significantly less able to put the photographs in order. Also, 7- and 8-year-olds gave analytic answers that demonstrated some knowledge of plot, in contrast to 5- and 6-year-olds, who gave descriptive answers. The English report concludes that, "there is a fair amount of support . . . for the suggestion that the nodal age for the comprehension of the film's story is between six and seven years [Noble, 1969, p. 16] ." Noble points out that plot comprehension skills do not devlop gradually, since 5- and 6-year-olds are similar to each other, as are 7- and 8-year-olds.

In terms of the reality—fantasy distinction, the English children thought the film to be significantly less real as they got older. The younger English children more often reported seeing objects not in the film. For the immigrant sample, errors include the belief among the younger children that there were more than two puppets and that the puppets also spoke. Noble suggests that the finding of a belief that there were more than two puppets might indicate that the concept of "puppet" as a permanent entity, independent of its environment, does not yet exist for some of the younger children.

The German report (Keilhacker, 1969) employed the same methodology as the English report and, with the following interesting asides, essentially comes to the same conclusion. The children cite the fact that "the biscuits are too hard" much earlier in age than that "the puppets were hungry." This implies, Keilhacker argues, that motives that link sequences of fact are grasped in ascending orders of abstractness. The concept "too hard" is tied to a concrete situation and a clearly perceptible action sequence, whereas "hunger" must be read out rather loosely over many action phases and must be mostly inferred. Another interesting aside occurred when seven German children answered yes when asked whether the puppets spoke. But several also added that "the speech could not be heard." This illustrates an interesting problem that will be encountered repeatedly when interpreting the results of research with preschoolers. Reality, for these children, seems to depend more on their own experience of speech or on the experience of a dialogue between the two puppets than on the physical perception of having heard nothing. Preschoolers have difficulty assuming the role of another; their ability to distinguish between subjective and objective experience is often blurred. As a general rule, then, especially when working with young children, it is critical that the researcher probe thoroughly and deeply into the meaning behind the response. All too frequently, a researcher may find the "obvious" interpretation to be incorrect and biased in the direction of an adult's perspective. The reports of other nationalities basically confirm the English and German findings.

Similar results are reported in an experiment conducted by Leifer, Collins, Gross, Taylor, Andrews, and Blackmer (1970). Children of three age levels (4, 7, and 10 years) were shown a 20-minute fairy tale and then presented with four series of photographs (sets of three, five, seven, and nine photographs). The photographs showed central incidents in the film, and the task was to place them in the correct order of occurrence. The 4-year-olds were generally unsuccessful: Only 20% were successful on the three-photograph set, with a marked decrease in performance on the longer sets. In contrast, all the 7-year-olds succeeded on the three-photograph set, and 55% succeeded on the five-photograph set. Preschoolers were generally "vague at best" in their responses to questions about the feelings or motivations of the film characters.

Another study, by Coates and Hartup (1969), showed 4-year-olds a movie of a man performing a series of novel acts, such as building a tower. The film was broken down into 20 critical behavior sequences. Unlike other studies, the children were told in advance that they would be required to remember what they saw. Four-year-olds did not recall much of what they observed. On average, they recalled only six of the model's novel acts.

Leifer and Roberts (1972), as part of a larger study on children's responses to television violence, report comprehension scores at five different age levels (kindergarten, 3, 6, 9, and 12 years). Children watched six half-hour television programs selected for their high levels of violence. A multiple-choice test inquired about children's understanding of motivations for and immediate and final consequences of violence and asked for ratings of characters in terms of good, bad, and good—bad. Consistent with previously reported results, kindergartners understood very little about motivations and consequences of violence, third- and sixth-graders had a moderate level of understanding, and ninth- and twelfth-graders had a high level of understanding. Character evaluations were generally in agreement at all age levels, but kindergartners were more likely to be confused about a character's nature than older children. The findings on children's comprehension of televised content are consistent. Starting with the preschool years, regular and predictable age-related changes in comprehension occur.

Academic research and commercial market research on children's comprehension of television programs have proceeded separately. Knowledge of what children understand of television presentations is valuable information that, if used correctly, can translate into important economic advantages. Market research—parallel to, and apparently largely independent of, academic research—has slowly discovered the specific qualities of the child viewer, not only as a direct consumer of products but also as a powerful lobbyist, easily swayed by television commercials. As the following discussion should make apparent, practices in commercial children's television reinforce the conclusions of academic researchers.

COMMERCIAL CHILDREN'S TELEVISION

History

A brief history of commercial children's television programming reveals that it has passed through three distinct phases of development (Melody, 1973, pp.

33–35). During the earliest phase—the promotional era—programming was mostly concerned with market development. Network children's programming was of high quality, extensive, and sustaining or largely presented without advertiser sponsorship. Network shows such as *Howdy Doody* and *Kukla, Fran, and Ollie* were shown for 27 hours or more per week in the late 1940s and early 1950s, and almost half were without advertising. Furthermore, children's programming was aired principally during prime viewing hours for children, between 6:00 and 8:00 P.M. In contrast, local stations were mostly concerned with immediate economic objectives. The broadcast hours not claimed by network option time (the time stations are required to devote to network programs) were frequently filled in with short animated films used as fillers in the adult movie market. Any special effort by local stations to market special programs designed exclusively for children was infrequent.

As television sets were sold and the market approached saturation, the second phase—the mass-marketing era—began. In this era "ratings determined broadcast revenues . . . [and] audiences were conceived of as reasonably homogeneous mass markets of 'eyeballs' [Melody, 1973, p. 54]." Thus, in the late 1950s the networks discovered that it was more profitable to shift to prime-time family programs (between 7:30 and 10:30 P.M.). Non-prime-time children's programming was dropped by the networks (between 4:00 and 7:00 P.M.) because it was no longer viewed as a profitable source of revenue. Local stations, however, continued children's programming in this time period, but substituted cartoons from recently opened film libraries and reruns of old network children's programs. At about this time, local sponsors discovered that spot buying on children's programs could reach a specialized audience of children at the extremely low cost of 25¢–50¢ per thousand (Melody, 1973, p. 45).

The rush to children's non-prime-time programming quickly exhausted the material in the film libraries. First-run animated material of Disney quality was prohibitively expensive to produce for this market. At this point, a much less expensive limited animation technique was discovered by William Hanna and Joseph Barbera (productions using limited animation include *Gerald McBoing-Boing, Huckleberry Hound*, and, for the adult audience, *The Flintstones*). Thus, the local station non-prime-time children's show featuring a host who introduced the cartoons and sold the products was born (Melody, 1973, p. 45).

One last development during this era was the shift from sponsor control of the time periods to network control. As production costs rose, the financial risks became prohibitive to individual sponsors, who eventually relinquished control over time periods and program content to the networks. The networks then assumed monopoly control over all programming.

Finally, in the last and current era, "children as a specialized audience were rediscovered in true economic terms, i.e., as a profitable product for sale to specialized advertisers [Melody, 1973, pp. 54–55]." The discovery of the profitable daytime housewife audience in the early afternoon hours shifted children's programming to the highly popular Saturday-morning time slot. A further marketing development, called routining, provided sponsors with greater audience specificity. On Saturday morning the earliest shows are designed for the youngest children. As the morning wears on, the shows are targeted for progressively older children. Routining assures a continuous and highly specialized audience for the advertiser's products (Melody, 1973, p. 52).

Programming

According to Melody (1973), production of children's television is dominated by three major and several small independent companies. Typically, a contract for a children's series is for "seventeen half-hour episodes, with a guarantee that each of these will be used six times over two years [p. 68]." Animated pilots are infrequently required from the major companies, as a practice of introducing new characters into established series is substituted.

The economics of children's programming have reduced production to "factory-line production scheduling, the churning out of standardized, homogeneous products, and the minimization of programming costs and risks [Melody, 1973, p. 70]." Characteristically, the plots of children's cartoons involve strong elements of action and adventure, with frequent aggressive or violent confrontations. Cost-plus programming for children's television means that "every word that's written, every foot that's shot, everything goes on the screen [Eisner, 1971, p. 34, cited in Melody, 1973, p. 70]."

Economics have dictated other practices that tend to lower program quality and diversity. Most Saturday-morning children's television is animated because animators, unlike actors, do not receive royalties. Animation is limited sometimes to as few as 4 drawings per frame, in contrast to the traditional 64. Producers rely on short, animated segments that can be used interchangeably in the series, creating charges that some new series are merely "spliced-together leftovers [Morris, 1971, pp. 180–181, cited in Melody, 1973, p. 71]." Mechanized animation, already widely used in commercials, when applied to children's animated programs, is expected to reduce costs still further by about half (Melody, 1973, p. 71). Perhaps even more devastating in terms of educational potential is the recognition of the world-wide market for the product and the consequent minimization of English-language words in favor of international expletives, such as "ooo" and "ah," as well as action substitutes (p. 72). These practices greatly reduce the possibility that a new, perhaps creative and innovative producer can break into network children's programming.

Melody concludes that:

> Unlike adult programming, most children's programs are rerun indefinitely, regardless of the success of the first run, because the child audience is not as discriminating as adult audiences, and consists of a hard core of cultivated time-slot rather than program viewers. Hence, total failures are infrequent, risks are minimal, amortization schedules can be based upon more showings, and there is generally a substantial market in syndication after first-run showings. The unique characteristics of children's programs make them ideal low-cost fillers of time-slots that can't be used for the profitable selling of other viewer audiences to advertisers [1973, p. 72].

Advertising

Those in control of program content and advertising are, to a large extent, influenced by current conceptions of children. Melody (1973, pp. 75–82) traces three successive stages in the development of children's advertising:

1. *Adult-Oriented Stage:* Adults are in virtually complete control of product-purchase decisions and have dominant control of selection of programs. Thus, explicit and exclusive advertising to children was viewed as unprofitable.
2. *Child-Oriented Stage for Child-Consumed Products:* Children have significant influence over the purchase of certain products to be consumed by them, toys, candy, cereals, etc. Thus, specific programming and advertising to children could be profitable. A major limitation was the realization that children rarely make the purchases themselves. Thus, children must be made to nag, to become active lobbyists for the products.
3. *Child-Oriented Stage for Family-Consumed Products:* The current idea emerging in advertising directed to children is that they may be the best targets for certain adult products, especially those adults without brand-name loyalty, because they can be induced to serve as extremely effective lobbyists for purchases.

This last approach is emphasized by Helitzer and Heyel (1970, p. 44, cited by Melody, 1973):

> Mothers surveyed indicate that because their children ask for specific products and brands, they spend an average of $1.66 more per household weekly. Thus, "child-power" adds at least $30 million weekly, or $1.5 billion annually, to grocery retail sales—just to make junior happy [p. 80].

In summary, Melody emphasizes the relative lack of selectivity of children to program content directed at them. Children's programs are primarily "attention grabbing" and use heavy doses of continuous action and violence. Endless reruns and repackaging of old material minimize costs. The new market strategy stresses

> the powerful triumvirate of advertising, television, and the intrafamily sales force, the children. As this new structure of marketing media is developed and improved, children can be expected to become more efficiently and effectively integrated into this marketing system [1973, p. 80].

The commentary on the history of commercial children's television just presented traces different conceptions of childhood. Children were once considered to have little influence on produce purchase decisions. They are now viewed as having considerable influence, even on products that are consumed by adults. Issues are not as clearly defined in the next topic under consideration, television and its effects on social behavior. Greatest controversy exists over the possible contribution that televised aggression plays in producing aggressive behavior.

TELEVISION AND SOCIAL BEHAVIOR

The Controversy over Televised Violence

It is charged that children's television uses violence excessively (see, for instance, Gerbner, 1972; Barcus, 1975a, 1975b), and that this use of violence causes an increased use of aggression by viewers. The following quotations, all from respected researchers, reflect the widest possible range of differences of interpretation of the evidence:

> The overwhelming weight of evidence . . . supports the thesis that exposure to filmed or televised violence tends to lead young children to a state of heightened excitability and to an increase in subsequent displays of aggression [Bogart, 1972–1973, p. 494].

> There is . . . a remarkable degree of convergence among all of the types of evidence that have been sought to relate violence viewing and aggressive behavior in the young; laboratory studies, correlational field studies, and naturalistic experiments all show that exposure to television can, and often does, make viewers significantly more aggressive as assessed by a great variety of indices, measures, and meanings of aggression [Liebert, Neale, & Davidson, 1973, p. 87].

> We are not comfortable with the present efforts of social science to determine cause and effect. The laboratory and field experiments we have cited reveal all too many limitations. The child has been measured for aggressive behavior after only brief exposures to selected television fare. While it is significant that there should have been discernable differences in behavior—more especially when one weighs the cumulative results of so many experiments—it is more important to know what

happens to the child whose television viewing norm is six hours a day, year in and year out. This is *the* significant phenomenon which makes television distinctly different from books, movies, and every other form of communication. Television has become an enveloping environment through which values and life-styles are transmitted. Somehow social science has got to develop better environmental measures if its findings are to be persuasive.[1]

In the cases of violence and obscenity, it is unlikely that social science can either show harmful effects or prove that there are no harmful effects. . . . These are moral issues and ultimately all judgments about the acceptability of restrictions on various media will have to rest on political and philosophical considerations [Wilson, 1971, p. 61].[2]

It is possible that people have been entirely too glib in discussing the negative social consequences of the depiction of television violence. Personally, the investigators find the constant depiction of violence on television repugnant. But that is quite different from saying it leads to antisocial behavior among its viewers. We have not been able to find evidence for this; for if television is on trial, the judgment of this investigation must be the Scottish verdict: Not proven [Milgram & Shotland, 1973, p. 68].

Thus, the two sets of findings (experimental and survey) converge in three respects: a preliminary and tentative indication of a causal relation between viewing violence on television and aggressive behavior; an indication that any such causal relation operates only on some children (who are predisposed to be aggressive); and an indication that it operates only in some environmental contexts. Such tentative and limited conclusions are not very satisfying. They represent substantially more knowledge than we had two years ago, but they leave many questions unanswered [Surgeon General's Scientific Advisory Committee, 1972, pp. 18–19].

Faced with the just-cited disagreements over the interpretation of the evidence relating violence on television to antisocial behavior, it seems advisable first to document the extent and form of violence on television, particularly children's television. Later, the evidence, which culminates in the Surgeon General's Report, will be reviewed.

The Extent and Form of Violence on Television

The most thorough documentation of violence on television has been performed by Gerbner (1972). There are three components to Gerbner's research: (1) estimates of the quantity of violence; (2) analysis of the quality of violence;

[1] Quoted from Douglass Cater and Stephen Strickland, *TV Violence and the Child* (New York: Russell Sage Foundation, 1975), pp. 133–134. © 1975 by the Russell Sage Foundation.
[2] This and subsequent quotes cited to Wilson, 1971 are reprinted with permission of James Q. Wilson from *The Public Interest*, No. 22, Winter 1971. Copyright © 1971 by National Affairs, Inc.

and (3) a theory concerned with the meaning and function of televised violence. Gerbner's content analysis covers the years 1967, 1968, and 1969. The following are the principal findings with regard to quantity of violence:

1. *High levels of violence exist on American commercial television.* About 8 out of 10 dramatic presentations contained violence; violent episodes had a rate of occurrence of about five per dramatic presentation and about eight per hour.
2. *Grossly measured, violence declined from 1967 to 1969.* Although the rate of violence was steady, a reduced proportion of characters participated in violence and with a reduction in killing.
3. *Children's television, especially cartoons, increased in violence.* The extent of violence on children's television is documented by Gerbner:

> Of all 95 cartoon plays analyzed during the three annual study periods, only two in 1967 and one each in 1968 and 1969 did *not* contain violence. The average cartoon hour in 1967 contained more than three times as many violent episodes as the average adult dramatic hour. The trend toward shorter plays sandwiched between frequent commercials on fast-moving cartoon programs further increased the saturation. By 1969, with a violent episode at least every two minutes in all Saturday morning cartoon programming (including the least violent and including commercial time), and with adult drama becoming less saturated with violence, the average cartoon hour had nearly six times the violence rate of the average adult television drama hour, and nearly 12 times the violence rate of the average movie hour [1972, p. 36].

It should be noted that level of violence varied by network; CBS had the lowest violence rate both overall and for children's programming.

The following are the principal findings with respect to the types (or quality) of violence on television:

- *Agents.* Humans are the primary agents of violence (70%). The proportion, however, of nonhuman agents of violence increased from 1 of 10 agents in 1967 and 1968 to 2 of 10 agents in 1969. Significantly, cartoon violence contains a much higher proportion of nonhuman agents of violence (about half in 1967 and 1968 to three-quarters in 1969).
- *Means.* Weapons were used in about half of all violent episodes. The use of weapons increased from 52% to 83% from 1967 to 1969 in all violent episodes in cartoons.
- *Consequences.* Fatalities and casualties decreased sharply. Discomfort by those injured was rarely depicted. However, in absolute terms in 1967 and 1968 almost every violent episode had an injury, and in 1969 this was reduced to 1 in 3; in 1967 and 1968 2 of 3 episodes had a death, and in 1969 the fatality rate was 1 in 10.

- *Time, place, setting.* Violence tends to occur on television in unfamiliar surroundings and is least common in familiar surroundings. Thus, violence occurs on television with greater frequency in the past or future, outside of the United States, and in remote places.

Finally, Gerbner attempts to fit the facts together into a theory that gives coherence, in terms of meaning and function, to violence on television. According to Gerbner, television represents what might best be called the national mythology of American culture. Typical situations, roles, and outcomes portrayed on television reflect, it is argued, the norms and values of American culture better than any other American institution, particularly because the presentations are offered as entertainment. The following are the types of roles and their frequency of occurrence:

- *Violence.* About two of three leading characters are involved in violence.
- *Victims.* There are one and one-half victims for every violent character.
- *Retribution and punishment.* Forty-two percent of violent characters were killed or injured in return.
- *Not being violent is no guarantee of safety.* Seventeen percent of nonviolent characters were victims of violence.
- *Violence is mostly committed by males free of responsibilities.* Violence is to a large extent committed by "strong" male types, middle-class or higher, and unmarried. Only 50% of females commit violence. Also, unlike the usual occurrence of violence in real life, television portrays violence as mostly occurring between strangers, for motives related to the acquisition of gain and rarely for broad social causes.
- *Nonwhites, foreigners, and persons of low socioeconomic status are more likely to be portrayed as violent.*
- *Ordinary work is underrepresented in television portrayals.* Only 5 of 10 major characters had any indication of employment.
- *Women are represented as: sexual attractors; marriage partners, lacking in social power and influence; and as victims.*

The period between 1967 and 1969 was one when networks were under great pressure to reduce violence on television. Violence was reduced overall. However, it was accomplished by eliminating killing by women but not by reducing the number of women victims. Gerbner argues that under pressure to reduce violence, the nonessentials, the details that serve only to embellish the norms and values of American society, are stripped away first, leaving the portrayal of violence almost exclusively within the domain of powerful and influential males. The women, given the values, remained victims.

Gerbner views violence as the special technique television employs to portray and designate power and influence. The fictional aspect of television is an essential ingredient in Gerbner's thesis. Through fiction, television represents the idealized, only lightly concealed as fantasy.

More recent studies by Barcus (1975a, 1975b) provide information regarding the content of children's television. The first study deals with weekend commercial children's television in the Boston area. Three network stations (NBC, ABC, CBS) and two independent local stations (Channels 38 and 56) were content-analyzed. About one-half of all program material was network-originated, another third was recorder-syndicated, and the rest locally produced. The network channels provide the most diversified programming, with NBC and ABC presenting as much as one-third of programming devoted to information for children. This is in contrast to the unrelenting 100% cartoon comedy of Channel 38. According to Barcus, 59% of the drama time had either no violence or only incidental violence, whereas 16% of the drama time was saturated with violence. The remaining 25% of drama time was subordinate to violence. Most violence occurred in comedy formats (one-third saturated with violence). Fifty percent of the violence was with weapons. More than 50% of the subject matter of the programs was devoted to five topics: interpersonal rivalry (winning over another) (14%), the entertainment world (sports, show biz) (13%), domestic topics (marriage, home, family) (10%), crime (robberies, police) (10%), and the supernatural (magic, occult) (10%).

Cartoon comedy remains the most popular with children 2–11 years. On the average, 11.5% of children were watching 51 cartoon segments (73% child audience). Other formats (nonanimated comedy–drama, action–adventure, variety–quiz, information) fare poorly by comparison.

Characters on children's television are predominantly male (about 75%), mostly adults (about 61%). Some anthropomorphic characters whose age and sex are indeterminate are included in the remainder. Minorities fared better in terms of representation. Eighty-nine percent of coded major characters were white, 7% black, and 4% other minority or ethnic groups. However, it is noted by Barcus that blacks are disproportionately portrayed as children.

Barcus compared the 1975 results with a similar study performed in 1971 (Barcus, 1971). He found that commercial time decreased from 11.3 to 9.5 minutes per hour, but the number of commercials decreased only from one every 2.8 minutes to one every 2.9 minutes. Thus, there were as many commercials, each of shorter duration. Toys, cereals, and candies provided almost all of the commercial advertisements. Host selling and program-character lead-ins and tie-ins have been discontinued as advertising practices since 1971. Program diversification increased in 1975 with a shift away from crime, interpersonal rivalry, and the supernatural (from 56% in 1971 to 34% in 1975) toward domestic subjects.

Changes in violence level are also noted by Barcus. Program time in which violence occurred decreased (from 31% to 16%), but the proportion of dramatic segments reported as saturated with violence remained the same (30% in 1971 and 29% in 1975). The explanation is that the number of short cartoon comedy segments saturated with violence increased, and the longer network and situation comedy programs contained less violence.

The other Barcus study (1975a) reports on a national survey of children's programming in the afternoon hours from 3:00 to 6:00 P.M. on UHF independent stations. Network stations do not provide children's programming at these hours. Not surprisingly, the local stations have become the after-school "kiddie" stations. The changes Barcus reports in network productions have not occurred in the afternoon hours on independent stations. Commercial time averages 20%, almost 96% of programming was recorder-syndicated, high levels of cartoon comedy are reported and the level of violence is higher than that reported for weekend broadcasting. The popularity of the different formats and nature of the characters represented remains about the same as for the weekend programming.

In brief, there is considerable agreement between Melody's conclusions (1973) and those of Gerbner (1972) and Barcus (1975a). Melody, working within a mass-communication framework, examines children's television and finds it primarily "attention grabbing," using high doses of continuous action and violence. He explains the history of children's television primarily in economic terms. Gerbner and, to a lesser extent, Barcus view the evolution of television programming, including children's programming, as a reflection of the norms and values of American culture expressed in idealized fantasy form. Violence, Gerbner argues, is the special device used by television to portray and designate power and influence. Melody's economic analysis and Gerbner's cultural analysis both predict high levels of violence; Melody, because violence attracts large audiences of potential purchasers; Gerbner, because violence has a special role in conveying the values and norms of American culture. Melody's economic analysis and Gerbner's cultural analysis complement each other in that Melody explains why violence is used whereas Gerbner explains why it is effective.

Another problem of considerable importance is the evidence, cited earlier in the chapter, which suggests that children have a limited comprehension of program content. Citizen's activist groups (particularly Action for Children's Television) assume that young children's limited comprehension make them particularly vulnerable to commercial announcements and more likely to imitate portrayed violence. Citizen protest has, to a limited extent, been effective in eliminating or reducing certain practices on commercial children's television, such as eliminating vitamin commercials, eliminating host selling and program-character tie-ins and lead-ins, reducing commercial time, and reducing violence levels.

Although many have already chosen their side, the evidence relevant to the relationship between televised violence and antisocial behavior is difficult to interpret. The next two sections critically examine the evidence for and against the thesis that televised violence causes antisocial behavior, particularly in children.

Evidence for a Relationship between
the Viewing of Violence and Violent Behavior

Advertisers would not spend money on commercials if they did not believe that commercials can create consumer preferences. Bandura (1973, p. 274) argues that the ability of television to effect aggressive responsiveness is not unlike its ability to effect consumer purchase decisions. Consider, for instance, a televised commercial for a particular brand of car. Many inducements, including social and economic ones, tempt the potential purchaser. Immediate purchases, however, are not the expected norm. Instead, advertisers realize that consumer purchases are multidetermined. They depend on such factors as the need for another car, the availability of money, the need for a larger car, the need for social prestige associated with a new car, etc. The rise in sales above an established baseline is a sufficient indicator in the industry that the advertising has been effective, despite the fact that each individual purchase decision is determined by a different set of influences. Bandura points out that advertisers continue to purchase commercial time even though the industry cannot specify in advance exactly who will be influenced, when, and how. The advertiser is primarily interested in the end result, a rise in sales.

In contrast, the networks and their sponsors recoil at the thought of accepting the same kind of evidence when confronted with the assertion that violent content on television should be controlled because it influences violent behavior. According to Bandura, the networks' evaluation of social science research "convey[s] the impression that only demonstration of instant direct effects on viewers would constitute convincing proof that televised modeling can be a contributing influence to aggression [p. 274]." Bandura's charge, put succinctly, is that the networks have a double standard.

The basics of Bandura's argument are derived from experimental evidence produced mainly by Bandura and his associates. The experiments involve observational learning, where a model performs a series of novel, aggressive responses while a child observes. Later, the child is given the opportunity to imitate the aggressive responses of the model. The extent and form of the child's imitative responses encouraged Bandura to posit the existence of a special type of learning, observational learning, which does not require either reward or punishment for learning to occur. Practice of the observed acts is also not required. Essential to Bandura's theorizing is the distinction between learning and performance. A response may be learned from observation, but may not be performed. Thus, even if imitation does not occur after observation of a model's aggressive actions, it is no guarantee that the aggressive responses have not been learned. Bandura argues that when conditions are more conducive to aggression, the learning, which has been acquired but never performed, is more likely to occur.

One particular experimental design, used frequently with variations by Bandura and his associates, has had considerable influence on other research efforts. Bandura's experimental procedures and standards of interpretation of the evidence of experimental results have been the standard for many and the standard of comparison for many others on how to conduct research on the effects of television on social behavior. A detailed description of the Bandura, Ross, and Ross (1963a) experiment follows. This experiment provides an excellent illustration of Bandura's experimental procedures and argumentation. Other variations on this experiment will be reported much more briefly.

Bandura, Ross, and Ross (1963a) explored the effects of film-mediated stimulation upon subsequent aggressive behavior. Subjects were 48 boys and 48 girls enrolled at the Stanford University nursery school. They ranged in age from 35 to 69 months, with a mean age of 52 months. There were three experimental groups and one control group of 24 subjects each. Prior to placement into groups the children were matched individually on aggressiveness using ratings of their aggressive behavior during social interactions in the nursery school that were determined by the experimenters and nursery school teacher together. Ratings included physical and verbal aggression; aggression toward inanimate objects; and aggression inhibition, or the extent to which aggressive reactions were inhibited in the face of high instigation. Inter-rater reliability was .80.

One experimental group observed real-life aggression, a second group was shown filmed aggression of the identical behavior by the same real-life models, a third group was shown a cartoon film of a female model dressed as a cat who performed the same behavior as shown in the other groups, and a fourth group, a control group, had no exposure to the model. After exposure, the children were slightly frustrated by being interrupted while engaged in play with attractive toys. It was assumed that the mild frustration would enhance the likelihood of aggressive displays in the test situation. The experimental groups were also divided equally into boys and girls with equal opportunity to observe same sex or opposite sex models.

The real-life aggression condition involved an opportunity for a child, alone in a room with an adult model, to observe the adult pummel an inflated Bobo doll. The Bobo doll was three feet tall, pear-shaped, and weighted at the bottom so that it popped up after being hit. The behaviors of the adult model were highly unique, unlikely to be imitated without recourse to the model. Specific model behaviors included: sitting on the doll and punching it repeatedly on the nose, pummeling the raised doll on the head with a mallet, and tossing the doll in the air and kicking it about the room. The sequence of behaviors of the model were repeated three times. Verbal responses by the model included such hostile remarks as "Sock him in the nose," "Hit him down . . . ," and "Pow." The filmed aggression sequences lasted 10 minutes and were in color. In the filmed human aggression condition, the film started after the experimenter left the child alone in the room; whereas in the cartoon aggression group the experimenter walked over to the television set, which was equipped with a glass lens screen and rear projection arrangement (hidden from the child by large panels), and remarked, "I guess I'll turn on the TV," then tuned in the cartoon program and promptly left.

The test room contained toys classified by Bandura as aggressive (Bobo doll, mallet, dart guns, tether ball hung from ceiling, etc.) and nonaggressive (tea set, crayons, coloring paper, dolls, etc.). Twenty minutes of play were observed behind a one-way mirror. Scoring was divided into 240 5-second response units categorized into imitative and nonimitative aggression, partially imitative aggression, and aggressive gun play. Inter-rater reliability was in the .90's.

The principal finding was that the experimental groups displayed increased aggressiveness, both physical and verbal, against the Bobo doll as compared to the no-model control. Imitative- and total-aggression scores were higher for children in the filmed and cartoon groups compared to controls. Boys displayed more aggression than girls in all categories, and aggression was generally higher when the model was male rather than female. The authors (Bandura *et al.,* 1963a) conclude, "The results of the present study provide strong evidence that exposure to filmed aggression heightens aggressive reactions in children. Subjects who viewed the aggressive human and cartoon models on film exhibited nearly twice as much aggression than did subjects in the control group [p. 9]."

In a variation of the above experiment (Bandura, 1965), children observed one of three consequences to a filmed model: The model received punishment for acting aggressively, the model was praised and rewarded for acting aggressively, the model received no consequences. Children who either saw the model praised and rewarded or saw no consequences to the model performed a greater variety of imitative aggressive responses. In all three conditions boys produced substantially more of the model's behavior than girls, especially in the condition when the model was punished. In a follow-up, rewards were offered for each response of the model the children could reproduce. Reward completely eliminated performance differences, bringing performance among all the groups to a high level. Thus, according to Bandura, the importance of the distinction between learning and performance is demonstrated. Children learn more from observing a model than they ordinarily display.

In another study Bandura, Grusec, and Menlove (1966) demonstrated high retention of the model's behavior when children were required to verbalize every aggressive action of the model, moderate retention when children passively observed the model, and low levels of retention when children were sufficiently distracted so that they could not think about and classify the model's responses into cognitive representations.

Hicks (1965, 1968a) demonstrated long-term retention of modeled behavior. Imitative behavior was measured immediately after exposure to aggressive models, 6 months later in one experiment and respectively 2 and 8 months later in the other. In the second experiment there was 60% retention after 2 months and 40% after 8 months. However, since the children practiced retention immediately after observing the model, it is not possible to determine whether the children recalled the model, their practice, or both. The results of the Bandura, Grusec, and Menlove study, which shows high retention with practice (required verbalizations of the model's behavior), suggests that the children may have recalled their practice and not the model.

Hicks (1968b) studied the role of social sanctions on modeled aggression. A child and an adult jointly watched a televised male model soundly pummeling an adversary. In three different conditions the adult either approved, disapproved, or did not comment. The sanctioning adult's behavior affected the children's subsequent imitative responses in the predictable direction, but only when the adult was present in the test situation. When the adult was not present, the children ignored the adult's prior social sanctions and displayed similar amounts of imitative aggression, irrespective of experimental condition. The requirement of the actual presence of the sanctioning adult severely limits the generality of the findings.

Madsen (1968) reports that children, especially boys, are more inclined to imitate a familiar aggressive model than an unfamiliar model. He also reports no effect of a 6 week nurturant relationship with a model on a subsequent test of aggressive imitation. A learning test, where children were encouraged and re-warded for recall of the model's behavior, reveals equivalence of groups, irrespec-tive of familiarity or nurturance.

Bandura (1973, p. 82) believes that the ability to generalize the findings of the modeling experiments is mistakenly questioned on the grounds that the targets are nonhuman and injurious intent is not present. For instance, he argues by analogy that recruits are taught combat skills in the army in simulated situations. If real military combat were necessary to teach soldiers to kill, training would be considerably more hazardous. Also, Bandura (1973, p. 83) presents other evidence supporting the likelihood that the research findings of the modeling experiments are generalizable to real-life situations. Walters and Brown (1963) trained boys to hit a Bobo doll using intermittent rewards. Later observation showed these boys to be more physically aggressive in a competitive situation than boys without training. Other evidence cited by Bandura is Chit-tendon's (1942) classic demonstration that assertive behavior in young children responds favorably to constructive training employing doll play. Trained children responded with less assertiveness in structured and regular social interactions. It should be noted that the evidence that Bandura uses to support the generality of findings using the modeling paradigm does not include modeling experiments. Both of the just cited experiments involve reinforcement procedures, in one instance positive reward for aggression and in the other sanctions and training of more socially acceptable alternatives.

Another study by Bandura, Ross, and Ross (1963b) demonstrates the importance of the consequences of aggression in determining a desirable model for children to imitate. Children watched a film on television showing either (1) Rocky playing with Johnny's toys because he beat Johnny; (2) Rocky thrashed by Johnny for trying to take away Johnny's toys; (3) a control group with highly expressive but nonaggressive models; or (4) no film. Later observations showed that children in the punished group did not imitate Rocky's behavior and when asked who they would prefer to be like, rejected Rocky as a model. However, the children in the group that observed Rocky's successful aggression readily chose him as a desirable model for imitation even though the children characterized him as harsh, rough, mean, and wicked. Bandura concludes that, at least for young children, the rewarding consequences of aggression can override value systems.

A later experiment typifies a change in direction away from studying specific, concrete demonstrations of imitation of aggressive modeled behavior. In a study of higher forms of modeling (Bandura, 1971), models were observed using a consistently successful approach in diverse situations. The approach, not any particular behavior, had to be abstracted as a higher order variable from the different observations of the model's behavior. Observers responded by imitating the abstract approach used by the model, even though the test situation did not permit exact modeling.

In summary, acceptance of Bandura's results for real life would force the conclusion that exposure to aggressive film models on television tends: (1) to reduce children's inhibitions against aggression; (2) to shape the form of children's aggressive behavior; (3) to produce imitation by children of the behavior of rewarded models rather than punished ones; and (4) to produce imitation by children of the model's aggressive behavior when specifically asked or rewarded for it.

The modeling experiments have been extremely influential in determining the climate of opinion surrounding the potential effects of the mass media. They have, however, also created considerable controversy as to their acceptability as evidence for real-life situations. There are those who accept these experiments at face value and who are reasonably certain that televised violence is causally related to violent behavior. There are others, however, who do not accept the modeling paradigm and who are opposed to the conclusions drawn from these experiments. What follows is a brief presentation of the objections to the modeling paradigm. Afterward, experiments that respond to these objections will be examined.

Objections to the Modeling Paradigm Experiments

One of the principal objections is that the Bandura-type experiments do not involve genuine aggression. Wilson (1971) has ridiculed Bandura on this point:

> Now if it were in the public interest to protect Bobo Dolls from being hit by children encouraged to play with them, and if hitting Bobo Dolls was a regular feature of television, then admonishing the media to refrain from such features might be in order. But what evidence is there from the Bandura experiments that aggression against dolls is ever transferred to aggression against people or even that the children in the experiments define hitting a doll as "aggression?" In the Bandura experiments there is no evidence on either score . . . it is not even necessary to have laboratory experiments to induce in children the kind of "aggression" Bandura observed—all that is necessary is to give them a football on a Saturday afternoon in October . . . [p. 50].

Bandura (Bandura et al., 1963a) considers it irrelevant whether the imitative responses obtained in the modeling experiments have any aggressive intent. He argues that

> the aggressive responses acquired imitatively while not necessarily mediating aggressive goals in the experimental situation, would be used to serve such purposes in other social settings with higher frequency by children in the experimental conditions than by children in the control group [p. 9].

The critical problem, then, seems to be with the definition of aggression. In Bandura's definition there are stimuli he labels as "aggressive" (e.g., mallets, dart guns) and responses he labels as "aggressive" (e.g., hitting a Bobo doll on the head with a mallet). For some, an adequate definition of aggression is the intentional infliction of hurt on another. Whereas this definition will not meet everyone's criteria for a definition of aggression, it does appear to focus on the central issue of concern with respect to mass-media influences: Do people intentionally inflict hurt on others as a result of watching violence on television? Bandura's reply is yes, but it is based only upon conjecture and not upon experimental evidence. He states that a response can be inherently aggressive (such as hitting, spitting, etc.) and, once learned through observation, is available whenever a situation that arouses aggression and a suitable target are present.

The fallacy of this argument will be demonstrated by using Bandura's own illustration from the training of army recruits. Bandura argued that troops are trained not in actual combat, but in simulated sessions and that, once "aggressive" responses are learned, they are successfully transferred to actual war settings. Bandura is accurate insofar as recruits must learn how to fire guns and must learn the essentials of war maneuvers, etc., in basic training. These are the required skills. However, no amount of proficiency in the basic skills of war, by itself, will make an aggressive soldier. Attitudes and beliefs should be consistent with being a soldier. For instance, it is desirable to believe that soldiering is an honorable profession, that violence is the only way to solve certain types of disagreements, that it is good to kill the enemy because their cause is evil, that the cause one is fighting for is just, and perhaps that God is on one's own side. Particular war skills are integrated into the cognitive framework of individuals. Although each recruit may be able to use a gun with identical proficiency, the meaning and justification for the act of shooting the enemy is different for each one. Shooting a gun is not inherently aggressive, it is the intent that makes an act aggressive.

Similarly, so-called portrayals of aggression on television are not inherently aggressive. They depend upon the interpretation given to them by the viewer. Most viewers consider the portrayal of violence mere "entertainment" and would never consider imitating the violence in real life. It is always possible that a few viewers might, for whatever bizarre reasons, ignore the entertainment aspect of portrayed violence and adopt it as a potential solution to one of life's problems. Notice that in neither case is the portrayed violence inherently violent, it depends upon how the individual assimilates the portrayal and upon individual predispositions.

In contrast to the evidence, statements by those supporting regulation of violence on television have been highly inflammatory. Incidents of tragedies and near tragedies have been innapropriately used as evidence; some examples follow:

> A six-year-old son of a policeman asked his father for real bullets because his little sister "doesn't die for real when I shoot her like they do when Hopalong Cassidy kills 'em' " [Schramm, Lyle, & Parker, 1961, p. 161, cited in Bandura, 1973, p. 102, and in Liebert et al., 1973, p. 3].

> A housemaid caught a seven-year-old boy in the act of sprinkling ground glass into the family's lamb stew. There was no malice in the act. It was purely experimental, having been inspired by curiosity to learn whether it would really work as well as it did on television [Schramm et al., 1961, cited in Bandura, 1973, p. 102, and in Liebert et al., 1973, p. 3].

Researchers who cite quotations such as these suggest that something is terribly wrong with television fare and that if the public does not demand immediate correction, then we are accomplices to the murder and maiming of our children, and incidentally of their pets (Bandura, 1973, p. 102). Again, the best reply comes from Wilson (1971):

Interlaced between paragraphs recounting experiments are ones of pure polemic in which the substantive arguments are advanced by asking rhetorical questions. For example, an account of a child who hanged himself apparently trying to imitate Batman leaping through the air moves Professor Alberta Siegel of Stanford to ask, "In what sense is television 'responsible' for this child's violent death?" No answer is offered to the rhetorical question, nor is any indication given of what one would do with any conceivable answer (perhaps ban costumed figures, from Peter Pan to Superman, from flying on television?) [p. 52].

Presumably, demands to "clean up" television would include Popeye, Bugs Bunny, Looney Tunes, Merry Melodies, Road Runner, Porky Pig, and other "violent" children's delights. If this were to occur, one might find, as in Prohibition days, a national underground network, but this time dedicated to showing cartoons to children and others who, for their own reasons, like them.

It is questionable where regulation would end. To be fair, every interest group would have to be appeased. Redl reports (personal communication in Schramm *et al.*, 1961, p. 143) that institutionalized disturbed and delinquent children lay awake and had bad dreams as a result of watching late-evening "programs showing loving parents and warm family relationships. . . . These family programs reminded the children of what was lacking in their lives."

The Bandura experiments have also been criticized in terms of their hidden "demand characteristics." That is, the children in these experiments might have correctly interpreted the experimental expectations and complied with them. An examination of the methodological details of the Bandura *et al.* (1963a) experiment indicates that this is a definite possibility. Bandura consistently fails to present interview or other questionnaire data in this experiment (or in others) that might provide an insight into the children's motives for imitating the model. The experimental procedures diverge considerably from the typical child's everyday activities—strangers devote considerable attention to the child and put on an unusual if not "bizarre" display, sometimes in extravagantly costumed settings. The children seem to accept these activities. What they think of them is another matter. Almost immediately after these displays, the children are provided with an opportunity to imitate the model with identical materials. The experimental children were from the Stanford University nursery school and were mostly middle class. Evidence indicates that middle class children have a high need to please. Noble (1975) cites one incident that reveals what might have been happening in Bandura's experiments: "One four-year-old girl was heard to say on her *first* visit to a Bandura-like laboratory, 'look, Mummy there's the doll we have to hit [pp. 133–134].' "

Another criticism of Bandura's experiments concerns the assumption that films and television can be used interchangeably. Noble (1975, pp. 36–64) considers movie viewing to be an identity-loss situation. Films seen at the movies are generally seen once, in darkness, in strange situations; and the viewer, when engaged, generally identifies with a major character. In contrast, television is viewed with lights on, at home, and frequently with other members of the family. The same characters often appear daily or weekly and become participants in what might be characterized as an extended family. The viewer is not encouraged to lose identity. Indeed, Noble considers television to be an identity-gain situation and reports high levels of verbal participation by children with television characters. The one-shot Bandura experiments, Noble argues, do not replicate the usual television viewing situation, and therefore conclusions drawn from them are, at best, speculative.

Long-term viewing effects on children were examined in an early, and major, study by Himmelweit, Oppenheim, and Vince (1958). Only one of the points that emerged from that study—the need to consider the functions of play developmentally—will be examined. In order to grasp the influence of television on children's play it is first necessary to understand how television stimulates fantasy activity and what functions fantasy has in the play of children. The Western is a good vehicle for this study. Televised Westerns were once shown to children very frequently. Permutations of plot, characterizations, motives, and situation in Westerns are easily learned by children. The good guys are easily distinguished from the bad guys. Children in the Himmelweit *et al.* study (p. 195) describe the good guys as clean-shaven, neatly dressed, having the best horses, handsome, kind to ladies, associated with one partner, infrequent patrons of bars, and possessors of pearl-handled guns. The bad guys are starkly contrasting. The perception of role is largely portrayed visually. Although young children may understand little of the details of plot, visual cues are sufficient so that an experienced child viewer feels no unease from observing the fighting in Westerns. Six or 7 appears to be the age when children cease being frightened by Westerns. Role playing of cowboy hero and villain in fantasy, either alone or with friends, is common between ages 6 and 10. Himmelweit *et al.* conclude that the role-playing fantasies of children are not aggressive "but are only versions of chasing and being chased—of cowboys and Indians, of cops and robbers—the oldest of childhood games . . . played long before television was thought of [pp. 195–196]." They further conclude that these games demonstrate the fondness for rules and a clear and explicit distinction between good and evil. Playing Western roles is useful to the child, as it provides a field of play, sufficiently divorced from reality, within which to test ideas of friendship and fair play. It should be noted that children are much more frightened by detective stories and supernatural thrillers, where plot and characters are much less easily stereotyped, than by Westerns. Regrettably, Bandura did not consider Guillaume's 1926 classic (Guillaume, 1926/1968) on imitation in children, or Piaget's study on play (Piaget, 1946/1951) or the monumental effort by the Opies (Opie & Opie, 1969), who doggedly recorded the natural street play of children in the United Kingdom. Had Bandura incorporated this body of information into his work, basic misunderstandings of children's imitative play in the laboratory might have been avoided.

Response to the Objections

The Surgeon General's Scientific Advisory Committee Report, *Television and Growing Up: The Impact of Televised Violence* (hereafter referred to as The Report), contains 23 research projects and over 40 technical papers in five volumes. The project was controversial from its inception. Five industry representatives participated on a 12-member committee advising the Surgeon General on research projects. Additionally, seven prominent researchers on the topic, including Albert Bandura, were vetoed by the industry. The project cost $1.8 million and took almost 3 years to complete. Despite Bandura's absence as a direct participant, much of the research was directed toward filling in missing links in the experimental evidence that was accumulated using the modeling paradigm. No attempt will be made to review all the research and technical papers in The Report. A selected review, concentrating on early childhood, follows. It is necessary first, however, to consider a research paper not contained in The Report.

Hanratty, Liebert, Morris, and Fernandez (1969, cited in Liebert *et al.*, 1973) used the Bandura format with 4- and 5-year-olds, but substituted, in the experimental group, a live adult dressed as a clown instead of the Bobo doll. The Bobo doll was used in the control condition. More aggression was exhibited toward the Bobo doll than toward the live model. However, there were, according to the authors, a fair number of imitative physical assaults against the human clown, including one bruised arm from a whack with a mallet. Liebert *et al.* (1973) believe they have countered the objection that live models were not used in the original Bandura studies. The study demonstrated aggression and infliction of pain on a live model dressed as a clown. The lesson learned from this study is reasonably clear: Adults dressed as clowns, posturing and provoking attack from young children, had better defend themselves. It is not clear that the children knew they could actually hurt the clown.

In another study—this one included in The Report—Liebert and Baron (1972, pp. 181–201) used a measure of aggression previously established by Berkowitz (Berkowitz & Geen, 1967; Geen & Berkowitz, 1966, 1967) with older subjects. The Berkowitz procedure involved subjects who were told they would participate in a learning experiment that required shocking another person. The other person was, in actuality, never shocked, though the subjects did not know this. The willingness to administer shock was used as the measure of aggressive responsiveness. This procedure has been criticized on the grounds that it does not elicit true aggressive responses, as the context is a learning experiment and many people believe punishment can stimulate learning. Liebert and Baron (1972) modified the design slightly to make it applicable to children between the ages of 5 and 9. One group of children watched a $3\frac{1}{2}$-minute scene on a television monitor from *The Untouchables* that contained a high level of violence while a control group watched an "exciting sports sequence." After viewing, each child was tested to determine number and duration of electric shocks that would be administered to a fictitious child in another room. It was explained to the children that pressing a green button would help the other child turn a lever and that pressing a red button would hurt the other child by making the lever hot. Liebert and Baron found higher levels of aggression, as measured by the frequency with which the red button was used, in the group that watched the scene containing violence. Criticism of the preceding study again centers about the genuineness of the aggressive responses, the demand characteristics of the decidedly artificial experimental procedure, and the lack of information provided about long-term effects of television viewing.

In a collaborative effort, Eckman, Liebert, Friesen, Harrison, Zlatchin, Malmstrom, and Baron (1972, pp. 22–58) studied facial expressions of emotion in an effort to predict subsequent aggression. The Liebert and Baron children were used in this study. The researchers hypothesized that positive emotions while watching violent television would correlate positively with subsequent aggression as measured on Liebert and Baron's button-pressing task and that a negative correlation would exist between negative emotions and subsequent aggression. The children tested were 30 boys and 35 girls, 5- and 6-year-olds. Essentially, Eckman *et al.* video-taped each child's face, without the child's knowledge, during exposure to Liebert and Baron's violent and control television programs. The findings were supported for the boys but not for the girls. No effects were found for the nonviolent television sequence. The results are interesting even though inconsistent. Unfortunately, the children were not interviewed about their feelings about and comprehension of the programs watched. In a hypothetical example, an observer rates a child as having high levels of the emotions of anger and happiness and low levels of disgust, fear, pain, and sadness while watching violence on television. Subsequently, the child is aggressive, as defined by Liebert and Baron. No effort has been made to try to determine what the child was thinking about while watching. The absence of such information, combined with inconsistent results, makes Eckman's rather interesting research difficult to interpret.

Leifer and Roberts (1972, pp. 43–180) used a paper and pencil test of willingness to aggress as their measure of aggression. The measure was validated against the Bandura modeling experiments for the younger children and the Berkowitz pseudo-electric-shock measure for selected groups of older children. Leifer and Roberts's results on comprehension were reported earlier in this chapter. Two principal findings are that violent programs produced higher levels of willingness to aggress than less violent ones and that understanding the motivations for and consequences of violence did not account for the extent of willingness to aggress. The conclusions provided by Leifer and Roberts are open to serious alternate explanations, because the willingness-to-aggress score was validated only against the previously described and criticized measures of aggression.

In summary, an effort was made to provide answers to objections to old research by supplying new evidence. Hanratty *et al.* (1969) used a human clown target instead of a Bobo doll in an effort to respond to criticism that Bandura's experiments did not measure genuine aggression. Liebert and Baron (1972) changed the measure of aggression to administration of pseudopain in a button-pressing task against an unseen target. Eckman *et al.* (1972) measured the facial expressions of the younger children in the Liebert and Baron experiment. Finally, Leifer and Roberts (1972) used a willingness-to-aggress measure and found little relationship between children's willingness to aggress and their comprehension of televised violence. Although the just-mentioned laboratory experiments provide a few additional insights, these appear to be of minor importance. The basic designs continue and the same objections remain applicable: The experiments are artificial; children may be responding to the demand characteristics of the tasks; the experimental measures do not appear to define genuine aggression; and brief experimental exposures to televised aggression probably have little relevance to the real-life conditions of television watching.

The most important field study to emerge from The Report was a longitudinal study set in rural, upstate New York. Lefkowitz, Evan, Walder, and Huesman (1972, pp. 35–135) used a peer rating of aggression in the classroom in the third grade (age 8) and a similar rating at age 19. Since subjects were no longer in school during the second rating, interviews were conducted from memory using class rosters. Preference for televised violence was measured at grade 3 from a parental questionnaire and in the second rating from an interview with the subject. The findings show: (1) a significant correlation between preference for television violence at age 8 and peer-rated aggression at age 19 ($r = .31$); (2) a significant correlation between peer-rated aggression at ages 8 and 19 ($r = .38$); and (3) a moderate correlation between preference for television violence and peer-rated aggression at age 8 ($r = .21$). There were no relationships between: (1) preference for television violence at age 19 and peer-rated aggressive behavior at age 8; (2) preference for television violence at ages 8 and 19; and (3) preference for television violence and peer-rated aggression at age 19. The joint finding of a relationship between preference for television violence at age 8 and peer-rated aggression at age 19 with the absence of a relationship between peer-rated aggression at age 8 and preference for television violence at age 19 is, the authors believe, important. It indicates that preference for viewing violence at age 8 is causally related to peer-rated aggression at age 19 and that peer-rated aggression at age 8 is not causally related to preference for television violence at age 19.

The Lefkowitz *et al.* findings are important because they provide the *only* evidence on the long-term effects of viewing televised violence. However, it must be remembered that this study is correlational and in addition has many methodological problems. A list of a few of them is appropriate:

1. Parental reports of television viewing tend to be inaccurate. For instance, Bechtel, Achelpohl, and Ackers (1972, pp. 274–299) compare self-reports of television viewing time obtained from volunteers who allowed electronic monitors, including video-tape cameras, in their homes. Overreports of viewing time range from 25% to 40–50%.
2. Attrition of the sample leaves considerable opportunity for bias. Only 63% of 735 subjects queried at age 19 responded to requests for interviews.
3. The last interview, carried out after the subjects had left school, required long-term memory of events and was therefore subject to unreliability.
4. The nine-item peer rating may not provide genuine measures of aggression. They include questions such as: who does not obey the teacher, who says "Give me that," who does things that bother others, and who says mean things?
5. The nine-item peer-rating was summed to provide a total-aggression score. This is a questionable procedure. A better procedure would have included correlating each item individually. It would, for example, be highly informative to know the correlations to the item "Who starts a fight over nothing?"
6. The use of identical questions at two widely different ages do not take into consideration changes in development of the individual. The identical behavior, separated by 10 years, may have a completely different meaning.

Lefkowitz's study has been given considerable importance in the Surgeon General's Report. Thought provoking as its findings may be, however, the study is hardly definitive, given the inadequacies cited above.

Stein and Friedrich (1972, pp. 202–317) examined the effects of television programs on preschoolers in a nursery school. After establishing a baseline of ordinary behavior through observations in the nursery for a period of 3 weeks, the researchers divided the children into three treatment groups. During a 4-week period the children viewed short television film episodes of (1) 6 aggressive *Batman* and 6 aggressive *Superman* cartoons; (2) neutral films that were neither aggressive nor prosocial; and (3) 12 prosocial episodes from *Mister Rogers' Neighborhood* that stressed the value of sharing, cooperative behavior, and self-discipline. After the treatment, children were observed for an additional 2 weeks, during which no television was shown. The principal findings were that:

1. Tolerance of delay and rule obedience declined in children in the aggressive condition.

2. In the aggressive condition, only children initially above the median in aggression showed increased interpersonal aggression.

3. More interpersonal aggression was displayed by those who saw the aggressive programs than by those who saw the neutral programs.

4. Children initially below the median in aggression displayed no effects on aggressive behavior as a result of watching televised aggression.

5. Children exposed to the prosocial treatment displayed higher task persistence, higher rule obedience, and greater tolerance of delay than children in the neutral condition. These results were especially pronounced for the higher-IQ children.

6. Lower socioeconomic status (SES) children displayed increased prosocial interpersonal behavior after treatment in the prosocial condition. No effect is reported for higher SES children.

7. Attention to programs and knowledge of content were unrelated to changes in behavior.

8. Home-viewing patterns were unrelated to baseline behavior.

An interesting effect reported by Stein and Friedrich was that self-controlling behavior, particularly tolerance for minor frustrations, declined for all children exposed to the aggressive television episodes. For higher SES children, the reduction in self-control was associated with increased social interaction, primarily of a cooperative kind. Stein and Friedrich postulate that aggressive television has a general stimulating effect for higher SES children that leads to increased social interaction with a concomitant reduction of self-control. This was not the case for lower SES children who were already aggressive. Not only did aggressive television lead to lower levels of self-control for lower SES children, but also produced increased levels of aggression.

It is unlikely that the head teachers could have influenced the behavior of the children in the direction of the treatment, since the viewings were held in rooms other than the classrooms, with the teacher absent. Thus, with some cooperative effort, the teaching staff remained blind to the experimental treatment.

This study overcomes many of the objections leveled at the Bandura-type studies. It was conducted under natural field conditions, controlled for different viewing contents, and measured changes in behavior from real-life observations. There are, however, certain limitations. Demand characteristics of the experimental conditions could have operated to produce the results obtained. The children must have been aware that they were in a "special" situation, given the extraordinarily high levels of observation and the meticulous procedure of going to a separate room each day to watch television. Consequently, an unknown percentage of the children may have felt that they were required to copy what they had seen on the television set. Thus, the observed behavior may have been compliance, in the sense that the children may have perceived that they were expected to play in the ways observed on the television. If this was the case, much of the recorded aggressive behavior may have been playful in intent. Insight into this possibility would have been obtained had the children been interviewed and had longer term follow-ups been arranged to test for the persistence of aggressive behavior.

One last methodological note is worth mentioning. The children were assigned to treatments randomly, with some control to equalize age and social class. Effort was not made to match children on important baseline measures and then to randomly assign them to treatments. There are statistically significant differences in baseline-condition characteristics of the children that might have affected the results. Initial differences between groups are reported in the following categories: frustration, object frustration, physical aggression, interpersonal aggression, cooperation, verbalization of feelings, rule obedience, tolerance of delay, and task persistence (Stein & Friedrich, 1972, pp. 242–243). The generality of the initial differences between groups casts doubt upon the randomization procedure, the comparability of the groups, and the accuracy of the findings. Despite these criticisms, Stein and Friedrich are to be commended for making significant breakthroughs in field experiments under natural conditions.

One last field study, although considerably smaller in scope and not in The Report, is worthy of mention. Steuer, Applefield, and Smith (1971, pp. 442–447) tested 10 preschoolers, average age 51 months, in groups of 2 each, with aggressive or nonaggrassive television programs over a period of 11 days. One child in each group saw either aggressive or nonaggressive television. The children were matched on parental ratings of television use at home. Three of five children who watched aggressive television increased in interpersonal aggressive behavior from baseline, compared to matched controls. In two cases in which interpersonal aggression hardly increased during treatment, no recorded observations of interpersonal aggression were noted in the baseline period. Accepting the results at face value, extreme individual differences are noted among preschoolers in their susceptability to influence from televised aggression. This topic has not received much attention in the research to date.

On Viewing Violence: Conclusions

From the research reviewed, the informed layman's opinion of what constitutes aggression appears to be very different from the working definition of many social scientists. Percy Tannenbaum, who used Berkowitz's pseudo-electric-shock procedure in his research, argues that the ordinary definition is of no consequence:

> The charge is made that we don't have good measures. But in experimental research, we use the same inadequate measure under the same conditions except the condition that the experimenter varied systematically—in this case, the kind of film

or TV show the kids have been exposed to. So if there are differences, what you want to account for is those differences. It's not adequate to say the measure wasn't good enough. Once you've accepted, say, that pseudo-electric shocks or how many times you kicked the Bobo doll is going to be used for the purposes of this study as an adequate measure of the term "aggression," then *what the statistics are about is the difference between the groups.*

When there is random behavior among the kids in my lab toward what buttons they push, there is the same chance of equally random behavior whether they saw an aggressive movie or a non-aggressive movie. If there are differences in the "mean" and around the "mean" in each group—greater than the differences among the children *within* a group—then we say that is a significant finding. It could have occurred by chance in only a small percentage of the cases.

I am dissatisfied that we measure aggression in different ways. But I am impressed when different investigators do indeed measure the relationship between TV viewing and aggressive behavior in different ways—each with its own flaws but each with its own rationale as well—and they come up with similar findings. That is impressive because the differences should contribute to a lower relationship, not a higher one. It gives increased validity to the random nature of the research projects [from an interview with Cater and Strickland].[3]

This author does not accept Tannenbaum's assertions. Social scientists using terms in common usage with generally accepted definitions should observe those definitions. Proving points by arbitrary definitions may satisfy a few researchers and others sympathetic to their position, but such practice is not likely to convince others of the usefulness of their findings. It is not impressive that research based on widely differing inadequate definitions achieves similar results. Rather, it is depressing to realize that the overwhelming body of research that purports to demonstrate a relationship between televised violence and violent behavior is shackled to untenable theoretical and methodological considerations that render the research findings virtually useless as evidence in social policy considerations.

Lastly, Tannenbaum asserts that the research projects in this area have a random nature. Randomness in social science research is only approachable, never obtainable. The decision to conduct an experiment or not, the definitions of the independent and dependent measures, the types of statistics employed, the assumptions used in the interpretation of the results—all present difficulties to randomization.

In summary, the evidence does not provide support for the theses that televised violence is harmful to society or produces antisocial behavior at an individual or group level. Efforts to alter the content of television offerings cannot at present be supported by social science research, because that research has been inadequate to respond to the issue.

[3] Quoted from Douglass Cater and Stephen Strickland, *TV Violence and the Child* (New York: Russell Sage Foundation, 1975), p. 43. © 1975 by the Russell Sage Foundation.

Prosocial Potential

One aspect of the prosocial potential of television has already been touched upon, namely the possibility of altering the behavior of young children toward increased task persistence, higher rule obedience, greater tolerance of delay, etc., as a result of watching prosocial television programs such as *Mister Rogers' Neighborhood* (Stein & Friedrich, 1972). Another prosocial possibility, opposed to the observational learning formulation, is that watching violence on television serves to provide an outlet for pent-up aggressive drives. According to the catharsis hypothesis, originally proposed by Aristotle, accumulated aggressive urges are supposedly drained after watching violence, with the result that the individual behaves less aggressively. The often uncritical acceptance of the catharsis hypothesis has been noted by Berkowitz (1973, p. 103). Critical reviews are provided by Berkowitz (1973, pp. 103–113), Liebert *et al.* (1973, pp. 44–48), Bandura (1973, pp. 148–154), Goranson (1970, pp. 15–22), Liebert, Sobol, and Davidson (1972), and Liebert, Davidson, and Sobol (1972). More sympathetic reviews are provided by Feshbach (1970), Singer (1971), and Feshbach and Singer (1972a, 1972b). The catharsis hypothesis is currently in general disfavor after passing through successive periods of uncritical acceptance and controversy.

The experiment around which greatest controversy centers was performed by Feshbach and Singer (1971). In a field experiment, subjects were 625 adolescent boys from three private residential schools for middle class boys and from four residential treatment homes for boys lacking in proper home care. Treatment consisted of watching a minimum of 6 hours a week for 6 weeks of either primarily aggressive television programs or primarily nonaggressive programs. Additional hours of watching were permitted as long as they involved the assigned type of material. All children were randomly assigned to treatment groups. A behavior rating scale was completed daily by a member of the staff familiar with the boys' activities throughout the treatment. The study was not without its problems. In three institutions the experimenters relented to protests that *Batman* was not included in their aggressive programming. The children watching the nonaggressive material displayed higher levels of physical aggression against peers, and a higher proportion of aggressive encounters were rated as unprovoked. The nonaggressive treatment group had twice as many fights, of which two-thirds were considered provoked, in contrast to a rate of one-half all fights considered provoked among the aggressive treatment group. Similar, but not as marked, differences occurred for pushing and shoving; rough, destructive handling of property; and verbal aggression. Aggression against authority figures was in the same direction, but the relationship was not as strong (Feshbach & Singer, 1971, pp. 68–72). An intriguing finding was that the differences were almost entirely attributable to the four "boys' homes." The boys in the public care facilities were "at risk," from mostly working-class backgrounds, with higher initial levels of aggression. Wells (1971) in an unpublished replication finds no catharsis effect with a sample of tuition-paying middle-class boys. This study is often cited as failure to replicate Feshbach and Singer's findings. Actually, it partially confirms them, since Feshbach and Singer report no catharsis effect for middle-class boys.

The Feshbach and Singer experiment has been thoroughly criticized in a specially commissioned technical paper in The Report (Liebert, Davidson, & Sobol, 1972). A few of the criticisms include: (1) There was an unknown amount of violence in the nonaggressive viewing material because selection was by program format and not by direct content analysis; (2) programs labeled aggressive by other researchers (e.g., cartoons) were in the nonaggressive material; (3) it is unknown how often and how attentively children watched television during treatment; (4) there was a breakdown of the treatment conditions (e.g., the *Batman* protests); and (5) frustration at being deprived of favorite programs assigned to the aggressive-material viewing group may have contributed to aggressive behavior among the nonaggressive treatment subjects.

In conclusion, Feshbach and Singer's demonstration of catharsis is subject to criticisms that are sufficient to place its major results in doubt. A distinction worth pursuing is the observed differences between the boys who were "at risk" and the middle class boys in the private schools. The strong form of the catharsis hypothesis, that catharsis operates equally well on all individuals, may not be correct. A weak form, selective to the individual and to the particular form of presentation, may be a more accurate representation of the facts. Only certain types of individuals may be drained of their aggressive tendencies by watching only certain types of observed violence, while the level of violence in others may be unaffected or increased.

Noble (1975, pp. 141–156), in a series of three superbly reasoned experiments, manages to reconcile Bandura and Berkowitz's results with Feshbach and Singer's. In the first experiment (Noble, 1973) a comparison between the effects of different types of filmed aggression was studied. Four different types of aggressive programs were shown to young children. Realistic or stylized aggression in which the victim was seen or unseen comprised the four types of presentation. Measurements of degree of imagination in play, number of minutes of destructive play, and percentage of time spent in social interaction were rated before and after viewing each type of film. Imagination in play was also used to infer the degree to which the child experienced anxiety or was disturbed by the film portrayal. The assumption was that the less time spent in imaginative play, the greater the disturbance. Stylized aggression was followed by greater imaginative play, fewer minutes of destructive play, and a greater percentage of time spent in social interaction. The results were particularly prominent for stylized aggression with the victim unseen. In comparison to the baseline control before viewing, the stylized aggression with the victim unseen had a cathartic effect, play was more imaginative, there was less destructive play, and social interaction was greater. The other conditions produced less imaginative play and less time spent in social interaction, especially in the realistic condition and in the condition where the victim was seen. In conclusion, Noble demonstrated that the type of film (realistic–stylized or victim seen–victim unseen) determined whether or not catharsis occurred.

In a second experiment, Noble and Martin (1974) presented four different types of televised films to different groups of Irish schoolboys. Three films were of three respective wrestling matches where the outcomes were clearly different: (1) the Irish wrestler won; (2) the English wrestler won; and (3) the match was drawn. The fourth film shown, as a control, was a neutral film on Bali. The children were rated on aggression and nonaggression by teachers highly familiar with them. Before and after the televised film, behavior was also rated on amount of imitation of the wrestling, amount of fighting, and degree of imagination in play. For the aggressive boys, viewing the home team win produced no imitation at all, almost no fighting, and high levels of imaginative play. From high levels of imaginative play it is inferred that the film of the home side winning produced little anxiety or disturbance in the aggressive children. In contrast, the aggressive boys who watched the home team lose exhibited high levels of imitation of the wrestlers, had high levels of fighting and low levels of imaginative play. Thus, watching the home side lose produced higher imitative and nonimitative aggression in aggressive boys, and from the low level of imaginative play it can be inferred that they were anxious or disturbed by the presentation. The results for the nonaggressive boys were markedly contrasting. The sight of the home team winning and especially of a draw produced high levels of imitation of the wrestling, much fighting, and a low level of imaginative play, from which it can be inferred that the children were anxious or disturbed by the presentation. When the nonaggressive boys saw the home team lose, they exhibited no imitation of the wrestling at all, little fighting, and a high level of imaginative play. It can be inferred that the nonaggressive children did not experience much anxiety or disturbance from watching the home team lose. In a 2-month follow-up, the effects of viewing the wrestling had completely disappeared for all children. The results showed a catharsis effect in two circumstances: when the aggressive boys saw the home team win and when the nonaggressive boys saw the home team lose.

In the last experiment, Noble and Mulcahy (1974) used realistic and stylized aggressive films shown on a television monitor to groups of children in their classrooms. The children were 6½-year-old boys, classified as aggressive and nonaggressive by teacher ratings. The teachers had taught the children for 2½ years previously. The boys were also observed, before and after treatment, on three dimensions of classroom behavior: (1) degree of imagination in play; (2)

amount of conflict with other boys; and (3) amount of social interaction with other boys. The stylized aggression was a Western and the realistic aggression was a wrestling match where the victim's pain was shown. Each child received both treatments, with an observation period after each treatment. Aggressive boys played more imaginatively after seeing the Western, but this was not the case for the wrestling. In addition, the aggressive boys' social interaction lessened after watching both the Western and the wrestling, but declined more for the wrestling. In regard to the third measure, interpersonal conflict increased for the aggressive boys after watching both the wrestling and the Western, but more so for the wrestling. In contrast, the nonaggressive boys exhibited different reactions to the same presentations. For the nonaggressive boys imaginative play decreased equally after watching both the wrestling and the Westerns; social interaction decreased, but more so after the wrestling; and interpersonal conflict increased sharply after the wrestling and only slightly after the Western. Noble argues that the results of these experiments reconcile Bandura and Berkowitz's results with those of Feshbach and Singer. Feshbach and Singer report a catharsis effect for initially aggressive children at high risk. Noble reports the same effect for aggressive children, but refines the effect as being stronger for stylized aggression, where the same-side hero loses and the victim is seen. Bandura reports an increase in aggression with middle-class children presumably initially low in aggression as a consequence of watching stylized aggression. Noble reports that stylized aggression produces less aggression but that imitation of a familiar model (an Irish wrestler for Irish children) is copied by nonaggressive children. Noble's results predict that Bandura would have obtained higher imitative aggression had he used realistic aggression rather than stylized aggression with his nonaggressive children. Berkowitz reports an increase in aggression for realistic aggression (a prizefight film, *Champion*) for an initially low-aggressive group of college students. Noble reports the greatest increase in interpersonal conflict for nonaggressive boys after realistic exposure (wrestling).

Noble's results require replication with more precise experimental controls. Replication with girls as subjects is also needed. Also, Noble does not examine long-term effects of viewing, and closer examination of the demand characteristics of his experiments is in order. The most important contribution of these experiments, however, is the forcing of a distinction of individual differences in aggressiveness by demonstrating differential responsiveness to different types of aggressive presentations. What remains is the unanswered question of fundamental importance: Why do aggressive and nonaggressive children respond differently to different types of presentations of violence? The research evidence presented next provides one possible explanation.

Children's responses to televised aggression should depend upon differences in their ability to internally transform what has been observed so that it is consistent with currently held beliefs and behaviors. In this respect Collins

(1973, p. 5) finds it useful to postulate the existence of a cognitive mediator, defined as "a cognitive state that is formed during observation ... [which] includes a representation of the modeled social behavior *and* the observer's inferences and evaluations about the action and motives and consequences associated with it." Collins considers only age-related changes in the cognitive mediator. However, the observation of differences in aggression for different types of aggressive programs that are not age-related also requires the postulation of an individual-difference dimension to the cognitive mediator.

Individual differences in imaginative play may, in part, account for the observed differences in aggressive responses to different types of aggressive programs. Biblow (1973, pp. 104–128) presented aggressive films, nonaggressive films, and a neutral task to 30 high- and 30 low-fantasy 10-year-old white middle-class children. The films were presented in the classroom on a television monitor. Level of fantasy was measured on the basis of the combined score of a movement response on the Holtzmann Inkblot Test and imaginative responses on the Torrance "Just-Suppose" Task (e.g., Just suppose clouds had strings attached to them that would hang down to earth. What would happen?). All children were frustrated in a task prior to exposure to the film. Level of aggression as well as mood were recorded before and after treatment. High-fantasy children displayed significant decreases in aggressive behavior after aggressive and nonaggressive films but no decrease in aggressive behavior after the neutral task. The failure of the neutral task to reduce aggression is explained, according to Biblow, as being so time-consuming that imaginative play was not possible during its presentation. All groups of low-fantasy children displayed no decrease in aggressive behavior and, in fact, displayed a slight increase. Changes in mood for the two different groups, while not as consistent as the changes in behavior, are consistent with these findings. If it is possible to infer that Noble's aggressive and nonaggressive children differed in level of fantasy activity, then observed differences in aggressive response are, in part, explained.

Evidence from other research supports the inference that differences did, in fact, exist. Smilansky (1968) and Freyberg (1973, pp. 129–154) demonstrate striking differences in fantasy play of children from different socioeconomic levels. Smilansky found that Israeli children from poorer home backgrounds had lower levels of "sociodramatic play." She found, for instance, increased role-playing behavior with more positive affect, less fighting and hyperactivity, and more verbal communication as a result of training. Freyberg obtained similar results with 5-year-old lower-class children. After training, children played more imaginatively, improved in verbal communication, were more sensitive to other children's behavior, were more spontaneous, used play material more creatively, were more inventive and original, labeled more, showed increased attention span, and expressed more positive emotions than an untrained control group. Although the results of training were dramatic, the level of spontaneous imaginative play after training for the best of the lower-class children in Freyberg's sample was still below the spontaneous imaginative play for an untrained sample of upper-middle-class children (Pulaski, 1973). Supporting evidence is provided by Burton L. White (Pines, 1969), who reports five times the level of role playing in middle-class children as opposed to lower-class children.

Freyberg concludes that spontaneous imaginitive play is a cognitive skill and that lower-class children are generally deficient in it. She also suggests that the origins of this deficiency may be attributable to different ways that lower-class and middle-class parents interact with their children. Lower-class parents seem to have much less awareness of their roles as tutors to their children and consequently display almost no such behavior.

The findings on social class differences in spontaneous imaginative play are striking. Of equal interest is the apparent ease with which successful training can be accomplished (in Freyberg's case eight 20-minute sessions in small groups). Long-term effects of training remain unexplored, as do effects of training on responsiveness to aggressive and nonaggressive televised film presentations. If the inferred relationships between spontaneous imaginative play, training, changes in aggressiveness, and responsiveness to televised aggression are confirmed, televised instruction in spontaneous imaginative play can provide an enormously useful skill.

Chittendon (1942) demonstrated that assertiveness in preschoolers could be constructively modified by symbolic doll-play training sessions. The dolls played the roles of preschool children who "participated in social situations similar to those in which the child frequently experienced difficulty [p. 73]." Child and experimenter analyzed each of 11 15-minute situations together to reach a decision as to which social responses were most appropriate. Preschoolers were gradually encouraged to make independent decisions and to work out, on their own, the socially desirable alternatives. Training was not unlike the training subsequently used by Freyberg to enhance spontaneous imaginative play in disadvantaged preschoolers. Chittendon reports greatest success from the symbolic training procedure in reducing dominance and more moderate success in increasing cooperative behavior. Persistence of these effects was noted in a 1-month follow-up. Limitations of Chittendon's study include small sample size and an unrepresentative sample of upper-socioeconomic-class children.

The aforementioned results demonstrate the effectiveness of training in spontaneous imaginative play and training in assertiveness control using symbolic presentation procedures. Such training may prove to be highly effective and efficient for use on television. Observational learning has been demonstrated by Bandura, although exactly how to interpret it is open to question. The one limitation of the symbolic training procedures for use on television is that both involve active participation of a child with an adult in a small-group interactive situation where gradual independence of performance is required. Remarkably, judgments made in the symbolic play situation transferred to behavior in real-life social situations. There is even some preliminary evidence that the behavior persists. Television instruction, devoted to training preschoolers in diverse constructive social skills, has a reasonable possibility of success if it can actively engage the child viewer. It is argued, and documented in later chapters, that there is a regular progression in the ability of children to solve problems, perform perceptual analyses, use language, and employ memorization techniques. Also documented is the fact that progression in these skills can be enhanced by appropriate training. Training in spontaneous imaginative play and assertiveness control through symbolic play modeling is only one example of the potential usefulness of well-conceived training procedures.

Another important point is that children from disadvantaged backgrounds are generally deficient in the just-mentioned skills. The curriculum and instructional techniques proposed in Chapters 4–7 provide appropriate training in these skills. The next two chapters are devoted to a survey of programs, including *Sesame Street*, designed to accelerate intellectual development. It is argued that the approach taken on *Sesame Street* tends to focus too much on teaching school content (such as number recognition and counting, letter and word recognition) in the hope that giving an early start to children, particularly the disadvantaged, might lead to success in school. It is countered that this approach ignores the underlying reasons why many children fall behind in school. Earlier and intensive drill on the content of the first-grade curriculum may have a limited positive effect upon learning, but it is not necessarily the best approach. An analysis of this approach, which seems representative of much of the televised teaching of young children, follows in the next two chapters. The outline of a proposal, concentrating on the development of fundamental skills, follows.

CONCLUSION

This chapter has examined the assertion that television exerts a considerable influence upon children's social perceptions of the world and, consequently, upon their reactions to it.

The most recent estimates of weekly viewing time indicate that first-graders average about 22–24 hours; sixth-graders, 30–31 hours; and tenth-graders, 27–28 hours. Preschoolers and first-graders watch about the same amount of television as each other, and they do so with considerable active involvement, such as playing games about shows viewed on the screen and singing commercials. Preschoolers can also identify major network characters. A study of urban poor black 6-year-old children indicates that their viewing preferences are more extreme than the typical white middle-class youngster of that age: They prefer cartoons overwhelmingly, to the almost total exclusion of educational programming.

Children's comprehension of what they watch is surprisingly low given the number of hours a day they devote to television viewing. Starting with the preschool years, age-related changes in comprehension are regular and predictable. The nodal age for comprehension of a story is about 6 or 7 years. The understanding of the distinction between reality—fantasy gets less blurred as children get older. Younger children, particularly those below 6 or 7 years, thought much of what they watched on television was real. Younger children are less able to reproduce the correct order of occurrence of major events in a story or to comprehend the feelings or motivations of film characters.

Commerical children's television has gone through three distinct periods. In the early years, before the market was saturated with television sets, children's programming was of high quality and largely without advertising. After market saturation was reached, networks switched to mass marketing, dropped specialized children's programs, and concentrated on family programs. Local stations became the children's outlets; low-cost animation techniques were perfected; the host-show cartoon format featuring a local host who introduced cartoons and sold products was born. Finally, children were discovered as a specialized market for certain products (e.g., candy, toys), and Saturday morning became the established children's time slot.

Children's programming is dominated by economic considerations. Programs are contracted with rerun guarantees, using factory-line production techniques and standardized plots with plenty of action and frequent aggressive confrontations. Some new children's series have even been accused of being "spliced-together leftovers."

Advertising on children's programs has gone through three distinct stages: (1) an adult-oriented stage, where advertising to children was viewed as unprofitable; (2) a child-oriented state, where advertising was directed at children for children's products; and (3) a child-oriented stage for family-consumed products. In the last stage, children are conceived of as active family lobbyists, easily swayed by commercials.

The incidence of high levels of violence on American television, particularly children's television, has been documented in this chapter. Controversy exists, however, about whether or not televised violence influences antisocial behavior in real life. One position is that violence is a reflection of the norms and values of American culture expressed in idealized fantasy form. This may explain why violence seems to attract large audiences. Since highly rated shows attract advertising, violence perpetuates violence on American television.

The evidence, which indicates that there is a relationship between viewing violence and behaving violently, comes from observational learning experiments.

The typical experimental design includes exposure of a young child to a model hitting an inflatable, pop-up doll (Bobo doll). The model employs highly novel procedures. Afterward the child is provided with an opportunity to imitate the aggression. Other experimental treatments involve rewarding or punishing the model for aggression. Imitative and nonimitative aggression is observed, recorded, and compared to a no-model control group's aggressive behavior. The conclusions from these experiments are, generally, that exposure to aggressive film models on television tends: (1) to reduce children's inhibitions against aggression; (2) to shape the form of children's aggressive behavior; (3) to produce imitation by children of the behavior of rewarded models rather than punished ones; and (4) to produce imitation of the model's aggressive behavior when children were specifically asked or rewarded for it. The final conclusion relates to the distinction between learning and performance. Aggressive behavior may be learned but not immediately performed. Later, when conditions are more encouraging, aggressive responses learned observationally may be performed.

The observational learning experiments have been criticized because they do not involve aggression in the usual sense but rather aggression generally against inanimate dolls that cannot be hurt or in other artificial experimentally induced situations. In reply it is argued that "aggressive responses" once learned, even though they may not mediate aggressive goals in the situation in which they were originally learned, are transferred to other situations. One example is that army recruits learn aggressive responses in artificial training situations and then transfer them successfully to battlefield situations. But it is countered that there is little evidence that indicates that aggressive responses can be stored in a literal sense and used at later, more favorable occasions. Rather, an aggressive act depends upon the way the individual assimilates the situation and upon individual predispositions. Acts, by themselves, are not inherently violent; they depend upon the perceptions and motivations of the person performing them. Also, the observational learning experiments may be producing results that are artifacts because of demand characteristics inherent in the experimental situation. That is, the children may have figured out the experimenter's expectations and merely complied with them.

Other criticisms of the observational learning experiments include: (1) no distinction is made between filmed and televised violence; (2) the long-term effects of viewing violence are not explored by the one-shot procedures; and (3) the developmental function of imitation in children's play is inadequately explored in the observational learning experiments.

Recent research, primarily from the Surgeon General's Report, has attempted to reply to some of the objections by using more realistic measures of aggression. However, it is argued that these experiments continue to be artificial, involve demand characteristics that children may be responding to rather than measure genuine aggressive responsiveness, use questionable definitions of aggression, and are short-term in nature. The only longitudinal study that reports an effect of viewing violence on subsequent aggressive behavior is correlational in nature, has many design inadequacies, and is therefore difficult to interpret.

Field experiments overcome some of the objections leveled at laboratory experiments, such as artificiality and inadequate definitions of aggression, but at the expense of less precise controls. In one field study, 4 weeks of either aggressive, prosocial, or neutral television watching by preschoolers was preceded by 3 weeks of nursery school observation and followed by another 2 weeks of observation. Interesting interaction effects in response to the different types of televised presentations were observed. These effects depended upon the initial level of aggression and social class of the children. Other experimental results, to be reported, show comparable individual differences in response to different types of televised presentations.

The overall conclusion from the research to date is that the evidence does not provide adequate support for the theses that televised violence is harmful to society or produces antisocial behavior at an individual or group level. Efforts to alter the content of television programming cannot at present be supported by social science.

The prosocial potential of television was the last major topic of discussion in this chapter. The catharsis hypothesis proposes that watching televised violence drains aggressive urges and, consequently, results in less aggressive behavior. A major field study of boys in public institutions examined and supported the catharsis hypothesis. Sufficient criticism has been leveled at this experiment to cast doubt upon its major conclusions. However, the controversy surrounding the catharsis hypothesis has generated additional valuable research projects that indicate that the catharsis hypothesis may be valid under certain conditions. Different types of presentations produce different effects on individuals differing in initial level of aggressiveness. Distinctions must be made between realistic or stylized aggression, whether or not the pain of the victim is seen, whether the home side wins or loses, and whether the child watching is himself rated high or low in aggression. These results confirm the individual-difference results, previously reported, found among preschoolers in a nursery school. Under some conditions catharsis does occur.

Children differ in their levels of imaginative play, and this may explain the observed individual differences in response to different types of televised aggression. Children high in imaginative fantasy play displayed decreases in aggression after watching aggressive and nonaggressive films, whereas children low in imaginative fantasy play displayed a slight increase. Furthermore, evidence indicates that imaginative fantasy play is a cognitive skill highly evident in middle-class children and that lower-class children are deficient in it. Lower-class children, after training in imaginative fantasy play, demonstrate less fighting and hyperactivity, more imaginative play, improved verbal communication, greater sensitivity to other children, greater inventiveness and originality in play, greater attention span, more positive emotions, etc. A comparison between individual differences in responsiveness to different types of televised aggression and individual differences in imaginative fantasy play indicates some striking parallels. It is suggested that one instructional function of television would be training in spontaneous imaginative fantasy play. Its result would likely include lessened susceptibility to televised violence in young children and an increase in an important cognitive skill basic to self-control and introspection in social situations. The increased ability to rework social experience in fantasy in more socially constructive ways, it is argued, is a basic skill, fundamental to later satisfactory performance in school.

2

The Limits of Instructional
Television for Young Children:
An Analysis of a Controversy

With the premiere of *Sesame Street*, educational television designed for preschoolers came of age—not only in this country, but around the world. It is the purpose of this book to examine this newly emerging phenomenon.

On November 5, 1970, the *New York Times* published an article by Andrew H. Malcolm titled, " 'Sesame Street' Rated Excellent: 2-Year Study Finds It Helped Children of the Poor Learn." Details from his article report that the popular television program that uses "fast-paced advertising techniques to instruct children in basic skills" had "an excellent educational impact on young viewers during its first year on the air."

Sesame Street is primarily aimed at teaching such school-related skills as letters, numbers, forms, relations, classifications, and body parts to disadvantaged 4-year-olds in urban ghettos, but its appeal is far more extensive. According to other details from Malcolm's article: (1) disadvantaged children who regularly watch the series show greater gains in learning than advantaged children who watch only infrequently, regardless of age, sex, or geographic location; (2) 3-year-old regular viewers learn more than 4- or 5-year-old viewers who watch less frequently; (3) children appear to learn equally well watching at home or in preschool centers, but children who learn the most "tended to have mothers who watched the show and discussed it with them later."

Sesame Street was reported in the article as having been viewed by approximately 7 million families over about 250 public and commercial television stations nationally. A more recent estimate made by Children's Television Workshop, the producers of *Sesame Street*, based on Neilson ratings is that 8 million children see the show every week and that there may be 6 million who

43

see three or more shows every week (Mayer, 1972, p. 134). On the international scene, an article by Michael Dann (*New York Times*, August 6, 1972), consultant for international distribution to Children's Television Workshop, reports that *Sesame Street* is broadcast in over 48 nations and territories. This figure did not include a scheduled premiere in the fall of 1972 in Latin America of a Spanish version called *Plaza Sesamo* to a potential audience of 22 million preschoolers. *Sesame Street* is broadcast, and in general received enthusiastically, around the world.

According to Dann, *Sesame Street* seems to have stimulated efforts in other countries. Dann mentions three new British-produced programs for preschoolers, two new programs in Germany, and a projected new program in Hong Kong. According to Dann,

> All the expertise from the original series is available to any country, any place, regardless of whether it is interested in carrying the original series or making its own show.
>
> By itself, the English-language version is probably seen by more people more times than any other show in the history of television, and the audience will be dramatically increased when the Spanish, Portuguese and German counterparts go on the air.
>
> In the inforseeable future, when *Sesame Street* and its offspring have run and rerun their courses, their impact will still be felt in the awakening of the universal medium of television to the possibilities of entertaining and educating young people in nations throughout the world.

In this country, the CTW production staff and researchers believe the effects of *Sesame Street* to be far reaching and educationally profound. According to Malcolm (*New York Times*, November 5, 1974), the workshop would like to study the effects of *Sesame Street* on the growing numbers of 2-year-old viewers and to determine whether the existence of *Sesame Street* necessitates changes for primary school curricula.

Barely 1 year after Malcolm's article another article appeared in the *New York Times* (September 8, 1971) entitled "BBC Orders Ban on 'Sesame Street.'" The announcement, made by Miss Monica Sims, head of children's television programming included the following:

> Educationalists in America have questioned the value of 2, 3, and 4 year olds acquiring knowledge in a passive, uninvolved fashion, and had criticized the program's essentially middle-class attitudes, its lack of reality and its attempt to prepare children for school, but not for life.
>
> I share some of these doubts and am particularly worried about the program's authoritarian aims. Right answers are demanded and praised and a research report refers to the program maker's aim to change children's behavior. This sounds like indoctrination and a dangerous use of television.

This announcement caused widespread anger among certain segments of the British educational establishment, even though *Sesame Street* was later scheduled to be shown on British commercial television and, according to Dann, is now received by more than 50% of the country. Furthermore, Dann reports that Nigel Lawson, former editor of *The Spectator*, wrote in the *Times* (London) that "*Sesame Street* is the most important program ever to have been shown on television."

The debate over *Sesame Street* has been most intense in Britain (Efron, March 11, 1972). Efron quotes more fully from Nigel Lawson's editorial of December 22, 1971, in the *Times* (London) as follows:

> "I have little doubt that *Sesame Street* ... is the most important programme on television. ... *Sesame Street* is, in its way, a minor miracle. It is genuinely educational. ... Small children watch it of their own free will. ... It wins the cooperation of parents. ... It has had a particularly enthusiastic reception from teachers of older but backward children from deprived homes.
>
> "There is one section of opinion, and one alone, that is overwhelmingly hostile to *Sesame Street*: the educational establishment. ... The BBC is totally in the pocket of the educational lobby. ...
>
> "*Sesame Street* is doubly important; both as a breakthrough in preschool education and for bringing out the rottenness of the educational establishment in Britain."

Initially, *Sesame Street* got a trial run in Wales on independent television. The published report [*Sunday Times* (London), April 25, 1971] showed nearly unanimous enthusiastic approval from British mothers. Another enthusiastic supporter was Nigel Pitman, chairman of the Royal Society of Teachers Education Trust, who showed *Sesame Street* before educators and Parliament. Monica Sims defended her ban at the fall 1971 meeting of the European Broadcasting Union. In turn, Joan Gantz Cooney, CTW president, replied to Monica Sims in the form of a five-page, single-spaced note (Efron, March 11, 1972).

The controversy over *Sesame Street* seems generated, by and large, from subjective evaluations. Conclusions of both parties are not, in general, supported by hard evidence. What is needed is a more substantial evaluation of the issue than that which appeared in the British press.

Mayer (1972, pp. 155–156) offers what appears to be an insider's view of the contracting with Educational Testing Service of the research evaluation of *Sesame Street*. CTW and ETS agreed on the areas of measurement about which *Sesame Street* would "go to the wall." According to Mayer (1972), "These were, inevitably, the items most easily taught and most easily measured—recognition of letters and numbers, knowledge of the names of the parts of the body, and the simplest sorting skills [p. 155]." Mayer adds that "over and above more general educational functions, *Sesame Street* hours were designed to improve

scores on the tests ETS would give at the end of the year. Under the circumstances, it is scarcely surprising that the ETS results were positive [p. 156]."

Curiously, Mayer supports the procedures CTW adopted with ETS. He argues
that all new tests are necessarily artificial. Whether or not the scores on a test
predict anything of importance in the future of the students can be determined
only after the test has been given for some time. Thus Mayer declares:

> At best, tests on the first year or two or three of *Sesame Street* could give no better
> than insufficient information about the value of the program; it is hard to see how
> the CTW researchers could in all scientific probity have done anything other than
> plan the tests to show off their work in the best possible light [p. 156].

Mayer adds that "what little evidence has turned up about the more complicated, unmeasured goals of the program—or about the children's ability to
transfer the very simple stuff for which ETS measured into more complicated
situations—does argue that the program has indeed made a difference [p. 156]."

Unfortunately, the ETS research, contracted by CTW, is so extensive that it
cannot be considered in detail until the next chapter. Briefly, Mayer's arguments
are not entirely accurate. What ETS and CTW seemed to be intent on doing was
constructing criterion-referenced tests that measured the same items taught on
Sesame Street (Hines, 1970). Apparently, CTW and ETS made little or no effort
to use tests of established validity. Hines (1970) has therefore criticized ETS on
test construction and validation procedures. Furthermore, Mayer's statement
that there is additional evidence supporting the accomplishment of the "more
complicated, unmeasured goals of the probram" is, as far as this author can
determine, incorrect. Analysis of the *Sesame Street* research claims in the next
chapter should clarify this issue.

There are surprisingly few well-formulated criticisms of *Sesame Street.* Critical comments have most often appeared in the popular press (Bronfrenbrenner,
1970; The Children's Television Workshop, 1970; Cooney, 1970; Culhane, 1970;
Hentoff, 1970; Holt, 1971; Johnson, 1971; Little, 1969, 1970; "Open *Sesame,*"
1971; Palmer, 1969, 1971a, 1971b; Palmer & Connell, 1971; Rosenthal, 1970;
Scott, 1969; Sedulus, 1970; "*Sesame* at One," 1970; "*Sesame Street* Evaluation," 1971; "*Sesame Street* Lights," 1971; "*Sesame Street*—What Next?,"
1970; "*Sesame* under Attack," 1971; Shayan, 1970; Trout, 1971; Woodring,
1970; Wylie, 1970). They offer surprisingly few new insignts into the educational effectiveness of *Sesame Street.* A review of the popular literature was
done by Rogers (1972). A few of the more salient remarks are abstracted from
her review:

> "If what people want is for children to memorize numbers and letters without regard
> to the difference between children, then *Sesame Street* is truly responsive [Culhane,
> 1970, p. 63, quote from Frank Garfunkel]."

"To give a child 30 seconds of one thing and then to switch it and give him 30 seconds of another is to nurture irrelevance and to give reinforcement to a type of intellectual process that can never engage in sustained and developed thought [Culhane, 1970 p. 63, quote from Frank Garfunkel]."

Sesame Street is far too removed from structured teaching[Culhane, 1970, attributed to Carl Bereiter].

Sesame Street borrows too heavily from the high pressure aspects of commercial television [Shayan, 1970].

Sesame Street is too much like a school and there is too much deliberate teaching [Holt, 1971].

Sesame Street establishes passive learning conditions. In contrast, active engagement is more favorable to learning [Sedulus, 1970; Woodring, 1970].

Sesame Street places too much emphasis on cognitive skills and not enough emphasis on social skills [Shayan, 1970].

Sesame Street should place more emphasis on preparing children for the broader aspects of life [Holt, 1971].

Sesame Street might replace other, more traditional efforts [Culhane, 1970]. In reply, Joan Gantz Cooney, president of CTW, states "*Sesame Street* was never intended to replace other educational experiences [Rogers 1972, p. 47]." Cooney adds "TV is a poor substitute for a comprehensive preschool program and that all the affective, and certain of the cognitive skills are taught better by a loving teacher [Rogers, 1972, p. 47]."

These comments from the popular press seemed to be only a prelude to more carefully worked out criticisms by several specialists in early childhood development. The most substantive critical comments about *Sesame Street* come from Herbert Sprigle (1971, 1972), who offers empirical data to support his claims. Another important general source of criticism comes from the Appalachia Educational Laboratory (Bertram, Pena, & Hines, 1971) and concerns itself with what appears to be limitations of the television medium as an educational device with young children. As part of a more general research on the development of a home-oriented preschool education program, Charles Bertram and his associates present extensive empirical data detailing the precise nature of these limitations. There are also three theoretical analyses of educational television and its possibilities (Kliger, 1971; G. S. Lesser, 1972; Fowles & Voyat, 1974). Unfortunately, these theoretical efforts do not extend to the empirically based criticisms of Sprigle and Bertram.

Alternative approaches to using television as an educational medium have, to date, been rare. One creative exception is the work of Terry Borton (1971). Borton attempted to overcome the passive educational qualities of the television medium by using a technique he called dual audio television. In this technique the standard television broadcast is "supplemented" by independent comments broadcast over a radio.

The remaining task of this chapter is to review, critically analyze, and integrate the comments of the researchers just cited. The ETS research on *Sesame Street* is so extensive, and the critical analysis necessarily so detailed, that it deserves a separate review and a separate critical analysis in the next chapter.

THE GOALS OF *SESAME STREET*

Gerald S. Lesser reports on the joint experience of researchers and television producers to develop television for children that draws upon current knowledge of how children learn. The most accessible source for his remarks appears in a rather lengthy article (G. S. Lesser, 1972) in a popular educational review. A briefer, less easily obtainable statement appears in an earlier article (G. S. Lesser, 1970) and most recently in Lesser's book (1974). His description of the evolution of *Sesame Street* from idea to fact is authoritative because he serves as chairman of the National Board of Advisors to Children's Television Workshop.

According to G. S. Lesser, *Sesame Street* was conceived as a supplementary educational experience designed to prepare children for school by "stimulating their appetite for learning." The program's goals include instruction in:

> (1) symbolic representation—letters, numbers, and geometric forms; (2) cognitive process—perceptual discrimination, relationships, classification, and ordering; (3) reasoning and problem solving; and (4) 'the child and his world'—concepts regarding the self, social units, social interaction, and the man-made and natural environment [p. 233].[1]

The goals are rather limited because of the mass nature of television communication. The producers hoped to be able to teach certain universals, such as reading and writing, and left other, more individually based objectives to more traditional educational forms.

Television is a limited educational medium. It has three major educational limitations (G. S. Lesser, 1972, p. 233): (1) Sequenced instruction is not possible; (2) it must entertain as well as educate; (3) the behavior of the child, or parent, is not controlled, as it is in the classroom. Accordingly, the premise upon which *Sesame Street* was produced was that

> television can serve only as one additional alternative to supplement other forms of educational experience, that its curriculum cannot cover the full range of preschool

[1] This and subsequent quotes cited to G. S. Lesser, 1972 are from G. S. Lesser, Learning, teaching, and television production for children: The experience of *Sesame Street. Harvard Educational Review*, 1972, *42*(2), 232–272. Copyright © 1972 by the President and Fellows of Harvard College.

objectives. Television must never be designed to replace or compete with other educational experiences. It can only aspire to complement whatever else the child has available [p. 233].

Children's Television Workshop brought together, for the first time, academics and nonacademics and set them to the tasks of defining general goals and writing a curriculum statement defining specific educational objectives. Normative data that indicated the child's initial level of competence and ultimate potential in a particular ability were not always readily available. These data were collected by a research staff (Reeves, 1970). Out of the seminars and research staff activities there emerged a general production strategy that script be tied to goals and priorities and that goals and priorities be put in behavioral terms.

When we spend some time watching children watching television, we come away impressed with the wide variety of styles of viewing. The research by Reeves (1970, p. 11) isolates several extremes of television viewing patterns. One "type" is called the "zombie viewer" because they can veiw television for hours with their eyes rarely leaving the set. Such viewing may reflect, in varying degrees, either intense concentration or stupor. Another type of viewing is described as "dual attention," where young children watch the set and also keep track of other events that might interest them. They seem to be able to switch from the television to another event and back again without discomfort. This type of viewing may represent, again in varying degrees, either distractibility or constant alertness that permits monitoring of several events simultaneously. Research on "dual attention" in young children seems to indicate that it is a characteristic of competent young children (Maccoby, 1967, 1969; Maccoby & Konrad, 1967; White, Watts, & Barnett, 1972). A third type of viewer might be categorized as the active participator. Such children, for instance, sing, dance, physically imitate, answer questions directed at them, play at being afraid, and even talk to the characters on the television screen. According to G. S. Lesser (1972, p. 237), little is known about what role these three patterns of viewing play in facilitating or inhibiting learning.

The CTW staff seems to operate on the principle, stated by G. S. Lesser (1972), that "Most children probably learn best what they want to learn [p. 238]." In this respect television can exert a favorable influence, since it is a nonpunitive medium. As G. S. Lesser (1972, p. 238) points out, children have no fear of turning it on and watching, experience no threat of humiliation, and have no sense of failure about meeting another's expectations. This operating principle leads naturally to an effort to combine education and entertainment in one content.

One method used to teach children in an entertaining way is through modeling or observational learning. Several different researchers seem to have demonstrated that by simply watching others (either live or on film) a child can learn a wide variety of desirable (e.g., Hoffman, 1970; Friedrich & Stein, 1973) and undesirable (e.g., Bandura, 1969; Feshbach, 1970) behaviors. Perhaps the most cited evidence from this body of research is the experiment by Bandura, Ross, and Ross (1963a), where children watched on film an adult pummel an inflatable rubber figure, weighted at the base so that it popped back up again after being hit. Filmstrips of the experiment show a child copying, in an exact manner, what had just been watched of the aggressive behavior of an adult toward the doll. All of this imitation is accomplished without any direct reinforcement of the child for learning—by simply watching others.

Children do considerable physical modeling and also quite a bit of verbal modeling of what they watch on television. Of course, the amount and type of modeling depends upon the child and on the particular material presented. For instance, when *Sesame Street* characters use their fingers or parts of their body to shape letters or numbers, children sometimes imitate them overtly (G. S. Lesser, 1972, p. 239). Many of the efforts to elicit modeling, however, have been designed to demonstrate effective verbal communication, by illustrating certain positive social attitudes, such as altruism, courage, kindness, and tolerance. G. S. Lesser (1972) illustrates what he considers successful modeling behavior when he cites the case of the young black child "who exclaimed while watching *Sesame Street,* 'Look! He's Black like me and he knows the right answers!' [p. 240]" However, the theoretical basis of modeling behavior is little understood and consequently offers as many problems as benefits to the dedicated producer of television shows for young children.

Another characteristic attributed to young children by the CTW team is that they have difficulty picking out the essential or relevant from the incidental or irrelevant in the intended message (G. S. Lesser, 1972, p. 241). In contrast, older children are much more capable of attending to the relevant or picking out what matters from what does not. G. S. Lesser labels this skill as "distinctive feature learning [p. 240]." A variety of special techniques are available to television producers to highlight messages so that the young child is more likely to understand them. One such technique is called stripping. Everything but the essential is eliminated from the message. Total stripping, however, involves certain risks (G. S. Lesser, 1972, pp. 241–242): (1) Children can sometimes learn the most from what adults consider to be irrelevancies; (2) total stripping may make the material boring to the child; additionally, when the material is repeated, children will look to the embellishments to supply new meanings and new interest to the repeated material; (3) it may not be possible to teach certain contents without adding some entertainment. The risk of possibly distracting the child from the central message is, in such cases, considered worth taking. G. S. Lesser (1972) argues that, whatever the risks, "television can provide for the young child a narrow, precise focus on central content, carefully eliminating irrelevancies and distractions [p. 240]."

Other special techniques for helping the child to "narrow focus" on the relevant characteristics of the message include: the use of special conventions, such as using speech balloons to teach letter names and a mind-at-work convention, where televised thoughts appear above a character's head to signal that the character is thinking before acting on a problem; zoom-in on the important characteristics of the message; slow motion to encourage the use of greater reflectivity; split screens to encourage the use of juxtaposing different objects or events and comparing them even when spatially separated; and cross-modal reinforcement, such as sound effects, to reinforce material visually presented.

There are two forms of teaching used by television: direct and indirect. According to G. S. Lesser (1972), "On television, direct teaching might be expressed by both telling and showing the children what you intend to teach them, then teaching them by telling and showing it to them, and finally by telling them and showing them again what you have taught them [p. 245]." However, most of the teaching done on television is covert and indirect. The situation comedies are the most blatant in sterotyping individuals, professions, and people of differing social and ethnic backgrounds. Messages about family life, sexual relations, education, consumer products, and attitudes about almost any imaginable aspect of life are illustrated by actions and seldom, if ever, taught directly. He points out that indirect teaching on television can be extremely effective, and we already know "that children can learn by modeling the behaviors of others without direct reinforcement, deliberate teaching or overt practice [p. 246]." Direct and indirect teaching are used to teach different things on *Sesame Street.* Indirect teaching methods are almost always used to teach social attitudes (e.g., kindness, courtesy, respect for racial differences, taking the point of view of others, modes of conflict resolution, and principles of justice and fair play). On *Sesame Street,* direct teaching frequently takes the form of teaching from the familiar to the unfamiliar, such as pointing out that a letter looks like a familiar object.

According to G. S. Lesser (1972, p. 247), *Sesame Street* tends toward sugar-coating reality (with just enough conflict to be realistic), but does not preach or directly lecture children on how they should behave. His arguments against preaching include: (1) We are not quite sure what is right for others, including children; (2) it is unjust to prevent children from working through to their own conclusions about right and wrong, (3) preaching on television does not work, probably because preaching requires a captive audience; (4) the first effort at preaching probably would be the last, since the children would stop watching. A strong effort was also made not to "talk down to children" or to trivialize a topic in an effort to make it simple enough for them to understand.

It was assumed that catching a child's attention would be much easier than directing or sustaining it. The assumption is that the child has a natural tendency to explore (G. S. Lesser, 1972, p. 249). What determines the direction of his exploration so that he watches one program and not another? There is much competition for the child's attention once he turns the television on. Most certainly, a determining factor will not be the good intentions of the producer of the educational television program. The programs on the other commercial channels are almost exclusively expensive, slick productions, using good actors, and advanced technical effects and are designed to attract, sustain, and direct attention. From the start, a guiding principle of the *Sesame Street* team was that it would have to compete successfully with the other offerings simultaneously available to the child.

Music is used extensively as an attention getting device on *Sesame Street*. The theory is that music has a different (and special) function for children than it does for adults. For adults music is mostly used as accompaniment to action and dialogue. But for children music functions as a signal—a familiar character reappears, something interesting is about to happen, etc. It is argued that children tend to drift in and out of attention to the television program, doing other things while keeping a peripheral eye or ear to what is happening on the set. That is, they use their special abilities of "dual attention" to "listen without quite listening, even when they are not actively watching [G. S. Lesser, 1972, p. 250]." Thus, we can see why using music as an attention getting device is considered so important by the *Sesame Street* production staff. It is directly based on the assumed way that children typically watch television. Music has additional functions on *Sesame Street*. It is used as an aid to memory. It is assumed that "Almost any child can more easily sing the alphabet than recite it [G. S. Lesser, 1972, p. 251]." Music and sound effects are also used as a direct way of teaching basic skills, such as auditory discrimination skills. For instance, in sound identification the child might be required to identify various animal sounds with the respective beast. Another reason for the assumed special importance of music with children "is its capacity to evoke physical participation [G. S. Lesser, 1972, p. 252]." It is assumed that the livelier the melody, the stronger the physical response of the child. As the child gets to know the words of the song better, his verbal response also improves.

However, there is one essential condition that must be met in the use of music with children for it to be properly effective as an attention getting device and consequently as a productive tool for the television educator. "A child's attention will be lost if the music is associated with static visual material. To be effective, music and sound effects must be integrated carefully with movement in the program's visual content [G. S. Lesser, 1972, p. 252]." It is assumed that music accompanied by a static visual display, such as a seated orchestra, or music accompanied by a static view of a nature scene will quickly lose the interest of the child. A possible reason for loss of attention by children to music accompanied by static visual displays is that it "violates a child's expectation that televised visual action will accompany what he hears [G. S. Lesser, 1972, p. 252]." Whatever the reasons for the above failure, however, a principle has been established for continued use by the *Sesame Street* production staff: "Synchronize sight and sound to provide cross-modal reinforcement [G. S. Lesser, 1972, p. 252]."

Another tactic for getting children's attention is through appropriate use of repetition. According to G. S. Lesser (1972, p. 252), repetition has the following positive attributes: (1) All new material is not desirable—children want sequences repeated; (2) the familiar recaptures children's attention; (3) the familiar provides opportunities for practice; (4) the familiar teaches television formats and conventions; (5) the familiar provides the bridge from the familiar to the unfamiliar.

Certain types of material seem to hold the child's interest better on repetition than others. Short films and animation that have a step-by-step buildup to an incongruous outcome seem to retain their interest when repeated. It is assumed that such material "permits a child to anticipate each step in turn, while still holding the denouement in abeyance, saving the humorous outcome for the end but giving the child the safety of knowing that it indeed will occur after the child has followed the episode through its earlier steps [G. S. Lesser, 1972, p. 253]." Repetition can also serve as a "mind-stretcher." According to G. S. Lesser (1972, p. 253), the child is able to explore new aspects of repeated segments, even for material that is repeated exactly. In this way the child is ultimately able to understand relatively complex concepts and situations that are beyond his comprehension on a single exposure. *Sesame Street* uses repetition by generally keeping the content constant while varying the format. For instance, the teaching of letter recognition involves having the same letter appear in many different styles and situations.

However, repetition must be used judiciously. According to G. S. Lesser (1972, p. 254), slowly paced and longer segments suffer more with repetition than faster paced and shorter segments. Also, segments with many facets that can be explored over repeated viewings hold up well, or at least until the child has exhausted the different possibilities.

Once the attention of the child is obtained, the next task is to direct the child's attention to the salient features of the material to be learned. The following techniques to direct attention (G. S. Lesser, 1972, p. 254) all depend upon the capability of television to narrow the child's focus: (1) the use of surprise and incongruity; (2) the use of animation and pixillation (speeded-up comic movements); (3) the inclusion of symbolic material to be learned within the televised dramatic action.

G. S. Lesser (1972, p. 254) attributes the effectiveness of surprise in directing children's attention to the following sequence: (1) Surprise violates expectations; (2) the violated expectations pose a puzzle; (3) this puzzle forces a confrontation and, hopefully, an integration of the surprising content with the expected contents. The production techniques for eliciting surprise include: slow-motion and fast-action techniques: pixillation; stop action; reverse or back action; sudden appearances and disappearances, unexpected close-ups; and long or telephoto shots. Comic slapstick segments have been adapted to these techniques. One such sequence shows two adults making a peanut butter and jelly sandwich. To the bewilderment of the adult actors, the ingredients wind up on the outside of the sandwich. Such sequences, he reasons, delight children because "the element of surprise is augmented by the special appeal to the child in knowing that he, for once, knows more than the adult seems to know [p. 255]."

Another device used for surprising the child lies in using the television screen as a magical drawing board. G. S. Lesser (1972) cites as an example the construction of magical line drawings of familiar objects, accompanied by correcting comments by unseen children. The television set seems to be "making mistakes and the children correcting these mistakes provide an unanticipated experience that seems to hold special appeal for young children [p. 256]." Another special technique that seems to attract children is clay animation, where clay is molded and photographed on successive frames of motion picture film so as to give the appearance that the clay has life and movement (p. 256).

Superimposed upon all of these production techniques is a philosophical statement that "All forms of television production for children must find functional ways to bind educational and visual events [G. S. Lesser, 1972, p. 256]." It is assumed that if the content is not related or is "superimposed or peripheral" to the visual events, then "that content surely will be ignored [p. 256]." This position is alternatively phrased by G. S. Lesser as, "Action then, is a key ingredient in children's television [p. 257]." It is assumed, then, that children will ignore inaction on the television screen. Examples of such inaction are "message monologue," where a stationary character speaks a message with no accompanying action, or "message dialogue," such as an interview.

Effective televised instruction requires that the child's attention must not only be caught and focused but also sustained. One method for sustaining attention while teaching involves the effective use of humor. A working tenet of the CTW team seems to be that "what seems funny to young children tends to be physical rather than verbal [G. S. Lesser, 1972, p. 260]." Thus, *Sesame Street* employs variants of slapstick humor, usually with a mild moral message, such as the depiction of villians being outsmarted by their innocent intended victims. For the most part, the harmful outcomes of most slapstick humor are eliminated, as it is assumed that slapstick's appeal to children lies mostly in its effective use of incongruity and surprise rather than in the use of violence (G. S. Lesser, 1972, p. 261).

Another type of humor found effective in sustaining children's attention involves a theme centered around "waiting for the incongruous to occur [G. S. Lesser, 1972, p. 261]." For example, a rocket blast-off is seen that starts off the same way each time, but on each repetition something different and unexpected occurs (except for one successful launching).

In a somewhat restricted sense, the CTW team found language to be another source of humor that could be effectively used to sustain attention. Catch phrases such as the well-known cry of "Cookie!" by the cookie monster seem to be effective. Alliteration and rhyming can also produce comic effects that are effective in sustaining the child's attention. The CTW team found that puns were not generally effective with children. G. S. Lesser (1972, p. 262) speculates that this is so because puns require an understanding of the double meaning of the words, and children do not yet possess a sufficient level of language sophistication.

Humor also serves an auxilliary function of catching the interest of older siblings and parents, who frequently control the use of the television set. In this respect, guest celebrities are also used.

Inducing anticipation, in many instances, produces active participation and is therefore effective in sustaining children's attention. For instance, reciting the alphabet, either very slowly or with hesitations reflecting uncertainty, seems to be effective in getting children to anticipate overtly the next correct letter and then recite it out loud themselves.

Reciting the alphabet, regarded by many educators as a relatively trivial skill, is taught on *Sesame Street* for the following reasons: (1) It becomes a badge of competence for the child; (2) every letter of the alphabet could be included in each show, demonstrating the entire list; (3) naming and visually presenting the letters provides both a review of letters already learned and a preview of letters not yet learned; (4) presenting all of the letters provides an additional opportunity to make difficult visual and auditory discriminations; (5) reciting the alphabet frequently elicits verbal participation by the child (G. S. Lesser, 1972, p. 264).

The CTW team assumes that children's attention is best sustained by the use of diversity in programming. G. S. Lesser (1972) states that "Children lose interest when the program dwells too long on one subject or remains too long at one pace or in one style [p. 265]." Consequently, most of the program format on *Sesame Street* is in brief skits, with little continuity between them. It is assumed by the CTW team that young children have a limited ability to sustain attention on a topic for more than a brief period of time. Maintaining a story line was abandoned after some early efforts appeared to fail in sustaining the children's attention.

According to G. S. Lesser (1972, p. 266), characters that appeal to children must have distinctive and reliable personalities. For instance, James Henson's well-known "muppet" puppets include a large cast of distinctive and reliable, yet diverse, characters. Across diverse settings, each character can be relied upon to be consistent with an assigned role.

In addition to using puppets to attract children's attention, the CTW team assumes that children's attention is also particularly strong when children are used as actors—especially when children are performing an activity, such as solving a problem that allows audience participation. Dubbing children's voices into the sound track also seems to improve children's interest.

Another important consideration in sustaining children's attention involves varying the pace and mood and is summed up by G. S. Lesser (1972) as:

> Both fast-paced and slow-paced material will hold children's attention . . . but a slow peaceful episode is more appealing when surrounded by fast moving episodes than when it follows another slow, quiet piece. Interest in any particular episode is higher if it creates a pace and mood that looks, sounds, and feels different from the one that preceded it [p. 269].

There have been several modifications of *Sesame Street* since G. S. Lesser wrote his article. Fowles and Voyat (1974, p. 69) indicate a change in emphasis of program objectives (greater concentration on symbolic functioning and social-affective development). However, a more recent article (Palmer, 1974) confirms that the general goals and the methods through which *Sesame Street* seeks to attain them remain the same. CTW still retains the same strong commitment to eliciting activity in order to stimulate intellectual development:

> Since it is patently obvious that television does teach, it seems desirable to explore how this capability comes about and in what proper and constructive ways it can be exploited. . . . In spite of the apparent passivity of television viewing, the medium's activity eliciting potential is perhaps the chief basis for whatever instructional value it possesses [Palmer, 1974, p. 322].

Critique

Gerald S. Lesser's description of *Sesame Street* marks the emergence of what might be called "a policy for educating young children by television." As a pioneering effort, greatest attention was devoted to exploring the feasibility of televised instruction for preschoolers. Consequently, there was a focus on principles, rules, and techniques of instruction rather than upon relating to televised instruction the latest knowledge of how children think and learn.

The following is a list, derived from G. S. Lesser's article (1972), of the principal procedures employed by *Sesame Street* to induce learning:

1. Learning may occur through modeling or observational learning. This is referred to as indirect teaching or the use of role modeling and situation shaping to elicit behavioral and attitudinal imitation.

2. Learning may occur through direct teaching, or showing and telling what you intend to teach; through teaching by showing and telling; and finally through showing and telling what was taught.
3. Learning may occur if you arouse children's motivation to learn. Lesser believes that "children learn best what they want to learn." He also believes that children will attend the most to what they best want to learn. Thus, the principal precondition in order for learning to occur is attracting, directing, and sustaining the child's attention. In this case then, attending is loosely equated with learning. In the next section this assumption will be carefully examined. Equating attending with learning may lead to serious errors in programming for young children.

G. S. Lesser also believes restrictions must be placed on programs directed at children because of the unique qualities of their thought processes. Presentations should be kept in tune with the following properties of children's thought:

1. The capacity to dual-attend or the ability to attend to more than one thing at a time.
2. The inability to pick out the essential from the incidental in the intended message.
3. The relative inability to follow extended messages or extended story lines.
4. The lack of ability to attend to programming that contains long periods of inaction, such as adult talk.
5. The inability to understand puns, but the ability to appreciate alliteration and rhyming.

Thus, G. S. Lesser (1972) lists conditions that enhance children's learning from televised presentations. These conditions were, for the most part, empirically derived. The most serious omission, however, is G. S. Lesser's lack of concentration on relating empirically derived conditions of televised instruction to knowledge of young children that is obtainable from current experiment and theory. This is understandable considering the ground-breaking nature of the effort and the consequent concern with more immediate and practical matters. However, with the absence of a sound base in research, *Sesame Street* retains the quality of a series of popular gimmicks with little understanding of whether, how, or why they work. Preliminary efforts have demonstrated the feasibility of televised instruction at the preschool level. The next stage must involve a more intensive effort to link knowledge about preschoolers to improved instruction and curriculum on television.

The focus on production techniques without a clear understanding of their theoretical implications can easily lead producers astray. For instance, the extreme concentration on obtaining high levels of attention will be used to illustrate the potential mistakes inherent in working without a sound theoretical base. Approximately three-fourths of G. S. Lesser's article (1972) is devoted to principles, rules, and techniques to attract, direct, and sustain children's attention. In fact, much of *Sesame Street's* research is devoted to testing the attention qualities of new material.

For instance, Edward L. Palmer, the director of research for CTW, subjects new program material to a distraction test of his own design. His apparatus consists of a TV set and a projector set up adjacent to each other. A different slide, of material considered interesting to children, is shown every $7\frac{1}{2}$ seconds on the slide projector while the program material to be tested plays on the TV set. The percentage of time the child looks away gives an index of distraction and hence a measure of the attention quality of the televised material. Percentages of attention approximating 90% are considered excellent. Program material that does not pass Palmer's distraction test is considered poor material for *Sesame Street.* Thus, the attention qualities of program material are extremely important for the CTW team.

Attention

Television is an immensely popular medium with children. Surveys in the late 1950s indicate that children watch television 1–2 hours a day; elementary school children watch 2–3 hours a day (Schramm *et al.*, 1961). A more recent survey shows that elementary school children watch television 3–4 hours a day and that television is widely available to preschoolers (Lyle & Hoffman, 1972a, 1972b). However, the basis of this attractiveness is little understood. Perhaps a better understanding will be obtained by exploring the mechanisms of attention in young children.

Yendovitskaya (1964/1971a, pp. 65–88), reviewing the Soviet literature on attention, distinguishes two types of attention in young children—involuntary and voluntary. Involuntary attention "depends on the intensity of external influences or on the direct attractiveness of objects"; voluntary attention "is evoked and maintained by motives not directly related to its object [p. 78]." Involuntary attention appears earlier and is, from a developmental point of view, primitive.

> A characteristic aspect of the child's attention during the pre-preschool and the beginning of the preschool age is its nonpremeditated, involuntary nature. Attention is entirely determined by the conditions of the primary qualities of objects, such as their newness, attractiveness, etc. The pre-preschoolers and the younger preschoolers cannot yet isolate various elements of a given situation on the basis of a designated goal corresponding to a given task. Purposeful, deliberate attention begins to form in the child only during the preschool age, becoming during this period more stable, wider in scope, and more productive [p. 68].[2]

[2] This and subsequent quotes cited to Yendovitskaya 1964/1971a are from T. V. Yendovitskaya, Development of attention. In A. V. Zaporazhets and D. B. Elkonin (Eds.),

Yendovitskaya (1964/1971a, pp. 72–75) reports an experiment on the growth in span of voluntary attention in the preschool child. The child views a card with six geometric figures on it for 3 seconds and is asked (1) to determine the most attentive way of examining the drawings so that he can give a verbal report (naming the figures) and (2) to actually select the figures previously presented, which are now mixed with other figures. The child is aftewards asked to lay out the figures in the same spatial arrangement as presented on the card.

There are three cards (five pictures are the same on each card and one is different) and the conditions of presentation are different for the three presentations. The first card is shown without any preparatory work with the child. Before the second card is shown, the child is given the figures and encouraged to identify them verbally. If the child cannot do so, the experimenter helps. Prior to showing the third card, the experimenter organizes a map of visual inspection of the figures for the child so as to facilitate both the examination of all the figures and the identification and spatial recording of the figures on the card.

All three presentations were beyond the grasp of the 3- to 4-year-olds. For the 4-, 5-, and 6-year-olds, attention span and number of correct responses on all tasks increased as the children got older. The organization of a visual map of the figures was the most effective condition (especially for the oldest children). The second presentation was also more effective than the first. Furthermore, distributed attention (attention to both the form and the spatial location of the figures) was accomplished only by the oldest children. Yendovitskaya (1964/1971a) concludes (both for voluntary and involuntary attention) that "the child's attention becomes not only more stable and wider in scope, but also more effective [p. 74]."

The ontogeny of the development of voluntary attention is such that "the adult, with the help of words, expressive gestures, and other actions, attracts the child's attention to various aspects of reality. Gradually, the child learns to utilize these means for organizing his attention, which as a result acquires mediating, voluntary character [Yendovitskaya, 1964/1971a, p. 79]."

The role of the indicatory (expressive) gesture was used successfully to attract the child's attention by Vygotsky (Yendovitskyaya, 1964/1971a, p. 79) in a series of experiments. However, the indicatory gesture is only an initial help in the genesis of voluntary attention. Speech is a decisive influence in this process.

Yendovitskaya (1964/1971a) cites an ingenious experiment by Martsinovskaya that shows that through verbal instruction "it is possible to direct the attention of preschool children to the components of the situation, which by themselves would not attract attention; by so doing they can be distracted from very potent stimuli [pp. 80–82]."

The Psychology of Preschool Children. Cambridge, Mass.: MIT Press, 1971. Reprinted by permission of MIT Press.

Yendovitskaya (1964/1971a) concludes that

> Attention regulation through speech, as early as preschool age, permits one to direct the child's attention somewhat independently of the direct stimulation of external influences, and therefore to make his behavior freer and more adequate to the situation. Verbal presentation of certain goals and tasks, which the child in turn learns to present to himself, assures the isolation of any elements of the situation and the reliance upon them during execution of the action [p. 82].

The use of speech to direct attention is progressive in that successful completion of a task is more difficult as the task becomes more abstract. It is more difficult for the child to direct his attention toward concrete objects according to verbal instructions. It is still more difficult for children to complete an action according to verbal instructions within a verbal scheme.

For instance, Yendovitskaya (1964/1971a, pp. 85–86) cites an experiment by Leontiev where children were required to answer questions concerning the color of seven objects (among other questions). The verbal restrictions were that (1) two colors given in the verbal instructions were not to be named, (2) no color was to be repeated twice.

This task was difficult for both preschool and early school-age children, but more difficult for the preschoolers. When a supportive device of nine colored cards was added, the older children were able to organize their attention around it and drastically reduce their errors. Typically, they would place the two banned colors on the side and inspect them before giving an answer, and turn over the other cards after giving an answer. The younger, preschool children could not use the cards even after being given instructions on how to use them.

Thus, there seems to be a progression in the use of either verbal instructions from an adult or autosignaling by the child. Autosignaling consists of self-initiated verbal designation to direct attention to the salient features of a situation for correct action. In general, increases in linguistic ability seem to be tightly tied to an increase in voluntary attention.

The development of voluntary attention is determined by how well the child's activities are organized.

> How clearly the task of action, its goals, and conditions are specified and whether or not the situational elements, which are significant for the fulfillment of activity, are adequately identified determines the level of the child's attention. The cultivation of voluntary, premeditated attention is one of the important problems of preschool pedagogy and one of the important conditions in the child's preparation for training in school [Yendovitskaya, 1964/1971a, pp. 86–87].

Some of the extensive evidence on the details of the development of attention presented by Soviet researchers might be easily applied in the design of programming for children's television. The two distinct categories of attention discussed by Yendovitskaya are involuntary and voluntary; both categories evolve toward becoming more stable, wider in scope, and more productive. The involuntary form is developmentally more primitive, and the development of the voluntary form is an important condition for the child's preparation for school.

Accepting this dichotomy of forms of attention, one notes that the child can be extremely attentive to a television program in an involuntary manner. For instance, he may watch primarily because of the newness and attractiveness of what is presented rather than because of any effort at deliberate attention, such as trying to isolate various elements of a given situation on the basis of a designated goal corresponding to a given task. This acceptance of an involuntary form of attention by the young child may perhaps be the basis for his extended viewing of television, and in particular of his favorite program—the animated cartoon.

The exclusive acceptance, and even cultivation, by most children's programs of a primitive basis for viewing television is most likely harmful to certain children. The proper approach would be to design television programming so that it continually pushes the child toward more and more developmentally advanced forms of voluntary attention while utilizing the natural growth in the stability, scope, and productiveness of involuntary attention.

Certain efforts in this direction are detected on *Sesame Street*, but CTW's efforts appear scattered and isolated, without theoretical underpinning that would give structure and consistency. *Sesame Street* has become extremely popular and has taken its place beside apple pie in American culture, yet the basis for its popularity may be at the expense of the more difficult, more persistent pedogogical goals essential for success in school.

Surprisingly, there has been very little research on the effects of television on cognitive growth in young children. A brief article by Friedlander, Wetstone, and Scott (1974) depicts a rather simple procedure for determining children's comprehension of television programs. A 3-minute segment of a program is divided into 20 identifiable bits; simple questions are devised about each bit; and these questions are presented to the child viewer in a standard, consecutive fashion as part of a conversation. The questions are divided up into those that demand information content (explicit lines of ongoing action, statements of fact related to the central educational theme, rapidly presented peripheral actions or "asides" not essential to the ongoing activity) and those that refer to modality of presentation (dialogue, visual action and sound effects, combination of dialogue and visual action). Results suggest that more than half the tested children demonstrated comprehension of less than half the tested material. Furthermore, Friedlander *et al.* (1974) state that "the children did comprehend the general flow of ongoing activity but failed to make contact with the central information theme of the program. Rapid action and comic turns calculated to mobilize attention also appeared to have low comprehension payoff [p. 564]."

Friedlander *et al.* suggest that comprehensibility of thematic material might be enhanced if action sequences are designed to embody thematic material rather than decorate it and if irrelevent distractions and details are eliminated from the thematic material.

A central tenet of CTW programming posits a loose correspondence between level of attention and amount of learning. This assumption, as we have seen, is a gross oversimplification of the issue. The distractibility test, by itself, is an insufficient indicator of comprehension and hence of learning. It would seem that what is required is a two-pronged approach using: (1) the distractor test, which measures the attention qualities of the material; and (2) a comprehension test (similar to Friedlander *et al.*) that holds attention constant by telling the child to attend and later measures comprehensibility of the material. The testing of the interaction between the attention qualities of the material and its comprehensibility should lead to important information about the capabilities of educational television for young children.

Some preliminary information regarding the interaction between the attention qualities of program material and its comprehensibility appears to be emerging for the older child (Fowles, 1973; Palmer, 1974). Comprehensibility testing was done by Palmer on segments of *The Electric Company*, using a "freeze" technique. He stopped the presentation at critical junctures and asked the children questions about various aspects of the thematic content. Fowles (1973) used a verbal report method in which children were induced to make comments while watching segments of *The Electric Company*. In both cases the verbal report measures appear to be more appropriate for older children than for the *Sesame Street* target audience. Clearly then, much work remains to be done in investigating the interaction between attention and comprehensibility for the younger child.

IS TELEVISION A PASSIVE TEACHER?

> It now appears that whenever the viewer can be induced to form an hypothesis which is later confirmed or denied on the screen, the learning experience involved is equivalent to that gained through actual two-way communication. Though this is not the kind of learning a child experiences in first-hand encounters with his environment, it is active learning in an intellectual sense [Palmer, 1971b, p. 21].

This comment, from CTW's director of research, is a testimonial to the hope that much of the passive qualities of the television medium will be overcome. Fowles and Voyat (1974) devote a considerable part of their article to this very issue and, in fact, state that television, under proper circumstances, can be an active rather than a passive medium.

> Depending on the content of the program . . . television . . . can be made more or less active. The kind of interaction that transpires between a child and a television set, and its success as instruction, is ultimately determined by the design of the program content and the degree to which it reflects understanding of the developmental process, rather than by inherent properties of the medium itself [p. 69].

Close inspection reveals difficulties in supporting this statement. The kind of interaction between a child and a television set depends not only upon the moods, dispositions, and characteristics of the child, but also upon the special properties of the medium itself. The interaction possibilities of television are specific and limited. Television is clearly a one-way medium—no matter how actively the child reacts to it. No effective conversation can occur between child viewer and television commentator. In fact, recognition of this limitation appears even in Fowles and Voyat's article.

> The issue here is . . . how to accomplish . . . teaching . . . within the peculiar limits of television, limits that preclude . . . active involvement which we have seen is one vital component of the learning process in young children [p. 74].

This contradiction in Fowles and Voyat's article seems to reflect hope on the one hand and apprehension on the other. In fact, neither position is as yet supported by definitive evidence.

Fowles and Voyat attempt to convince the skeptic that television can be effective in inducing conceptual learning and cognitive growth. They do this by first concentrating on the distinct properties of young children's thought processes as derived from Piaget's work (i.e., Piaget & Inhelder, 1966/1971).

Piaget's Theory of the Thought Processes of the Young Child

Preoperational Thought

The young child who is within the target-population age range for *Sesame Street* is considered preoperational by Piaget. The terms preoperational and operational will be used extensively throughout this discussion. Piaget and Inhelder (1969a) define the terms *operational* and *preoperational* as follows: An operation is "that which transforms a state A into a state B leaving at least one property invariant throughout the transformation and allowing the return from B to A thereby cancelling the transformation [p. 156]." At the preoperational level "the transformation is conceived as modifying all the data at once without any conservation. This makes it impossible to return to the point of departure without a new action transforming the whole once more (recreating what has been destroyed, etc.) [p. 156]."

It is important to recognize that there are both an external, or objective, aspect and an internal, or subjective, aspect to these types of thought. A child may fortuitously return an object to its starting point but believe the action to be an entirely new one. Another child may do the same thing, but recognize the action is the same, but inverted. The first instance is an example of preoperational thought and the second of operational thought.

Preoperational children tend to concentrate on the initial and final states of an object rather than its transformation between states. Transformation is defined as a process by which an object undergoes a change of state (i.e., from one shape to another, from one location to another). For example, a young child is shown water being poured from a short fat glass into a tall thin glass. Next to both glasses is another short fat glass, identical to the first short fat glass, containing an identical amount of water. This glass is used as a comparison, so no water is poured from it. Four- and 5-year-olds typically believe the amount to drink has changed. Usually they believe that the tall thin glass has more to drink because it is "higher." Less frequently, they believe the short fat glass has more to drink because it is "fatter." Sometimes they vacillate between the two choices. Children of this age rarely recognize that the quantity of water remains invariant across the transformation. Piaget believes that the 4- to 5-year-old child compares the initial and final states of the water and ignores its transformation. However, children of this age are not ignorant of transformations. Preoperational children might understand there is the same amount of water to drink only if they pour it themselves. They conceive of transformations as creative actions that depend on their own actions. Therefore, a transformation performed by someone else has results that cannot be calculated. In contrast, the older children understand that the amount to drink remains the same regardless of the who pours. For older children, a reversible action has taken place in an objective space, one which can be canceled (poured back) or compensated (taller but thinner). Piaget believes that the remarkable fact of preoperational thought is that it fails to coordinate states and transformations and not that it is static in all its aspects: "Consequently the conception of states is too static, and transformations are endowed with a spurious exaggerated dynamism [Piaget & Inhelder, 1966/1971, p. 369]." In the last analysis, preoperational thought is centered on personal action and hence comprehends all action on the basis of personal action. Only when children finally conceive of actions as taking place in a space that is independent of their own acts can they think of the actions or objects as capable of reversibility and compensation. When this occurs, children can concentrate on a process of change taking place in more than one dimension simultaneously (e.g., height increases but width decreases). This increased ability to concentrate on the general coordinations of actions raises thought to the level of operations.

What this means is that children from about 2 to 7 years of age are fundamentally egocentric—they look at the world from their own point of view. For instance, young children, when asked to construct a display of toys from another child's point of view, will typically say that they cannot do it, or else they will construct it from their own point of view (as if there is no other point of view than their own).

It is also true that the distinction between subjectivity and objectivity is not yet clear in peroperational children. Consequently, their understanding of events and ways of communicating with others tend to be idiosyncratic. For instance, most children believe that the moon follows them around at night, that dreams are real external events, and that mountains were made for little children to climb.

Preoperational children also have a tendency to concentrate or "center" on one aspect of an object or situation and not to concentrate on two or more aspects of a situation simultaneously. They do not integrate the parts into a more comprehensive understanding. For instance, when preoperational children are presented with many flowers—a few roses and many daisies—and are asked, "Are there more daisies than flowers?" they typically respond, "More daisies." They do this in spite of the fact they know that daisies and roses are both flowers.

This is also the period when behavior based upon symbolic processes appears. For instance, children at this time become increasingly occupied with representing reality through fantasy (symbolic play or make-believe) and through drawing, which at this age is more an attempt to represent a personal understanding of reality than an attempt to copy it exactly. Piaget feels that children's activities such as symbolic play and drawing primarily assimilate reality to the needs of the child. In contrast, activities of the child such as imitation and deferred imitation (copying the model after the model has left) primarily accommodate the child to reality. Activities like symbolic play and imitation complement each other; both are necessary for the full expression and development of thought by the child. Consequently, implications from Piagetian theory would suggest that educational television should devote itself both to fantasy activities that encourage make-believe and drawing and to imitative activities that encourage direct copying.

The Transition to Operational Thought

Most school-related tasks require operational thinking. Thus, it is important to discover the conditions that encourage the transition to operational thought. This can best be illustrated by discussing the development of the conservations of substance, weight, and volume. If a ball of clay is transformed into a sausage shape, young children will usually indicate that the sausage has more substance than the ball (in the child's terms, more to eat). Children may give as their reason the fact that the sausage is longer. Furthermore, children tend to believe that the sausage is heavier and will displace a greater volume of water than the ball. Eventually, children discover that something is conserved in the transformation. The first discovery is that substance is conserved. Much later children discover that weight is conserved. Their last discovery is that volume is conserved.

What seems most amazing is that the earliest acquired understanding of conservation is not measurable by the child and that the other two, although they are acquired later, can be easily measured. The child can readily weigh the clay shapes or pick them up and estimate their weight and volume. Yet, substance is not in any way measurable—it is purely a product of reasoning.

To formalize the idea still further, Piaget (1971) draws upon the concept of logicomathematical experience to explain such acquisitions.

> In logicomathematical experience the information is drawn not from the object but from the subject's coordination of his own actions, i.e., the operations that the subject effects on the objects [p. 7].

Piaget (1971) describes a childhood experience of a great mathematician:

> While counting some pepples, he arranged them in a line, counted them from left to right and found that there were ten. He put them in a circle, counted around the circle and found there were still ten. With mounting enthusiasm, he counted around from the other direction and there were still ten. It was a great intellectual experience for him [p. 7].

This description of a child's first understanding of the concept of number represents a powerful advance in thought. Thought at this level, however, is still restricted to what Piaget refers to as the stage of concrete operations. That is, thought at this stage is still restricted to operations on actual objects only. In the final developmental stage, the stage of formal operations, the person does not require actual objects. For instance, the person can deal with the formal properties of numbers in thought alone.

Thus, operations depend for their development on logicomathematical experience, and this experience requires active, engaged exploratory activity among the world of objects. For Piaget, action represents the soil from which thought blossoms.

Conflict and the Development of Thought

Piaget argues from numerous experiments that cognitive growth is most likely to occur when children are presented with conditions that create cognitive conflict in them. In other words, children must be able to partially understand an experience. This partial understanding creates conflict, and the effort to resolve it induces cognitive growth. This suggests that cognitive conflict must be specific to the intellectual level of children, since what the children partially understand is determined by their level of intellectual development. Children must recognize the problem and actively engage themselves in its solution. Kohlberg (1968) concurs on the need of the experience to fit the child:

> Piaget's theory suggests that the child's sensitivity to environmental stimulation tends to increase with development. Each level of cognitive development represents the capacity to be stimulated by, or to experience something new. The child can only be stimulated by events or stimuli which he can partly assimilate, that is, fit into his already existing cognitive structures [p. 1046].

Bower (1974) supports Piaget on the key role that conflict plays in generating cognitive development.

> We have followed Piaget in arguing that conflict is the motive force in development. Conflict arises whenever the infant has two incompatible ways of dealing with the same situation. The conflict thus engendered produces the step to the next stage of cognitive functioning [p. 235].

Piaget and Instructional Television

Deductions from Piaget's theory may facilitate the search for effective educational television for young children. Optimal use of television implies developing program material that reflects the special characteristics of young children's thought. The main thread of the argument is as follows:

1. The television experience must constitute an intrusion on the child's existing cognitive structure.
2. Activities of the child that lead to a resolution of this intrusion generate cognitive growth.
3. Once cognitive growth has occurred, subsequent television experiences capable of generating further cognitive growth must match the more advanced coping capacities of the child.
4. Thus, cognitive growth is seen as gradual but progressive, and the child's sensitivity to televised events is seen as limited but increasing.
5. Therefore, the critical issue is the extent to which televised instruction can induce cognitive conflicts in children.

From previous discussions in this section and in the section devoted to attention it is apparent that children are restricted in the type of events that they perceive as conflictual. The prototype of conflict at this age involves a choice of behaviors involving objects and their successful manipulations. Eventually, through active manipulation of objects, the child discovers rules that generate a more general understanding of objects and their states and transformations.

The main problem, then, is that the prototype of learning for young children involves goal-oriented activity mostly at the level of behavior. Television is not eminently suited for initiating this type of behavior in the child.

However, there might be ways of bypassing this dilemma. Young children seem to be extremely robust in the ways in which they learn. Gouin-Decarie (1969) reports that limbless Thalidomide infants were approximately normal in sensorimotor development at the age of 2 years. These children, in order to perform the tests concerned with the concept of permanent object, would lift cloths with their teeth to discover objects hidden beneath them. Thus, if the normal path to cognitive development is blocked, the infant seems capable of developing cognitively through other paths.

A similar argument may apply to televised instruction. Learning from watching television might substitute for more active forms or engagement with the world of objects and people. However, there are a number of reasons, centered in the young child's thought processes themselves, why this argument might not be valid:

1. Children's thought is characterized by *animism*. For instance, a child might believe that the sun and moon are alive in the same sense that people are alive.
2. Children's thought is characterized by *artificialism*. For instance, a child might believe that the sun was formed by an outside agent, such as adults, and not by a natural process.
3. Children's thought is characterized by *participation*. For instance, a child might believe in some continuing connection between the activities of things and people, such as a belief that the sun started when people became alive.
4. Children's thought is characterized by *syncretism*. That is, children have a tendency to connect a series of separate ideas into one whole, without recognizing that the ideas are not logically connected. They fail to recognize that there is a difference between an objective connection between two events and a subjective, purely personal, way of connecting two events. For instance, children have been observed to respond to an ambiguous figure that can be perceived alternatively as a pair of scissors or a human face (but not both at the same time) with the following comment, "It's a man and somebody threw a pair of scissors in his face [Piaget & Inhelder, 1966/1971, p. 40]."
5. Children's thought is characterized by *juxtaposition*. That is, they have a tendency to describe events and parts of objects as isolated, ignoring the relationships between them. For instance, a child may draw a bicycle showing the pedals, chain, and wheels but not connect them.

These characteristics of preoperational thought indicate that for young children almost any event that does not involve direct contradiction at the level of behavior is considered possible. In its early stages children's thought is characterized by a failure to recognize contradiction and conflict, especially in events that do not involve consequences affecting ongoing activities with objects and people. Events occurring on a television screen do not, in general, affect a child's ongoing activities among objects and people. Consequently, television is weakest in the exact spot where children need the most help.

The progression of children's thought requires a successful transition from preoperational thought to concrete operational thought. This transition requires, as a major component, the actions of the child on the world of objects. It is felt by some that television ought to excel in facilitating this transition. According to Fowles and Voyat (1974),

> television can bring a whole arsenal of visual and audio-visual "tricks" to bear to create surprising, incongruous, and conflictual situations which are likely to elicit active responses. And these responses, given appropriate stimuli, can be of a sort to contribute to major changes in cognitive structure [p. 78].

Children's Television Workshop (CTW) is also committed to this belief, as is indicated by the following:

> One significant form of activity television can elicit is intellectual activity. . . . Some examples of intellectual activities include integrating separately presented items of information, anticipating upcoming events, forming new concepts, imputing motives and intentions to characters, following progressively developed dramatic and instructional presentations, and guessing answers to questions. The viewer may also take an active role in evaluating relationships between premises and conclusions, between information given and interpretations made of it, and between behavioral ideals and the actual behaviors carried out by the performers, or he may relate televised information to his own previous experiences and his future plans.
>
> The notion that certain activities containing a motoric component can be learned only through direct experience is also questionable. For example, learning how to construct alphabetical characters may be more dependent on practice in scanning over the configuration of the letter, on extended or repeated exposure to the letter, and on having an occasion to make and correct the more common errors than on motor activity itself. . . . We need to know more about the possibilities television offers for simulation of learning conditions in which direct, "hands-on" experience has traditionally been considered essential [Palmer, 1974, pp. 322–323].

Palmer is hopeful that television can elicit intellectual activity but presents little confirming evidence. Furthermore, Palmer does not seem to be distinguishing between the capacities of 3- to 5-year-old children and older children. The examples Palmer gives of hoped-for intellectual activities are, in many instances, well beyond the capabilities of the average child in the younger age range.

It might be argued that the goal of instructional television is to help children initiate such activities. There is an important distinction between eliciting and initiating intellectual activities. In eliciting advanced intellectual activities, the activities are presumed to exist in the child in a latent form. It is the task of the television producer to stimulate the child to use them. In initiating advanced intellectual activities, the child is presumed not yet to have the capability of performing certain activities. The child must be instructed in how to generate these for himself. The foregoing quote shows Palmer's emphasis on the eliciting capability of instructional television, with a corresponding lack of emphasis on the capability of television to initiate intellectual activities. To initiate advanced intellectual activities, it is necessary to determine the ways in which they are formed and then to attempt to duplicate them via television instruction. It is a lack of research in this area that holds back current efforts at instructional television for young children.

The ways children develop intellectually in the nontelevision environment may not be subject to duplication via television. There is no evidence that television, given its passive qualities, can prove effective in accomplishing this goal with young children. Given the evidence of how children develop intellectually, there would have to be a massive shift away from the typical ways children learn from their own activities and toward the ways that are possible through television. Perhaps this can be accomplished, but it remains to be proven.

Since Piaget has never explored in detail how television might affect cognitive growth, deductions from his theory by others are necessarily speculative. Palmer, and Fowles and Voyat are optimistic. I am cautious. A careful scrutiny of the literature on early child development (including the Genevan and Soviet literature) leads to a cautious conclusion that televised instruction of preschoolers is possible given lots of intensive planning. If one accepts the Piagetian position, those attempting to teach young children through television must work very hard indeed to generate cognitive conflicts in their young viewers. It has yet to be established that such generation of conflict is even possible. If such conflicts are generated, children must then find appropriate ways to test, revise, reconstruct, and reformulate these conflicts on real objects and people. All of this is necessary because this is the way children learn.

The analysis of the preoperational nature of young children's thought leads to the likelihood that television instruction, in most instances, will be grossly insufficient. Good pedagogical technique seems to involve much more than is easily obtainable from a television set. Duckworth (1964), writing within the Piagetian tradition, concludes that good teaching

> must involve presenting the child with situations in which he himself experiments, in the broadest sense of that term—trying things out to see what happens, manipulating things, manipulating symbols, posing questions and seeking his own answers, reconciling what he finds one time with what he finds at another, comparing his findings with those of other children [p. 2].

Dual Audio Television

Terry Borton (1971) is experimenting, with modest success, with a new phenomenon he calls dual audio television. He is concerned that a child can watch television for hours, day after day, observing life and listening to language, and yet learn so little. Borton quotes Courtney Cazden (1966), who speculates on the reasons:

> "Why isn't this extra language stimulation from TV more beneficial? Is the critical difference passive listening to a monologue versus active participation in a dialogue? If so, what is the supposed benefit of listening to stories? Is attention to language reduced when it is embedded in the context of constantly changing stimuli [p. 65]."[3]

Borton believes that we must transform TV into an active medium. He seems to have accomplished this in a limited way.

> Program related information and individualized feedback can be provided for young children by supplying a dual audio track for all commercial broadcasting. The child's part of such a system would be a simple, cheap, steel-encased transistor radio, equipped with an ear-bug and preset for a few special wavelengths . . . for each TV channel—the child would hear a broadcast aimed at helping him understand whatever happened to be playing. . . . The dual audio announcer would weave his commentary in between the verbal script and music of the commercial program. His function would not be to be a school-teacher. Instead, he would provide a rich variety of incidental information relating child and TV program [p. 66].

Through a variety of techniques the dual audio feedback announcer brings the child into active participation with what is being watched. As Borton (1971) indicates, "the dual audio announcer can help children to deduce inferences by asking, 'What happened?' or he can generate expectations by, 'What's going to happen?' [pp. 69–70]" Questions can be phrased that are answered later in the program, although the child answers immediately. Introspection can be enhanced by asking, "Would you do that?" The announcer can even be wrong sometimes.

Pilot studies made in group settings demonstrate the active nature of watching TV with dual audio track. Borton observes that children are no longer sitting in front of the television set as if hypnotized. They hold a dialogue with the announcer and ask each other, parents, and siblings for assistance in answering the questions. Increased movements, and imitations of the facial expressions and bodily movements of characters are observed.

Borton reports a consistent general pattern of results from some very brief

[3] This and subsequent quotes cited to Borton, 1971 are from T. Borton, Dual audio television. *Harvard Educational Review*, 1971, *41*(1), 64–78. Copyright © 1971 by Terry Borton.

laboratory experiments. Students using dual audio made half as many mistakes in replying to questions concerning program content as those without it. The dual audio students were also considerably more active and made many more comments and gestures related to the content of the program. They also seemed to enjoy what they were watching more than the children without the dual audio. Borton reports more laughing and giggling as the children were helped by the announcer to make connections between their lives and the show they were seeing.

There are, of course, many problems in determining the exact meaning of these results. This author visited Borton's laboratory and found his research intriguing. Borton's work is just beginning, and there are many hypotheses to be tested, such as the effect of dual audio on attention and comprehension. It would be interesting to determine how much of the effects are produced by novelty and also to determine what effects different audio strategies would produce. However, given the preliminary data that Borton has collected, dual audio television seems to be a logical development.

TELEVISION AND THE DISADVANTAGED CHILD

The extent to which disadvantaged children do poorly in school is best illustrated with the data obtained from the Coleman Report. In 1966 the Coleman Report, whose actual title is *Equality of Educational Opportunity*, hit the educational community like a storm. In the process it shattered the belief that our schools exert a strong effect independent of the child's background and general social context. The data were gathered from 4000 public schools, and more than 645,000 pupils were involved. Analysis was made at the kindergarten, third-, sixth-, ninth-, and twelfth-grade levels. In comparison to previous efforts, the Coleman Report is by far the most massive survey ever undertaken in this field.

Coleman analyzed differences in school environment and related them to academic achievement among the disadvantaged. He concluded that differences between schools accounts for only a small fraction of the differences in pupil achievement.

The academic achievement of the minority groups in comparison to the white population is illustrated in Table 2.1. Minority-group children are far behind at the different grade levels. There is a progressively increasing deficit in all three areas Coleman examined: verbal ability, reading comprehension, and math achievement.

I quote what I believe is the most important of Coleman's conclusions:

> Taking all of these results together, one implication stands out above all: That
> schools bring little influence to bear on a child's achievement that is independent of

TABLE 2.1

Number of Grade Levels Behind the Average White in the Metropolitan Northeast, for All Groups

Race and area	Verbal ability			Reading comprehension			Math achievement		
	Gr. 6	Gr. 9	Gr. 12	Gr. 6	Gr. 9	Gr. 12	Gr. 6	Gr. 9	Gr. 12
White, nonmetropolitan									
South	0.7	1.0	1.5	0.5	0.8	1.0	0.7	9.0	1.4
Southwest	.3	.4	.8	.1	.3	.5	.3	.3	.8
North	.2	.4	.9	.2	.3	.5	.2	.1	.8
White, metropolitan									
Northeast	—	—	—	—	—	—	—	—	—
Midwest	.1	.0	.4	.1	.1	.3	.1	.0	.1
South	.5	.5	.9	.3	.3	.4	.4	.6	1.2
Southwest	.5	.6	.7	.4	.7	.4	.6	.7	.6
West	.3	.3	.5	.2	.5	.8	.3	.3	.8
Negro, nonmetropolitan									
South	2.5	3.9	5.2	2.7	3.7	4.9	2.6	3.7	6.2
Southwest	2.0	3.3	4.7	2.4	3.3	4.5	2.4	3.2	5.6
North	1.9	2.7	4.2	2.2	2.6	3.8	2.2	2.8	5.2
Negro, metropolitan									
Northeast	1.6	2.4	3.3	1.8	2.6	2.9	2.0	2.8	5.2
Midwest	1.7	2.2	3.3	1.8	2.3	2.8	2.1	2.5	4.7
South	2.0	3.0	4.2	2.1	3.0	3.9	2.4	3.1	5.6
Southwest	1.9	2.9	4.3	2.1	3.0	4.1	2.3	3.0	5.7
West	1.9	2.6	3.9	2.1	3.1	3.8	2.4	3.1	5.3
Mexican American	2.0	2.3	3.5	2.4	2.6	3.3	2.2	2.6	4.1
Puerto Rican	2.7	2.9	3.6	3.1	3.3	3.7	2.8	3.4	4.8
Indian American	1.7	2.1	3.5	2.0	2.3	3.2	2.0	2.4	3.9
Oriental American	.9	1.0	1.6	1.0	.9	1.0	1.0	.4	.9

his background and general social context; and that this very lack of an independent effect means that the inequalities imposed on children by their home, neighborhood, and peer environment are carried along to become the inequalities with which they confront adult life at the end of school. For equality of educational opportunity through the schools must imply a strong effect of schools that is independent of the child's immediate social environment, and that strong effect is not present in American schools [Coleman, 1966, p. 325].

The middle-class child has done well in school before educational television, or for that matter before television. The minority child has, in general, done poorly in school and a significant question is, "Can quality instructional television designed for preschool years improve his chances of success?"

CTW believes that their approach, embodied in *Sesame Street* and *The Electric Company,* can achieve some modest measure of success. Essentially, they teach those skills that are directly necessary for school (i.e., numbers, letters, basic reading skills, etc.) plus a smattering of skills in the social-affective domain. However, the conclusions of the Coleman Report imply that such an approach might not be effective. It is not school skills that the minority child is deficient in but inequalities imposed on children by their home, neighborhood, and peer environment. Instructional television would have to overcome these effects. Coleman reports that our schools fail to overcome these effects. Can instructional television for disadvantaged preschool children do better?

Instructional television has advantages that our schools do not possess: (1) It reaches the child at a very early age, before neighborhood and peer environment influences solidify and (2) it enters directly into the home, where it is possible to affect the home environment. It seems, then, that a direct implication of Coleman's findings would be the need to exert every possible influence on the home atmosphere at the earliest possible age with the hope that this will eventually reverse the statistics showing school failure. Notice that this implies instructional television for young children *and* for parents.

The CTW approach to instructional television implicates the schools as the direct cause of failure for minority pupils. Pointing the accusatory finger is clearly not logical, and at the very least not productive. Unless we are willing to posit a national plot against minority pupils or some national form of racism or some genetic inferiority, it is difficult to explain how our schools can successfully educate one class of pupils and do so miserably with others. The clearest and most logical argument is that success in school depends more on what the child brings to school than what the school brings to the child.

Therefore, the approach adopted by CTW, which is to teach these early school skills and give the child a "head start" and hopefully propel him into later school success, does not seem logical. The Coleman Report indicates that this model is deficient and does not work for our schools. There is little evidence that a model that fails for our schools will work when applied from a television set. The burden of proof lies with CTW. Their research efforts are analyzed in Chapter 3. The efforts of others to test instructional television designed for the disadvantaged will be presented next.

The Evidence Against *Sesame Street*

Herbert Sprigle (1971, 1972) tested the following two hypotheses suggested by the research department of Children's Television Workshop: (1) *Sesame Street* can prepare poverty children for first grade; (2) *Sesame Street* can substantially narrow the achievement gap that now exists between the poor and the middle-class child.

In his earlier study Sprigle took 24 pairs of poverty children 1 year before entering first grade and randomly selected them into an experimental and a control group, matched by Binet IQ, age, background, parent education, and income defined by OEO guidelines for low-income families. The experimental children (E1) were exposed to *Sesame Street* each day for 1 year as the educational component of their kindergarten program. Additionally, their teachers used the follow-up activities suggested by Children's Television Workshop and also sent home activities recommended by CTW for parents. The control children (C1) were exposed to educational activities in a game format, four children per group, 15 to 30 minutes a day, with a teacher, with equal or more emphasis on emotional and social development. They were not exposed to *Sesame Street*. The differences between these two groups were evaluated 3 weeks after the start of first grade, as well as after the completion of the 130 *Sesame Street* programs for the experimental group, with a similar time gap for the control group. The Metropolitan Readiness Test, which measures many of the items *Sesame Street* purports to teach as well as readiness for first grade, was used. The comparison on the six subtests and total of the Metropolitan is reported in Part A of Table 2.2.

In Part B of Table 2.2, the scores of the same experimental group (E1) are compared with those of their more advantaged classmates (C2) in first grade, who are children from above the poverty guidelines and thus not eligible for Head Start, with parents who mostly have a high school education or slightly less and are employed as blue-collar or white-collar workers.

Sprigle also had available a sample of children in the same kindergarten as the *Sesame Street* children (E1), but 1 year before *Sesame Street* was available. These children (C3) were selected in exactly the same way as the *Sesame Street* children (E1), went to the same classroom, and had the same teacher. The only difference was "the teachers did not have *Sesame Street* and had to fill that gap doing other things [Sprigle, 1971, p. 207]." When these control children (C3) went to the first grade, they were given the Metropolitan Readiness Test (1 year

TABLE 2.2

Mean Scores on the Metropolitan Readiness Test, Administered in the Third Week of First Grade to One-Year Exposure Group[abc]

	Comparison	Word meaning	Listening	Matching	Alphabet	Numbers	Copying	Total
(A)	E1: *Sesame Street* versus	4.76***	6.38***	5.57***	6.76***	7.42***	3.42***	34.38***
	C1: No *Sesame Street*, game-format school program	7.75	11.04	10.08	15.70	16.08	9.70	70.37
(B)	E1: *Sesame Street* versus	4.76***	6.38***	5.57 N.S.	6.76*	7.42**	3.47***	34.38***
	C2: Middle-class first-grade classmates of E1	7.52	9.52	6.32	10.41	11.00	7.70	52.41
(C)	E1: *Sesame Street* versus	4.76 N.S.	6.38 N.S.	5.57 N.S.	6.76 N.S.	7.42 N.S.	3.47 N.S.	34.38 N.S.
	C3: No *Sesame Street*, same classroom and teacher, but 1 year earlier	5.45	7.45	5.80	6.30	8.00	3.90	36.70

[a]This and the tables on pages 78 and 79 are adapted by permission from the following articles by H. Sprigle: Can poverty children live on "Sesame Street"?, *Young Children*, 1971, 26(4), 202–217, and Who wants to live on "Sesame Street"?, *Young Children*, 1972, 28(2), 91–109. Copyright © 1971 and 1972, respectively, National Association for the Education of Young Children, 1834 Connecticut Avenue, N.W., Washington, D.C. 20009.

[b]Comparisons are between (E1) poverty children exposed to *Sesame Street*; (C1) poverty children exposed to a game-format cognitive-enrichment program; (C2) middle-class first-grade classmates of E1; and (C3) poverty children not exposed to *Sesame Street* but in the same classroom with the same teacher 1 year earlier.

[c]N.S. = not statistically significant

* $p < .05$
** $p < .01$
*** $p < .001$

before the E1 children). The comparison between the E1 and C3 children is given in Part C of Table 2.2.

Sprigle (1972) followed the progress of the original sample children through the first grade. At the close of first grade Sprigle tested the children using the Stanford Achievement Test, which measures the major goals of the first-grade curriculum. The post-first-grade comparison between the E1 children and the C2 children appears in Part A of Table 2.3; and the post-first-grade comparison between the E1 children and the C3 children appears in Part B of Table 2.3.

Sprigle (1972) conducted a second study, whose major purpose was to examine the effects of length of viewing of *Sesame Street.* As in the first study, he selected 24 pairs of poverty children, matched as in the earlier sample. One group of children (E2) watched *Sesame Street* each day in their day-care program for 2 consecutive years (the same treatment as the E1 children who watched for 1 year); the other group (C4) were exposed to 2 years of a structured curriculum as the cognitive component of their program, which was similar to the program described for the C1 children. The comparison between the E2 and C4 children is presented in Part A of Table 2.4; the comparison between the E1 and E2 children in Part B of Table 2.4; and the comparison between the E2 children and their middle-class classmates (C5) in Part C of Table 2.4.

Neither of the two hypotheses Sprigle tested was supported by the results of his research. The children who viewed *Sesame Street* for 1 year (E1) scored substantially lower on the Metropolitan than did the game-format children (C1), or their middle-class first-grade classmates (C2). Furthermore, the *Sesame Street* children (E1) who viewed only 1 year had comparable scores on the Metropolitan to a control group of children (C3) who were in the same classroom and had the same teacher 1 year earlier. The only difference between E1 and C3 was that *Sesame Street* was not yet available for the latter group.

The Metropolitan's validity as an indicator of first-grade performance has been questioned. The follow-up results indicate that the Metropolitan is valid for Sprigle's sample. At the conclusion of first grade the E1 children do less well on the Stanford Achievement Test than their middle-class first-grade classmates (C2). They also show no difference from the C3 children, who were 1 year ahead of them and had the same classroom and teacher but no *Sesame Street.*

Sprigle (1972) notes teachers' comments (concerning the Stanford Achievement Test) that "half of the *Sesame Street* graduates could not read or perform simple arithmetic problems. Many of them marked the test booklet indiscriminately [p. 95]." Also, the teachers report that "these same children did not seem to know what school was all about; they just did not have the affective, social and cognitive tools to cope with a first grade classroom [p. 95]."

Sprigle's later study (1972) gives additional support to his earlier findings (Table 2.4). *Sesame Street* children who viewed for 2 years (E2) still do less well

TABLE 2.3
Mean Grade Scores on the Stanford Achievement Test, Administered at the End of First Grade[a][b]

	Comparison	Word meaning	Paragraph meaning	Vocabulary	Spelling	Work-study skills	Arithmetic
(A)	E1: *Sesame Street*	1.3***	1.2***	1.3***	1.3***	1.4***	1.3***
	versus						
	C2: Middle-class first-grade classmates of E1	2.1	1.9	2.4	2.3	2.8	2.2
(B)	E1: *Sesame Street*	1.3 N.S.	1.2 N.S.	1.3 N.S.	1.3 N.S.	1.4 N.S.	1.3 N.S.
	versus						
	C3: No *Sesame Street*, same classroom and teacher, but 1 year earlier	1.4	1.4	1.4	1.3	1.5	1.5

[a]Comparisons are between (E1) poverty children exposed to *Sesame Street*; (C2) middle-class first-grade classmates of E1; and (C3) poverty children not exposed to *Sesame Street* but in the same classroom with the same teacher 1 year earlier.
[b]N.S. = not statistically significant
* $p < .05$
** $p < .01$
*** $p < .001$

TABLE 2.4
Mean Scores on the Metropolitan Readiness Test, Administered in the Third Week of First Grade to Two-Year Exposure Groups[a,b]

	Comparison	Word meaning	Listening	Matching	Alphabet	Numbers	Copying	Total
(A)	E2: *Sesame Street*, 2 years versus	5.41 N.S.	5.91 N.S.	3.29**	7.95**	6.83 N.S.	2.33**	31.75**
	C4: No *Sesame Street*, structured cognitive curriculum, 2 years	4.79	7.00	5.54	11.50	8.29	5.33	42.45
(B)	E1: *Sesame Street*, 1 year versus	4.76 N.S.	5.95 N.S.	5.14 N.S.	6.76 N.S.	7.42 N.S.	3.52 N.S.	34.38 N.S.
	E2: *Sesame Street*, 2 years	5.41	5.91	3.29	7.95	6.83	2.33	31.75
(C)	E2: *Sesame Street*, 2 years versus	5.42***	5.91***	3.29***	7.95***	6.83***	2.33***	31.75***
	C5: Middle-class first-grade classmates of E2	9.42	10.62	8.08	13.37	10.45	7.04	59.00

[a]Comparisons are between (E2) poverty children exposed to *Sesame Street* for 2 years; (C4) poverty children exposed to 2 years of a structured cognitive curriculum; (E1) poverty children exposed to *Sesame Street* for 1 year; and (C5) middle-class first-grade classmates of E2.
[b]N.S. = not statistically significant

* $p < .05$
** $p < .01$
*** $p < .001$

on the Metropolitan than control children (C4) who were exposed to 2 years of a structured cognitive curriculum; and these *Sesame Street* children also do less well than their middle-class first-grade classmates (C5). Furthermore, no difference on the Metropolitan is reported between those children who watched *Sesame Street* for 1 year (E1) and those who watched for 2 years (E2).

Critique

Gerry Ann Bogatz and Samuel Ball (1971, Vol. 1, pp. 20–21) have replied to Sprigle's 1971 study as follows:

1. There are only 24 matched pairs in Sprigle's experiment. This might be enough for a pilot study, but not enough, by itself, to challenge the *Sesame Street* research results.

2. The Stanford–Binet IQ was used at pretest and the less reliable Goodenough Draw-a-Person Test IQ at posttest. Both groups were matched on the Stanford–Binet IQ. The posttest IQ scores for Sprigle's first sample were:

	male	female
Sesame Street viewers	84	82
Sesame Street nonviewers	120	110

The posttest difference in IQ scores could reflect two possibilities, and Bogatz and Ball question both of them. They ask whether such a large decline in IQ could occur as a result of 130 hours of exposure to *Sesame Street* over a 6-month period. They also ask whether Sprigle's game-format alternative to *Sesame Street* could cause such a startling IQ improvement. On this basis, Bogatz and Ball doubt the credibility of Sprigle's results. They speculate that: (a) Sprigle's initial matching was unsound; (b) Sprigle's random pairings of children into experimental and control groups may not have been sound. As Bogatz and Ball state, "Hopefully, the pairs were systematically matched, and then randomly one member was assigned to one group and the matchee to the other group. It does not seem as though this was done [p. 21]."[4]

3. In Sprigle's study the children are 5- and 6-year-olds. *Sesame Street* is aimed at 4-year-old children, and the CTW research data indicate that the program is most effective with 3- and 4-year-old children.

4. Sprigle's comparison is specious. Sprigle's control group received an intensive small-group experience. *Sesame Street* was never intended as a substitute for Head Start enrichment programs.

[4] This and subsequent quotes cited to Bogatz and Ball, 1971 are from G. A. Bogatz and S. Ball, *The Second Year of Sesame Street: A Continuing Evaluation*, Vol. 1. Princeton, N.J.: Educational Testing Service, 1971. © Children's Television Workshop, 1971.

5. Sprigle's sample is not within the *Sesame Street* target sample. *Sesame Street* is intended for at-home preschoolers. Sprigle's sample were school-children, most likely receiving excellent educational experience during viewing.
6. In conclusion, Bogatz and Ball interpret Sprigle's results (assuming faith in the matching procedures) as meaning that "*Sesame Street* as a preschool TV show is not as educationally effective for 5- and 6-year-old children viewing in classroom groups as the alternative of an educational program presented by an experienced adult working with groups of four children [p. 21]."

Reply to Critique

These criticisms were leveled before Sprigle's second study (1972) was available. Sprigle has responded to some of these criticisms in his later research.

Although Sprigle's sample is small, he has doubled it with his second study. It does not seem that any individual researcher will have the resources to test *Sesame Street* using a large sample, stratified appropriately on a national scale. Therefore, all such studies as Sprigle's will be subject to such criticisms.

Sprigle's use of the Goodenough Draw-a-Person Test seems to have been motivated by other considerations than obtaining a posttest IQ score. The Draw-a-Person Test measures the child's awareness of himself. It is also a measure of imagination and creative expression. The results on the Draw-a-Person Test in Sprigle's (1971, p. 100) study, for children who watched *Sesame Street* 1 year and 2 years, respectively, reveal:

	IQ		Raw score	
	male	female	male	female
Sesame Street viewers for 1 year	84	82	12.33	12.43
Sesame Street viewers for 2 years	83	82	11.35	12.38

These differences are not statistically significant. The raw scores indicate the average number of body parts the children drew and are a measure of body image. A score of approximately 17 for boys and 21 for girls is considered normal. The conclusion is that both groups have a poor body image.

Sprigle has not stated in either of his articles on *Sesame Street* exactly how he matched subjects. This remains to be clarified.

The criticism that Sprigle's subjects were too old ignores the fact that *Sesame Street* is intended for preschool children in general. The *Sesame Street* research results indicate that the most favorable educational effect is with the 3-year-olds, but the show is also intended for older preschool children. If Sprigle had used younger children, he would have had to wait 2 to 3 years to test them when they entered first grade. However, we note in Sprigle's later study (1972) that he used 4-year-olds who watched *Sesame Street* for 2 years, and his results are still highly unfavorable.

The contention that Sprigle's comparisons are specious because he used a control group of children who received a small-group experience ignores the totality of his findings. Sprigle demonstrated that the *Sesame Street* children were not prepared for first grade. In comparison, Sprigle argues that the game-format children were better prepared, and their middle-class classmates were, in general, also prepared for first grade.

It is also unfair to criticize Sprigle's sample as being outside the target sample of at-home preschoolers who watch *Sesame Street*. If anything, Sprigle's sample is biased against himself (in comparison to the CTW research sample) in that the children watched under ideal learning conditions. The fact that Sprigle's subjects failed in their preparation for school, even under these ideal conditions, raises serious questions about the educational applicability of *Sesame Street*.

Sprigle's second study (1972), which includes a post-first-grade follow-up of the original sample, indicates fairly conclusively that these *Sesame Street* children did not receive a sufficient educational experience to change failure to success in their school work. This is a critical issue, and limiting Sprigle's conclusion to the particularities of his sample only serves to obscure the basic questions that he asks: (1) Does *Sesame Street* prepare poverty children for first grade? (2) Does *Sesame Street* narrow the achievement gap that now exists between the poor and the middle-class child?

Sprigle's answer to both of these questions is a clear no.

Comprehensive Intervention

The Home-Oriented Preschool Education Program (HOPE) is an instructional system developed by Appalachia Educational Laboratory (AEL) designed for use with Appalachia's poor (Bertram *et al.*, 1971a). The program, intended for use with 3-, 4-, and 5-year-old children, has three parts: (1) 30-minute television lessons broadcast into the home each day; (2) weekly home visits by a paraprofessional who discusses the program with parents and children and who delivers instructional materials; (3) group instruction provided once a week in a mobile classroom. The program underwent 3 years of field testing (1968–1971), and summative evaluation involved tests in language (the Illinois Test of Psycholinguistic Abilities), cognition (the Peabody Picture Vocabulary Test and a criterion-referenced instrument produced by AEL, the Home-Oriented Preschool Test), psychomotor development (Marianne Frostig Developmental Test of Visual Perception), and social skills (using a specially designed interaction technique).

The HOPE project was designed for a regional population of 25,000 preschoolers. In the summative evaluation the children were divided into four treatment groups: (1) TV, home visitor, and mobile classroom (TV–HV–MC); (2) TV and home visitor (TV–HV); (3) TV only; (4) control. There were, respectively, 95, 130, 66, and 103 children in each group.

At the conclusion of the 3-year field test there were significant treatment effects favoring the TV–HV group. A brief summary of cognitive growth in the four treatment groups at the conclusion of field testing indicates that the TV–HV group did best (mean = 30.68); next best was the TV–HV–MC group (mean = 29.85); next best was the control group (mean = 27.53); and last was the TV-only group (mean = 23.70). The test used in the calculation was a subtest of the Home-Oriented Preschool Test.

AEL's overall conclusion is that TV alone does not provide sufficient intellectual stimulation, but TV combined with other home-oriented treatments can provide positive effects. For the convenience of the reader a listing of AEL's *Technical Reports* is given at the end of the references.

Critique

It is impossible to compare AEL's results with CTW's because their program, called *Around the Bend*, differs greatly form *Sesame Street*. *Around the Bend* focuses on a young woman who becomes a friend of the viewer and who has experiences that children are also likely to encounter in their own homes. According to AEL, the activities of the young woman are designed to create a strong personal bond with the child viewer.

Another important difference is that AEL's regional audience only includes poor whites from Appalachia and mostly from rural areas. The CTW national sample includes a high percentage of minority children who live in poverty in large cities.

Nevertheless, it is important to note the rather limited success AEL achieved with TV-only instruction.

CONCLUSION

This chapter begins with the controversy generated by Monica Sims when she banned *Sesame Street* from the BBC. Sims objected to *Sesame Street* because of its middle-class orientation; its lack of reality; its attempt to prepare children for school and not for life; its teaching in a passive, uninvolved way; its authoritarian objectives; and its aim to change children's behavior.

An examination of some of these issues has been attempted in this chapter. The concentration has been on whether the instructional objectives are possible rather than on the moral righteousness of attempting these objectives. The issue of morality will be examined in the concluding chapter.

There are two major sources of the empirical evidence that place limits on the possibilities of instructional television for young children. Sprigle concludes that (1) *Sesame Street* does not prepare poverty children for first grade; and (2) that *Sesame Street* does not narrow the achievement gap between the poor and the disadvantaged. Appalachia Educational Laboratory finds instructional television, by itself, insufficient to improve the educational and social–affective development of Appalachia's poor.

In contrast to these results there are the claims of educational effectiveness published by CTW. Chapter 3 consists of a close look at the research supporting *Sesame Street.* The present chapter has analyzed the theoretical bases for such claims.

The first theoretical issue is concerned with what happens when a young child attends to a television program. Obviously, if a young child does not attend, he cannot learn. No so obvious, however, is the fact that a young child can attend intensely and still not learn. This point was demonstrated in the Soviet literature when the development of attention was reviewed. Young children can attend to a televised presentation in an involuntary manner. Involuntary attention depends only on the intensity of external influences or on the direct attractiveness of objects and does not require that children comprehend what attracts them. This, perhaps explains why young children can sit transfixed to a television set and afterward demonstrate that they have learned so little. Quite clearly, a goal of televised instruction is to prepare the child for comprehending ever more advanced presentations. First, more data are needed on what young children comprehend of televised material and the conditions that facilitate this understanding. Second, there is a need to relate these data to the type of program material that attracts the child.

Another related issue is whether TV is a passive teacher. A proper analysis of this issue requires an understanding of how young children learn. Adults can learn from passive television watching, much as they learn when listening to a classroom lecture. Young children, however, display unique qualities in their thought processes that seem to require an inordinate amount of active engagement with the world of objects and people for their development. Furthermore, the involvement of young children with experiences that they only partly understand, which in turn leads to intense conflict, seems to be a primary pathway for their intellectual development. However, television experiences do not tend to produce situations that produce conflict in young children. The prototype of conflict for young children seems to involve a choice between two behaviors, with one alternative leading to success and the other not. These choices, involving active engagement with objects and people, get progressively refined until the child can handle situations in more abstract terms—such as presentational learning, which occurs on television. The issue, then, is not whether television is a passive teacher, but whether television, when combined with the unique qualities of young children's thought, can initiate the development of thought to progressively higher forms.

Television instruction for disadvantaged preschool children poses special problems in addition to those already elucidated. The Coleman Report strongly implicates the home, neighborhood, and the peer environment and indicates that the schools exert only a minimal influence on the outcome of the educational process. Given these findings, the issue is not how many school skills can be taught to the preschool child, but how best to use television to influence positively the home, the neighborhood, and the peer environment. Television has two major advantages over schools: (1) It reaches children at early ages; (2) it enters directly into the home. Coleman's findings imply that every effort should be made to influence both the young child and his parents in their home. The traditional model, which fails with the disadvantaged poor in our schools, is equally likely to fail when applied from a television set.

It must be emphasized that instructional television for young children is at a very early stage of development. Theoretical obstacles are just that—theoretical. The approach that CTW takes is to concentrate on teaching school skills in the hope of obtaining early school achievement that might then lead to long-term success in school. There are, as has been indicated, other possibilities for instructional television. These alternatives will be examined in later chapters.

3

Sesame Street:
A Reassessment

The research supporting the educational effectiveness of *Sesame Street* is elaborately documented. The support attained by *Sesame Street* from the American public is unparalleled in the history of television programming—educational or otherwise. However, in spite of the supporting research and public acclaim, it is possible that *Sesame Street* is substantially less effective educationally than reported.

It is with great reluctance that this reassessment of *Sesame Street* is undertaken. *Sesame Street* is a well-intentioned and worthwhile endeavor, an alternative for young children to what has been called "the great American wasteland" of commercial television. But if the claims are grossly exaggerated, expectations must be revised, reasons for failures explained, and modifications proposed. The research sponsored by the producers of *Sesame Street* claims in its conclusions that *Sesame Street* is highly beneficial—especially for its target population of preschool disadvantaged children. It is precisely this conclusion that will be critically examined.

Research sponsored by *Sesame Street* has attributed to the program observed gains in performance by viewers. These gains may be attributable instead to special characteristics of the home backgrounds of the children and to influences on the home backgrounds that occurred incidental to the research. It is the purpose of this chapter to examine this thesis in detail. In later chapters another curriculum for educational television for preschoolers will be proposed.

The impact of *Sesame Street* on the consciousness of the American public, its educators, and its child psychologists is nothing short of phenomenal. Since the inception of its planning in the summer of 1968 the evaluative research on

Sesame Street has been, with few exceptions, virtually uncriticized in professional sources (Kliger, 1971; G. S. Lesser, 1972; Meichenbaum & Turk, 1972; Rogers, 1972; Sprigle, 1971; Stevenson, 1972b). For instance, Stevenson (1972b) after first stating, "The ETS study showed what we all know but need to be reminded of: children can learn a great deal from viewing television," then poses some questions that he believes remain unanswered from the study:

> Would children who did not watch *Sesame Street* frequently have shown comparable gains if some external motivation existed for watching it? Were children more expressive in their use of language after watching *Sesame Street?* How critical were variables such as parental interest and the home's educational environment in producing the gains found from viewing *Sesame Street?* What effect has *Sesame Street* had on children's performance in kindergarten and first grade? Are these effects lasting? Will attendance at preschool coupled with viewing *Sesame Street* produce greater gains than either alone? Does the cognitively oriented *Sesame Street* influence the child's social behavior and personality development? Is racial tolerance influenced by viewing the interracial cast of *Sesame Street* [pp. 355–356]?

But, he does not dispute the claims by Children's Television Workshop (CTW), the producers of *Sesame Street,* that *Sesame Street* is effective. It is precisely these claims that will be examined at this time.

There are several reviews of the literature on the topic of educational television for preschool children (Bernbaum, 1972; Meichenbaum & Turk, 1972; Rogers, 1972). With one exception (Cook, Appleton, Conner, Schaffer, Tamkin, & Weber, 1975), criticisms are offered within the framework of the research conclusions offered by CTW from the ETS study. The following is an independent assessment of the CTW research claims.

THE EDUCATIONAL TESTING SERVICE EVALUATION

Children's Television Workshop contracted with Educational Testing Service for an evaluation of the effectiveness of *Sesame Street* (Ball & Bogatz, 1970a, 1970b; Bogatz & Ball, 1971). The research was started during the planning stage of *Sesame Street* and allowed for an exchange of ideas between researchers and programming staff. Each group affected and modified the other. Program content was based upon knowledge about the abilities of children before they watched *Sesame Street,* obtained from the ETS evaluation and from an in-house formative evaluation group that participated in program adjustments (Gibbons & Palmer, 1970; Reeves, 1971).

The overall first-year conclusions of Samuel Ball and Gerry Ann Bogatz (1970b), coauthors of the ETS evaluation, are:

> Three- to 5-year-old youngsters from a variety of backgrounds acquired important simple and complex cognitive skills as a result of watching the program. Those who watched the most gained the most. . . .
>
> Educational television as an effective medium for teaching certain skills to very young children has been demonstrated by *Sesame Street* [p. 1].[1]

The stated purpose of the research (Ball & Bogatz, 1970b, p. 1) into the effectiveness of *Sesame Street* was to try to answer the following questions: What is the overall impact of *Sesame Street?* What are the moderating effects of age, sex, prior achievement level, and socioeconomic status (SES) on the impact of *Sesame Street?* Do children at home watching *Sesame Street* benefit in comparison with children at home who do not watch it? Do children in preschool classrooms benefit from watching *Sesame Street* as part of their school curriculum? What are the effects of home background conditions on the impact of *Sesame Street?*

Analysis of the First-Year Research

The research evaluated the first season of 26 weeks and, according to CTW,

> showed that television can be an effective medium for teaching 3- to 5-year-old children important simple facts and skills, such as recognizing and labeling letters and numerals, and more complex higher cognitive skills, such as classifying and sorting by a variety of criteria. The ETS research results reveal that *Sesame Street* benefits children from disadvantaged inner city communities, middle class suburbs, and isolated rural areas—all the groups studied in this evaluation [Ball & Bogatz, 1970b, p. 3].

According to the authors, there are three primary findings: (1) Children who watched most gained the most; (2) the skills that received the most time and attention on the program itself were, with rare exceptions, the skills that were best learned; and (3) the program did not require formal adult supervision in order to promote learning in the areas the program covers.

The authors support these findings with additional facts:

1. There was some transfer of learning, such as recognizing full words or the ability to write their own names. These skills were not taught on the program.

---

[1] This and subsequent quotes cited to Ball and Bogatz, 1970b are from S. Ball and G. A. Bogatz, *A Summary of the Major Findings in "The First Year of Sesame Street: An Evaluation."* Princeton, N.J.: Educational Testing Service, 1970. © Children's Television Workshop, 1970.

2. That children learned more the more they watched holds across differences of age, sex, geographical location, socioeconomic status, mental age, and whether the children watched at home or at school. This result is generally true in all eight goal areas, with differences in gain recorded in each area. There are also differences in gain for different groups of children.
3. The 3-year-old children gained the most, 5-year-old children gained the least. "Three-year-old children who viewed the show a great deal had higher attainments at posttest than those 4- and 5-year-olds who viewed the show less, even though the younger children scored lower at pretest than the older children [Ball & Bogatz, 1970b, p. 4]."
4. Disadvantaged children started out with considerably lower achievement scores on the skills taught on the program. However, those who watched a great deal surpassed the achievement scores of those middle-class children who watched infrequently.
5. A tentative finding is that the show may be highly effective with children whose first language is Spanish.
6. The variability of success suggests, in some cases, that there was either an initial underestimation or initial overestimation of the skills of the children.
7. Skill learning was greater when skills were presented in direct fashion on the show.

First-Year Sample Children

Excluding pilot testing, the first-year sample included 1124 children. Of these, 181 were lost on the initial testing to quality control. Of the 181 children lost, 173 came from the disadvantaged, and only 8 from the advantaged. Of the remaining 943 children, 774 came from disadvantaged backgrounds.

ETS First-Year Test Results

Eight major tests were developed by ETS specifically for the first-year CTW evaluation (see Table 3.1). Results were tested for significance with analysis of variance technique.

Comparison of the Content Analysis of the First Year of
Sesame Street *to the Test Questionnaires*

The percentage of time a particular item was taught should be related to how well it was learned. Inspection of the content analysis done by ETS reveals the information given in Table 3.2.

The percentages are based on a content analysis of 130 shows. An inordinate amount of time was devoted to naming letters (4.9%), initial sounds (4.9%), and recitation of numbers (5.4%).

TABLE 3.1
Classification of Items on ETS Test of *Sesame Street*[ab]

Test items	Number of items
Body parts total	32
Pointing to body parts	5
Naming of body parts	15
Function of body parts (pointing)	8
Function of body parts (verbal)	4
Letters total*	58
Recognizing letters*	8
Naming capital letters*	16
Naming lower case letters*	8
Matching letters in words	4
Recognizing letters in words*	4
Initial sounds	4
Reading words	6
Forms total*	20
Recognizing forms*	4
Naming forms*	4
Numbers total*	54
Recognizing numbers*	6
Naming numbers*	15
Numerosity	6
Counting	9
Addition and subtraction	7
Matching subtests*	11
Relational terms total*	17
Amount relationships	9
Size relationships	2
Position relationships	5
Sorting total*	6
Classification total*	24
Classification by size*	2
Classification by form*	6
Classification by number*	6
Classification by function*	9
Puzzles total*	5
Grand total*	203

[a]From S. Ball and G. A. Bogatz, *The First Year of Sesame Street: An Evaluation.* Princeton, N.J.: Educational Testing Service, 1970. © Children's Television Workshop, 1970.

[b]An asterisk indicates that a statistically significant effect was found on the test.

TABLE 3.2
Content Analysis of *Sesame Street*

Item	Percentage
Body parts total	4.0
Letters total	13.9
Forms total	2.5
Numbers total	9.9
Relational terms total	4.9
Sorting total	1.9
Classification total	.7

Analysis of the test itself reveals a strong emphasis on body parts (32 items), letters (58 items), and numbers (54 items). Naming body parts (20 items) is also strongly represented. In the letters total, naming capital letters accounts for 16 items, recognizing letters and naming lower-case letters accounts for 8 items each. In the numbers total, naming numbers accounts for 15 items, and counting accounts for 9 items. The classification total accounts for 24 items. Clearly, the largest part of the test is devoted to questions involving letters and numbers and, in particular, naming them.

Comparing the percentage of time devoted to a particular area on *Sesame Street* with the test results yields some unexpected findings. Naming letters and words yields statistically significant results, yet something that seems to be so easily acquired as naming body parts or pointing to body parts is not statistically significant (possibly because the children could already do this on the pretest, but from Figure 3.1, it is not certain that this is a ceiling effect). The sorting total is significant, as is the classification total. But, sorting has only 1.9% (278 items) and classification only 0.7% (91 items) of the total viewing time devoted to it. How does a child acquire these last two skills when sorting accounts for only slightly more than two items a show and classification less than three-quarters of an item per show? One possibility is that these are skills learned outside of direct teaching from *Sesame Street.* This result is not expected and requires further study. If there is a high correlation between the sorting and classification results and the letters and numbers results, it might imply that much of the learning was taking place outside of the direct teaching on *Sesame Street* and that even the learning that might most easily be attributed to watching *Sesame Street* (letters and numbers) could have been influenced by this outside learning. To put it directly, the children who learned sorting and classification had to learn it somewhere, and it is unlikely that it was learned from *Sesame Street,* because so little time was devoted to it. The *Sesame Street* show may have influenced the parents to either teach or provide games related to sorting and classification while they were drilling their child on the letters and numbers tasks emphasized on *Sesame Street.* If this is so, then the strongest effect would be due to home environment and only indirectly to the teaching provided by *Sesame Street.* The *Sesame Street* research is not directed to exploring this possibility fully. A home environment effect, however, could provide an alternative explanation of the obtained results.

Another interesting possibility is that the gains obtained may be attributable to familiarity with test taking or with the tester or maybe attributable to teaching to the test. ETS reports that the pretest took about 2 hours and the posttest took about $1\frac{1}{2}$ hours. Many of the questions were also the same. These last possibilities pose serious questions when interpreting the results.

Particularly disturbing is the possibility that teaching to the test may have a strong influence in effecting gains. For instance, we know that many teachers in deprived areas raise children's scores on standard aptitude tests by teaching the test items just before the test is administered. At a somewhat more sophisticated level, the same possibility (although unintentional) may apply to the retest used by CTW. The test items are, in many instances, exactly the same items that are drilled on *Sesame Street* (number and letter items account for 112 items out of a total of 203). Many of the responses required of the children are of the recognition type, with little testing of comprehension, and in many instances the responses do not require verbalization. Under these circumstances, it is quite possible that the reported gains reflect something other than increased general abilities in the area tested.

Another Evaluation of the First-Year ETS Research

The significance of the tests in relation to the amount of viewing falls into several interesting patterns, but, as the authors state, "The educational significance of the result is, of course, a matter of subjective judgment [Ball & Bogatz, 1970a, p. 334]." With this in mind, a descriptive analysis will be performed. The CTW sample is divided into viewing quartiles:

Q(1): Children who viewed rarely or never
Q(2): Children who viewed two–three times per week
Q(3): Children who viewed four–five times per week
Q(4): Children who viewed more than five times per week

Half the children in the Q(1) group never viewed the show, and the other half viewed on the average of only one time per week.

A display of the *Sesame Street* report card is presented in Figure 3.1. It is particularly important to notice that children who watched the show more often have consistently higher initial scores. The children were not preselected into viewing quartiles, but rather they selected viewing quartiles themselves. That is, *Sesame Street* was made available and the children selected how often they desired to watch it. The researchers either expected (or hoped) that there would

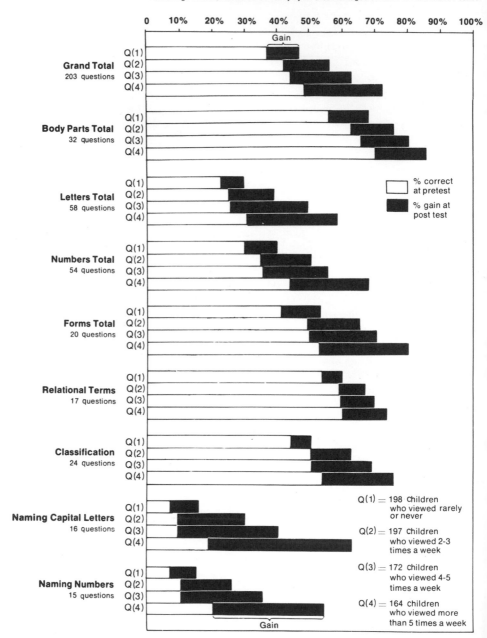

Figure 3.1. *Sesame Street:* First-year report card. [From S. Ball & G. A. Bogatz, *A Summary of the Major Findings in "The First Year of Sesame Street: An Evaluation."* Princeton, N.J.: Educational Testing Service, 1970. © Children's Television Workshop, 1970.]

TABLE 3.3
Test Scores of Disadvantaged Children

		Pretest		Gain	
		Mean	S.D.	Mean	S.D.
Q(1)	N = 198	75.62	24.73	18.63	20.04
Q(2)	N = 197	84.42	27.60	29.11	22.51
Q(3)	N = 172	87.74	27.63	37.97	25.29
Q(4)	N = 164	97.54	32.16	47.36	26.15

be no difference in initial scores for the children in the different viewing quartiles. This was not the case, however, and this created difficult problems of interpretation of the results. Because of this finding, the results could be interpreted to mean that children who watched more had greater gains because their initial abilities were greater than the less frequent viewers. The interpretation the researchers would like to demonstrate as correct is the simple conclusion that children who watch more, gain more. Much of the analysis will center about this critical issue.

The Disadvantaged Children. On the 203-item test (each item counting one point) the grand totals (mean figures) for all the disadvantaged children are shown in Table 3.3. Notice that as the data advance from Q(1) to Q(4) (with commensurately higher initial scores), the variability of the scores increases. This is an indication that the assumption of homogeneity of variance required in order to perform an analysis of variance might be violated. It is likely that the children in the different quartiles are not drawn from the same populations. The mean point differences in scores of the four groups of disadvantaged children (N = 731) in the different quartiles are shown in Table 3.4. Final-gain point differences of groups, corrected for initial differences between groups, are shown

TABLE 3.4
Differences in Test Scores between Viewing Quartiles for Disadvantaged Children

Pretest	Posttest
Q(4) − Q(1)=21.92	Q(4) − Q(1)=50.65
Q(3) − Q(1)=12.12	Q(3) − Q(1)=31.46
Q(2) − Q(1)= 8.80	Q(2) − Q(1)=19.28
Q(4) − Q(2)=13.12	Q(4) − Q(2)=31.37
Q(4) − Q(3)= 9.80	Q(4) − Q(3)=19.19
Q(3) − Q(2)= 3.32	Q(3) − Q(2)=14.14

TABLE 3.5
Differences in Test Scores between Viewing
Quartiles for Disadvantaged Children (Corrected
for Initial Differences)

Posttest		Pretest		Final gain
Q(4) − Q(1)	−	Q(4) − Q(1)	=	28.73
Q(3) − Q(1)	−	Q(3) − Q(1)	=	19.34
Q(2) − Q(1)	−	Q(2) − Q(1)	=	10.48
Q(4) − Q(2)	−	Q(4) − Q(2)	=	18.25
Q(4) − Q(3)	−	Q(4) − Q(3)	=	9.39
Q(3) − Q(2)	−	Q(3) − Q(2)	=	10.86

in Table 3.5. When calculated, with the range of final gains having been corrected for initial scores in percentages (based upon a total possible score of 203 points), the maximum percentage gain is about 14%. This percentage gain represents the largest gain, made by Q(4), less the gain made by the Q(1) group. Since the authors state that the gain by the Q(1) children must be attributed to maturation or other learning (it certainly is not attributable to watching the show, since they hardly watched it), then gains have been severely reduced among the disadvantaged children to a small percentage gain.

Also, the Q(1) viewing group started at a much lower level of ability than the Q(4) viewing group *and* finished at a level of ability that was still less than the initial level of ability of the Q(4) group. In spite of the fact that all the children are labeled disadvantaged in this sample, the wide range of initial abilities in the different viewing groups creates a strange impression that the children in the lower viewing groups have generally lower abilities and that this may possibly be due to poorer backgrounds, among other things.

Another important point is that the percentage of correct answers to the 203-item test remains low even after the rather lengthy (6 months) viewing period. Most experiments do not have as intensive a training period as was employed in this design. Assuming five viewings a week for 6 months for the Q(4) group, or a minimum of 130 viewings, the percentage correct goes from about 97.54/203 to 114.90/203 (48% to 71%). So, for the best group (in terms of initial ability *and* greatest amount of viewing) the most that they can answer correctly is about 71%. It is difficult to interpret this result, particularly when the test is so strongly keyed to the 6 months of intensive drill.

The Advantaged Children. Employing the same descriptive analysis with the advantaged children, the grand total (mean) results on the 203-item test for all the advantaged children are shown in Table 3.6. The findings are that the

TABLE 3.6
Test Scores of Advantaged Children

		Pretest		Gain	
		Mean	S.D.	Mean	S.D.
Q(1)	N=16	95.44	23.90	26.69	16.04
Q(2)	N=31	102.13	21.65	38.65	17.02
Q(3)	N=57	112.77	24.36	40.46	18.82
Q(4)	N=65	110.83	25.63	45.25	22.87

advantaged children have lower final-gain scores (which are corrected for initial scores) than do disadvantaged children. The posttest minus the pretest for the Q(4) − Q(1) minus Q(4) − Q(1) comparison is 18.56 points, a gain of about 9% (based upon a total possible score of 203 points). This is the largest percentage gain, with the amount of the other percentage gains decreasing steadily. Thus, in terms of gains that may be (but may not be) attributable to watching *Sesame Street*, we find the changes slight for the advantaged children. We might attribute this to the fact that initial means for the advantaged group are much higher than for the disadvantaged group.

Paradoxically, the amount of viewing for each quartile differs in the two groups. Going from Q(1) to Q(4) among the disadvantaged children yields 198, 197, 172, and 164 children, respectively. Doing the same thing with the advantaged children yields 16, 31, 57, and 65 children, respectively.

Clearly, many more advantaged children are, on the average, watching *Sesame Street* than are their disadvantaged peers. On the other hand, the disadvantaged children are, on the average, getting more out of the show. It is in this context that the previously stated conclusion that "children who watched the most gained the most" should be examined. Although this result obtains for both groups of children, the gains are somewhat smaller for the advantaged children. The gains are somewhat larger for the disadvantaged children, but a very large percentage of these children had low viewing rates. Should it be concluded that disadvantaged children will perform better if they can be induced to watch *Sesame Street*? This is an extremely tempting conclusion, but it may not be correct. The disadvantaged children may not be watching *Sesame Street* for a wide variety of reasons. For instance, they may not comprehend the program content; or, differences in the initial scores of the two groups may mean that the advantaged group has previously learned much more than the disadvantaged group; or, the advantaged group watches more because the show is more entertaining (perhaps more middle-class oriented); or, there is greater pressure for educational experiences in the middle-class home.

The Cohort Study

The conclusions of the first-year report largely stand or fall depending on the validity of the Cohort Study. As the authors, Ball and Bogatz (1970a), state

> One of the problems in the earlier descriptions of the data was that of the confounding of important variables. High viewers in a real sense selected themselves. When compared with the lowest viewing quartile they were seen to be, even on the pretest, more proficient in those areas measured by the test battery. Results from the parent questionnaire also showed that the heavy viewers, even within the inner-city areas, came from homes that were relatively more affluent and where the parents were somewhat better educated [p. 283].[2]

The problem, then, is to separate the effects of amount of viewing from the effects of initial ability and home background factors. That is, granted that high viewers gain more than low viewers, "is this due solely to amount of viewing or is it due to an interaction of amount of viewing, previous achievement, and a more affluent home background? [p. 283]"

Covariance analysis was considered, but, "fortunately," the authors state, "a less controversial and more efficient alternative was available [p. 284]." The authors state that the reason they rejected a covariance analysis on the posttest scores, using pretest scores as covariates, was that "there was no way of determining from the data the appropriate regression coefficient to use [p. 307]." They further add that they did not use covariance analysis for technical reasons, associated with Lord's Paradox, the natural confounding of the data, and interpretational problems (p. 307).

In the cohort design, the authors took two groups of children, cohort 1, 53–58 months old at pretest, and cohort 2 53–58 months old at posttest. That is, group 1 had not yet watched *Sesame Street* and group 2 had. Viewing records for both groups of children were available, as both groups of children were part of the original study. On this basis, the children were assigned to the four viewing groups, as previously described. The two groups of children were independent, as no child in group 1 could also be in group 2. The groups were further limited to at-home children from disadvantaged areas. There were 114 children in the pretest group and 101 in the posttest group. A further clarification of the cohort design is presented in Table 3.7.

The ETS researchers argue that if viewing is the effective variable, then small differences are expected between the pretest and posttest scores in Q(1), and these differences should increase as viewing level is increased to Q(4). This is because at viewing level Q(1) neither group 1 nor group 2 has had much

[2] This and subsequent quotes cited to Ball and Bogatz, 1970a are from S. Ball and G. A. Bogatz, *The First Year of Sesame Street: An Evaluation.* Princeton, N.J.: Educational Testing Service, 1970. © Children's Television Workshop, 1970.

TABLE 3.7
Basic Outline of the Cohort Analysis Design

Cohort status	Cohort 1	Cohort 2
Viewing level	Q(1), Q(2), Q(3), Q(4)	Q(1), Q(2), Q(3), Q(4)
Age	53–58 months	53–58 months
Dependent variable	Pretest scores	Posttest scores

exposure to *Sesame Street* and at viewing level Q(4) only group 2 has had much exposure to *Sesame Street*. Since the two groups being compared are about the same age, and separate ETS analysis reveals no discernible differences on a wide range of factors between the two groups, such as SES, home-background factors, initial abilities, and IQ, the authors state that "it is sufficient to indicate that this study design overcomes the confounding problems of amount of viewing with prior attainments, SES, IQ, and home background [Ball & Bogatz, 1970a, p. 288]."

The statistical treatment of the data used multiple analysis of variance, with the dependent variables being pretest for cohort 1 and posttest for cohort 2. The independent variables were cohorts 1 and 2, the viewing quartiles, and age (linear, quadratic, and cubic). The authors state, "The major question being asked was whether an interaction effect existed between amount of viewing and cohort status. A subsidiary question was whether age in the restricted range of this particular study was related to gains and, if so, how—linearly or curvilinearly [pp. 341–342]." The most important effect, the interaction between viewing and cohort status, was significant, demonstrating that the higher the viewing quartile, the greater the difference between test scores for cohorts 1 and 2. Linear age did not produce a significant effect. There were two other significant but apparently unimportant interactions. A subsequent breakdown of the viewing by cohorts interaction employing a univariate analysis of variance for each skill area reveals significance in the areas of letters, numbers, sorting, and classification. The authors conclude, "It was clear from the age cohort analysis that high levels of viewing of *Sesame Street* brought about gains in the major goal areas. Thus, the success of *Sesame Street*, in terms of its major goals and within the target groups of children that were of most concern, is well documented [p. 345]."

Criticism of the Cohort Study

The criticism will be divided into three parts. The first part is concerned with whether or not the Cohort Study actually separates the effects of initial abilities from the level of viewing. The second part examines whether or not home-background factors between the two cohorts are similar. The third part examines

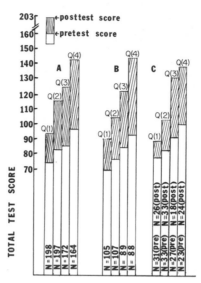

Figure 3.2. Pretest and gain on total test score, by viewing quartiles. A = all disadvantaged children; B = all disadvantaged at-home children; C = cohort children. [Adapted from S. Ball & G. A. Bogatz, *The First Year of Sesame Street: An Evaluation.* Princeton, N.J.: Educational Testing Service, 1970. © Children's Television Workshop, 1970.]

the effects of another study, called the High- versus Low-Learning Study, done by the authors, on the Cohort Study.

   Does the Cohort Study Separate the Effects of Initial Abilities from the Level of Viewing? In view of the significant interaction between viewing level and cohort status, the viewing-level effect is not independent of cohort status. This is a correct statement as to what the significant interaction means. Figure 3.2 presents in graphical form a display of the pretest and posttest scores of (A) all the disadvantaged children; (B) all the disadvantaged at-home children; and (C) all the Cohort Study children. A comparison of the samples, indicates in each case that as viewing level increases, initial score increases in a similar manner. The basic problem in the Cohort Study is still retained. It is still true that the more the children watch, the greater their initial ability. Even though the authors report that cohort 1 and cohort 2 are similar in age and home back-ground, it is not clear merely from a significant interaction between cohort status and viewing level that "high levels of viewing of *Sesame Street* brought about gains in the major goal areas." In Figure 3.3 the interaction effect is graphed in a new form that should make it more convenient to study. Please note that the more any two lines are parallel, the less they contribute to a significant interaction effect. Viewing level 3 and viewing level 4 are almost exactly parallel, so it can be seen that their comparison does not contribute to a

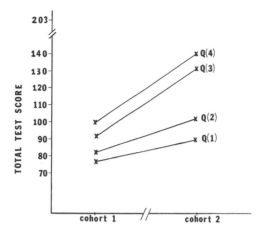

Figure 3.3. Pretest and gain on total test score for cohort sample children, by viewing quartiles. [Adapted from S. Ball & G. A. Bogatz, *The First Year of Sesame Street: An Evaluation*. Princeton, N.J.: Educational Testing Service, 1970. © Children's Television Workshop, 1970.]

significant interaction effect. Those groups that do contribute the most are precisely the groups with large initial differences in scores. Clearly, the Cohort Study does not separate initial ability from viewing level. In order to do so, all the children in the Cohort Study would have to be about equal initially. Since they are not, it is most important to find out why. The authors have not done so, either in the first-year report or in the second-year report. The authors report that the Age Cohort Study provided a "rigorous control of previous achievement, IQ, and home background factors and allowed the effects of viewing to be assessed without these confoundings. The results were very clear. Children who viewed learned. This learning could not be attributed to the effects of normal growth, IQ, previous achievement, or SES [Ball & Bogatz, 1970a, pp. 365–366]." With regard to the separation of the effects of initial achievement from viewing level, this statement is not correct.

In the Cohort Study it is correct that previous attainments are about the same within each viewing level and, on the average, for each cohort as a whole. That is, for all the cohort 1 and cohort 2 children, at viewing level Q(1), previous attainments are about the same, and this is also the case at viewing levels Q(2), Q(3), and Q(4). However, between viewing levels this is not the case. As viewing increases, pretest scores get higher. This issue appears to be confused in the ETS analysis. Because initial scores are about the same for both cohorts within each viewing level, this does not mean that the Cohort Study does away with the confounding problem, which is essentially related to the fact that as viewing increases, the initial scores of each successive group get higher. This difficult condition is still retained in the Cohort Study!

Are Home-Background Factors between the Two Cohorts Similar? Ball and Bogatz (1970b) state, "One might argue that group 2 was somehow systematically different from group 1, and that this was accentuated in the high viewing groups [p. 287]." The authors then present tables (pp. 295–298) that give parent questionnaire items for the two age cohorts. Their conclusion is, "It can be seen that there are no apparent background differences between the two groups [p. 287]." After examining the parent questionnaire, this conclusion is in doubt. To begin with, the parent questionnaire as presented is not at the same point of time in the experimental treatment for both cohorts. The authors present the pretest questionnaire for cohort 1 and the posttest questionnaire for cohort 2. One group of mothers has gone through the experimental procedure with her child and the other group of mothers has not. From the data presented, there is no way to separate the effects on the mothers' responses of having not yet participated in the study from the effects of having already participated in one. So, the data presented do not give adequate information to determine whether or not the two groups are alike. In spite of this, the data were of interest.

Differences exist in the parent questionnaires that are presented for the two cohorts. These differences have to be examined cautiously, as the cohort 1 mothers are responding before their children watched *Sesame Street*; and the cohort 2 mothers, afterward.

The authors present a statistical analysis that shows essentially no differences within each cohort on the parent questionnaire items. This author performed an additional chi-square analysis on the between-group differences. Significant between-group differences are presented in Table 3.8.

It is noted that in the highest viewing group, in answer to "What do you usually do when you are with your child?" more cohort 2 mothers respond that they read to him, watch TV alone, or watch TV with child than do cohort 1 mothers. Also, at the highest viewing level, in reply to "How often is your child read to?" the findings are that cohort 2 mothers reply "once a day" or "several times a week" more often than do cohort 1 mothers. The highest viewers in cohort 2 also watch more TV and local ETV than do cohort 1 children. Thus, there are important differences, especially at the highest viewing level, between the two sets of parent questionnaires.

It is not possible to determine whether or not these differences reflect changes in the mothers' attitudes as a result of participating in the experimental treatment. In order to do so, both pretest and posttest parent questionnaires for each group would have to be presented. If it is the case that parental attitudes were altered as a result of participation in the study, and mostly for mothers who fall within the higher viewing groups, then this is a significant finding. Since this is a likely possibility, it will be pursued further. One possible interpretation of this effect is the following:

(1) Children who select themselves as high viewers of *Sesame Street* have greater initial abilities than children who select themselves as low viewers.

(2) There are many possible explanations for why the high viewers of *Sesame Street* have greater initial abilities than the low viewers. One plausible explanation is that the higher viewers have better home backgrounds, where greater emphasis is placed on creating new and using available educational experiences.

(3) Thus, it is quite possible that participation in the ETS study had a much stronger effect on some mothers than it did on others. For instance, within some economically disadvantaged homes, *Sesame Street* became available under conditions where mothers were already informed that it was a positive educational experience for their child. Under such circumstances, mothers who were already providing better home-background conditions, including many diverse educational experiences for their children that enhance cognitive development, may have exerted a stronger influence on their children to watch *Sesame Street.* The

TABLE 3.8
Selected Parent Questionnaire Items for Age Cohorts[ab]

Question	Response	Cohort 1	Cohort 2	p
What mother	Reads to him	Q(2) = 53%	Q(2) = 76%	.10
usually does	Reads to him	Q(4) = 41%	Q(4) = 73%	.05
with child	Watches TV	Q(4) = 9%	Q(4) = 35%	.10
	Watches TV with him	Q(4) = 64%	Q(4) = 92%	.05
How often	Once a day	Q(2) = 32%	Q(2) = 9%	.05
child is	Once a day or	Q(4) = 32%	Q(4) = 66%	.05
read to	several times a week			
Hours child	Two or more	Q(1) = 47%	Q(1) = 81%	.05
watched TV	Two or more	Q(2) = 51%	Q(2) = 74%	.10
yesterday	Two or more	Q(4) = 46%	Q(4) = 84%	.02
Does child	Yes	Q(2) = 29%	Q(2) = 97%	.01
ever watch	Yes	Q(3) = 41%	Q(3) = 100%	.01
local ETV?	Yes	Q(4) = 55%	Q(4) = 96%	.01

[a]Adapted from selected parent questionnaire items for age cohorts (S. Ball & G. A. Bogatz, *The First Year of Sesame Street: An Evaluation.* Princeton, N.J.: Educational Testing Service, 1970. © Children's Television Workshop, 1970).

[b]Group 1:53–58 months at pretest time
Group 2:53–58 months at posttest time
Q(1): N = 32
Q(2): N = 34
Q(3): N = 27
Q(4): N = 22

mothers also watch and discover what it is important for their children to learn. They question their children and give additional instruction. They cue children as to what is important. Possibly they expand the curriculum to more advanced skills.

(4) Thus, it is a distinct possibility that *Sesame Street* serves mostly as an initial stimulus and only in homes that are prepared to use it. Favorable home-background conditions, for the most part, may determine how well prepared the home is to use *Sesame Street* as a new educational resource. However, if this is the case, *Sesame Street* might very likely be both self-fulfilling and self-defeating. Children from favorable background conditions will learn with or without *Sesame Street*, while children from less favorable home background conditions will get little but entertainment from it.

(5) Many mothers seem to believe that Sesame Street is an important educational resource for their children and that their children are learning *directly* from it. However, the above analysis indicates that the most important teaching influence might have been provided by the mother and associated favorable background conditions. Appearances may be deceiving.

(6) The analysis by CTW, based upon the ETS research, claims that *Sesame Street* is effective in teaching disadvantaged children. This, if incorrect, may lull the educator and child psychologist into a feeling of complacency concerning the enormous tasks to be accomplished with disadvantaged children. It is quite possible that *Sesame Street* has not gotten through to the core of what it means to be educationally disadvantaged. The foregoing analysis indicates that appearances are not proven and need further study.

Effects of the High- versus Low-Learning Study on the Cohort Study. The mean total gain for all Q(4) children was 48.15 points, with a standard deviation of 25.44. This means that about two-thirds of the children had gains of between 23 and 74 points. Using at-home, disadvantaged, high-viewing children as the sample in the High- versus Low-Learning Study, the researchers tried to determine what differentiated the high learners from the low learners, all with Q(4) viewing levels. The final sample consisted of 43 children who were Q(4) and in the top category of gain and 11 children who were Q(4) and in the bottom category of gain. There was only one statistically significant difference between these two groups and that was in the degree to which the mothers talked to the children about *Sesame Street*. Small differences existed in: socioeconomic status, educational level, number of people in the home, number of rooms in the home, male-head employment record, amount of children's possessions, and parental attitudes. However, Ball and Bogatz (1970a) conclude that, "Aside from the small differences catalogued above, there seem to have been no consistent differences between the high and low learners in the areas of home background covered in the Parent Questionnaire. In addition, comparison of these groups'

Peabody Picture Vocabulary Test (PPVT) IQ's shows no significant differences [p. 302]."

The authors state that a vital assumption of the Cohort Study is that the two cohorts are the same on all important factors. To test for possible differences, the parent questionnaire was used. But the parent questionnaire did not detect differences between high and low learners in the High- versus Low-Learning Study, where the children were matched at the Q(4) viewing level (except for the degree to which mothers talked to their children about *Sesame Street*). Thus, the authors' statement that "there were no apparent systematic background differences between the two groups in the Cohort Study [p. 288]" must be modified in light of the fact that the parent questionnaire was insensitive in the most extreme circumstances (in the High- versus Low-Learning Study) in predicting differences in learning while holding viewing constant. Incidentally, it would be interesting to conduct the same High- versus Low-Learning study with low-viewing children.

Final Comments on the First-Year Report

After a great expenditure of time and money, the results of the first-year study appear to be inconclusive. That is, while a general relationship is clear that the more the children viewed, the more they gained, no causality can be inferred. The frequent viewers had higher attainments and came from more affluent home backgrouns at the outset of the study. Therefore, while frequent viewers gained more, the greater gains could have been a result of influences other than frequent viewing. The previous analysis shows why the cohort study does not separate viewing level from previous attainments and home-background factors. The main problem seems to be that the authors felt that they were not in a position to experimentally assign subjects to different viewing groups. They tried to do so by an experimental manipulation—namely, encouraging one group and not encouraging another. Unfortunately, this procedure broke down, but in a rather interesting way that deserves further exploration. What happened is that large numbers of children who were not encouraged were in the higher viewing quartiles. In addition, these higher viewers had greater initial abilities and came from more affluent home backgrounds. Furthermore, it seems that there may have been important changes in attitudes among parents in the higher viewing groups as a result of participating in the study. Thus, there are at least two elements of doubt introduced into the interpretation of the results. The first is that a definite causal connection between higher viewing and gains has not been established, and the second is that there is evidence to suspect that alternative causal relations between level of viewing and gains are operating. In this situation there is no way of isolating the contribution of viewing to gains. Although the two cohorts are similar in initial abilities, the viewing levels of the children are still self-selected. It is the relationship of initial abilities, home backgrounds, viewing levels, etc., to gains; how much these factors *contribute* to gains; and the combined effect of these factors that are of interest. More rigorous experimental procedures are needed to answer these questions. Therefore, the claims made in the first-year report regarding the effectiveness of *Sesame Street* are not only not proven but are also subject to equally plausible alternative explanations that provide possible influences other than *Sesame Street* as a direct cause of the reported gains.

The Second Year of *Sesame Street*

The second year of *Sesame Street* is basically divided up into the "New Study," and the "Follow-up Study." The New Study sampled disadvantaged, at-home children, so that the experimental group mostly viewed *Sesame Street* and the control mostly did not view *Sesame Street.* This was accomplished through the experimental manipulation of an encouragement or nonencouragement condition. In the Follow-up Study the major goal was to assess the continuing effects on at-home, urban, disadvantaged children from the first-year sample of viewing over a 2-year period. In order to retain continuity within my analysis, the Follow-up Study is considered first.

The Follow-up Study

The major inferential analysis was called the Follow-up Cohort Study. The design considerations are similar to the previously described and criticized first-year Cohort Study. Cohort 1 children had viewed *Sesame Street* in the first year and summer, and cohort 2 children had, in addition, viewed during the second season. Cohort 1 was 63–68 months old at pretest and cohort 2 was the same age at posttest in Year II. The statements of Bogatz and Ball (1971) regarding the findings should be viewed with caution because this design does not permit causal attribution of the type "the greater the viewing, the greater the gains." The major findings of the Follow-up Cohort Study are:

1. "The descriptive analyses showed that the high viewers in Year I gained more than the low viewers, that the high summer viewers gained slightly more than the low summer viewers, and that the high Year II viewers gained less that the low Year II viewers. At the end of the two year study high viewers had maintained their initial advantage over low viewers [pp. 173–174]."

2. "Cohort 2 children performed better on the more complex goals than

Cohort 1 children. There were eleven subgoals where significant effects were noted and, of these, eight were new or revised from the first year. Conversely, differences in most old and simple goal area scores were not significant. The second year of teaching to the same goal areas was seemingly less effective because much was already learned in the first year [pp. 174–175]."

3. "Cohort 2 children (eighteen months' exposure to the show) had significantly more positive attitudes to school and to race of others than cohort 1 children (twelve months' exposure to the show). Attitude change was not a goal of the show [p. 175]."[3]

Teacher Rankings of the Follow-up Cohort Study Children. There were 302 follow-up children. About 160 went on to Head Start, kindergarten, or first grade. Of those who went to school, 112 teacher rankings were obtained in the fall of 1970 and 84 in the spring of 1971. Authors Bogatz and Ball (1971) preface their conclusions on teacher rankings with the comment that "no causality can be inferred [because] the frequent viewers were also somewhat younger and had somewhat higher attainments at the outset of the study [p. 176]." However, they do find that the children who are the most frequent viewers of *Sesame Street* were ranked by their teachers in the fall of 1970 as being highly qualified in the areas of general readiness, quantitative readiness, attitudes toward school, and peer relationships. These results fade out in the spring 1971 teacher rankings. The disappearance of these differences is hard to explain.

It should be pointed out that the positive teacher rankings of the high-viewing *Sesame Street* children are consistent with the hypothesis concerning greater initial achievement and better home backgrounds for the higher viewers. The fade-out of these results is not consistent with this hypothesis. What can be stated at this time is that this issue needs further study.

The New Study

Bogatz and Ball (1971) state that

a direct comparison between the results of the New Study and those obtained in the first year of *Sesame Street* cannot be made. The children studied in the second year had somewhat lower pretest attainments than the children studied in the first year. As well, the two series of *Sesame Street* were different, the second year being somewhat broader in scope and containing greater difficulty levels in many of the continued goal areas [p. 164].

---

[3] The original quote erroneously reversed the number of months' exposure to the show for cohorts 1 and 2. The figures have been corrected here.

Table 3.9 presents in summary form the total pretest and gain scores for the three major groups of children in the New Study according to viewing status. In this study, amount of viewing was again a matter of self-selection by the viewer. We note a consistency with the first-year results when comparing H(1) viewers with H(2) viewers. H(2) viewers have initial abilities that are greater than H(1) viewers. Looking at the non-viewers, we find some surprisingly large pretest differences between those who were not encouraged to view and those who were encouraged to view (*t*-test, almost significant at the .05 level, two-tailed). This might mean there was some unknown difficulty in the sample selection process. We also note that the encouraged nonviewers have larger gains than the not-encouraged non-viewers. Also, encouragement seems to be important among the H(1) and H(2) viewers.

A sophisticated inferential analysis was done on these data in order to determine the effects of encouragement and the subsequent viewing of *Sesame Street*. One analysis was a multivariate analysis of variance (MANOVA) of all

TABLE 3.9
Grand Total Pretest and Gain Scores for Children in the New Study[a][b]

		Pretest		Gain	
Group[c]	N	Mean	S.D.	Mean	S.D.
All children, nonviewers	108	72.9	29.0	9.0	27.9
All children, H(1) viewers	89	63.8	27.5	23.7	28.0
All children, H(2) viewers	86	71.7	30.2	32.3	25.5
Not encouraged, nonviewers	99	74.4	29.0	7.8	26.9
Not encouraged, H(1) viewers	46	64.0	25.2	19.8	25.8
Not encouraged, H(2) viewers	8	83.1	38.0	13.9	25.0
Encouraged, nonviewers	9	56.9	25.3	22.0	36.1
Encouraged, H(1) viewers	43	63.6	30.0	27.8	30.0
Encouraged, H(2) viewers	78	70.6	29.3	34.2	24.9

[a]Adapted from G. A. Bogatz and S. Ball, *The Second Year of Sesame Street: A Continuing Evaluation.* Princeton, N.J.: Educational Testing Service, 1971, Vol. 2, Tables 30, 33a, and 33b. © Children's Television Workshop, 1971.

[b]Children in the New Study include: (a) all children in the New Study; (b) not-encouraged children in the New Study; (c) encouraged children in the New Study. Maximum possible score = 214.

[c]Encouraged were visited once a month by tester who told the parents and children about the show and its importance, distributed CTW publicity, *Sesame Street* buttons, and souvenirs.

H(1) Viewers watched two–three times per week for one-half hour (average).

H(2) Viewers watched four times a week for 1 hour (average).

total test gains, with encouragement, sex, and age as independent variables. In addition, a multivariate analysis of covariance (MANCOVA) on total test gains was run for the same independent variables where pretest total scores, pretest Peabody IQ, and SES were covariates.

The authors' overall conclusion from the analysis is that encouragement is a significant factor. Age was also significant in the MANCOVA analysis, indicating, state the authors, that the show benefited each of the age groups to a significant degree. The problem with this design again rests in the sample, which was self-selecting into viewing groups. The authors are correct when they state that the two groups are comparable at pretest, but within these two groups there are indications that as viewing increases, initial abilities also increase.

In Table 3.10, a within-group chi-square analysis was performed on selected parent questionnaire items between the posttest—not-encouraged and posttest—encouraged New Study groups. It was found from the posttest questionnaire that more positive responses were received from the encouraged group to questions concerning whether mother watches *Sesame Street* with child, whether mother and child talk about *Sesame Street*, whether child plays games based on *Sesame Street*, and if *Sesame Street* is rated as being helpful. These are hopeful results and they reinforce earlier arguments concerning the importance of home-background factors. Indications are that home-background factors may be of primary importance. It might well be the mother who is doing the teaching and, if so, she can be convinced to teach what is presented on *Sesame Street*.

Overall Conclusions

Contrary to CTW's claims, the data are inconclusive. The designs used in the research do not allow determination of the causal basis of the gains reported. What are needed are additional studies despite the fact that Bogatz and Ball (1971) indicate in a postscript that "this is our second and probably our last major evaluation of *Sesame Street* [p. 178]." The types of studies needed are ones that isolate the effects of various important factors on gains. To start out, a design has to be employed that experimentally manipulates level of viewing, initial achievement, and encouragement. In the early stages of the evaluation of *Sesame Street* it was satisfactory to allow children to select their own viewing level. Even in the New Study, where the experimental manipulation using encouragement was fairly effective in sorting viewers from nonviewers, there are indications that initial ability and home-background differences are contaminating factors.

Before the range of educational possibilities for children through television can be accurately assessed, more must be known about what affects children's learning and in what ways they learn through the normal course of development.

TABLE 3.10

Selected Parent Questionnaire Items for the Posttest—Not-Encouraged and Posttest—Encouraged New Study Groups[a][b]

| Question | Response | Percentage positive responses | | |
		Group1	Group 2	*p*
Mother watches *Sesame Street* with child	Almost always Usually Sometimes OR Hardly ever No *Sesame Street*	15%	68%	.01
Mother and child talk about *Sesame Street*	Almost always Usually Sometimes OR Hardly ever No *Sesame Street*	18%	67%	.01
Child plays games based on *Sesame Street*	Almost always Usually Sometimes OR Hardly ever No *Sesame Street*	11%	42%	.01
How helpful *Sesame Street* is for child	Very Somewhat OR Not at all Don't know No *Sesame Street*	23%	86%	.01

[a]Adapted from selected parent questionnaire items for all encouraged and not-encouraged children (G. A. Bogatz & S. Ball, *The Second Year of Sesame Street: A Continuing Evaluation.* Princeton, N.J.: Educational Testing Service, 1971, Vol. 2, Table 18. © Children's Television Workshop, 1971).

[b]Group 1: *N* = 152 not-encouraged
Group 2: *N* = 130 encouraged

The studies done by Samuel Ball and Gerry Ann Bogatz represent an excellent start. However, these studies present many more problems than they solve. They seem more exploratory than conclusive.

Sesame Street Revisited

The recent popularity of "commissioned" evaluation studies in the social sciences has lead to the formation of a new discipline, namely evaluations of evaluations. To a great extent public policy hinges on the results obtained from evaluations. This being the case, independent assessments of the accuracy of these evaluations assume critical proportions. With the support of the Russell Sage Foundation series "Continuities in Evaluation Research," Thomas D. Cook and associates (1975) have performed an evaluation of the ETS evaluation of *Sesame Street*. The Cook *et al.* evaluation took several years to complete and disagreed sharply with Ball and Bogatz's conclusions (Ball & Bogatz, 1970a, 1970b; Bogatz & Ball, 1971). The disagreements resulted in a dialogue between Cook and his associates and the ETS–CTW groups that delayed publication 2–3 years. It is impossible to review thoroughly the Cook *et al.* findings in a few pages. What is attempted is a brief review of the most important points of the Cook reevaluation. Cook *et al.* had available the original data for re-analysis. The preceding analysis was conducted by this author solely from the published ETS reports. All analysis was conducted from the limited data they provided. With the publication of the Cook *et al.* monograph, a decision had to be made whether to revise and incorporate Cook *et al.* into this author's already completed evaluation or to treat it separately. The latter course was deemed desirable. First, there are many objections to the method of analysis Cook *et al.* employed in the re-analysis of the ETS data (see Ball & Bogatz, 1975, in Cook *et al.*, 1975, pp. 387–404). Second, the Cook *et al.* manuscript devotes considerable attention to the broader social issue of *Sesame Street* as "public good," which was not the intent of this author's analysis. Third, the analysis performed by this author approached the data differently than did that of Cook and associates. A separate discussion serves to highlight these differences.

Sesame Street is usually viewed in real life by children without experimental manipulation that seeks to encourage viewing. This being the case, Cook *et al.* feel that the findings for not-encouraged viewers are of greatest interest. The following are the findings on the effects of viewing without encouragement:

1. In the first-year evaluation statistically reliable gains were found for letters and numbers, and marginally reliable gains were found for object relations.
2. In the second-year evaluation statistically reliable gains were found in object relations and in the grand total (heavily weighted on letters and numbers).

3. On five of eight individual first-year tests, and six of nine second-year tests Cook *et al.* did not find statistically signficant results that were replicable across different modes of data analysis. However, most of the effects were in the direction of *Sesame Street* having taught the skills in question.

4. "The data . . . suggested to us that one season's viewing . . . was not caus-ing as generalized or as large learning gains as those that were attributed to 'Sesame Street' in the two ETS reports. When we considered effects that met statistical criteria of social significance, the series seemed to have practical consequences only for gains in letter-related skills." Furthermore, "these skills may not have included learning to recite the alphabet any more quickly than would have happened in the course of the child's maturation [Cook *et al.*, 1975, p. 264]."

5. The above conclusions apply only to economically disadvantaged children.

6. The above results depend upon a valid measure of viewing. Cook *et al.* question the viewing measures used in the ETS evaluation but find the post-test parent questionnaire the most useful. The degree to which it is valid is unknown.

7. The samples of not-encouraged children were small in both the first-year and second-year evaluation (not exceeding 110 children in either year). This precluded extensive and sensitive analysis of the data.

In summary Cook *et al* (1975, pp. 326–327) conclude that *Sesame Street* taught letter, number, and object relations skills. Cook *et al.* also find that *Sesame Street* is viewed more frequently by children of higher income, better educated parents. It is in this pessimistic context that Cook *et al.* find econo-mically disadvantaged children making greater gains from viewing *Sesame Street* than advantaged ones.

Cook *et al.* (1975, pp. 241–245) cite an unpublished dissertation by Minton (1972) that corroborates their findings. Minton obtained the Metropolitan Readiness Scores (MRT) of 482 preschoolers in 1968, 495 in 1969, 524 in 1970. The Metropolitan measures readiness for first grade. *Sesame Street* was not on the air until 1970. The preschoolers were between the ages of 58 and 70 months. Minton was able to divide the sample into three distinct groups: (1) affluent surburban white children; (2) economically disadvantaged children previously enrolled in a Head Start program (50% black, 10% Spanish-speaking, 40% white); and (3) working-class middle-income children from all socioeconomic levels who later went to a parochial school. Data collected by Minton indicated substantial levels of viewing of *Sesame Street* by all three groups in 1970, the first year *Sesame Street* was available. Out of six subtests on the Metropolitan, only the alphabet subtest was statistically significant in the direction indicating that *Sesame Street* had been effective. The matching subtest was significant in the opposite direction.

Minton employed an ingenious design to control for the possibility that the kind of child entering kindergarten in 1970 differed from the kind of child entering kindergarten in 1969. The design employed a sibling control. Minton found all children in the 1969 and 1970 samples who had an older sibling. Next, differences in MRT scores between siblings, where available, were compared for the 1969 and 1970 samples. The rationale of this procedure is that neither the 1969 children nor their older siblings could have watched *Sesame Street*, so that any differences in MRT scores between younger and older siblings when they entered school could not have been due to *Sesame Street*. However, such differences might be due to the younger siblings having watched *Sesame Street*, while their older siblings could not have watched the program. If the 1970 children were to be found to know more than their older siblings had upon entering first grade and if this difference were larger than the difference between siblings in the 1969 sample, then this would be strong evidence than *Sesame Street* caused learning and not that some unknown difference existed between the 1969 and 1970 children. Only the alphabet subtest of the MRT was statistically significant confirming the Cook *et al.* reexamination of the ETS data. Further analysis reveals that the economically advantaged children outperformed the other two groups on the alphabet subtest. There were no statistically significant effects for the economically disadvantaged children. Thus, in the Minton data there is no support for the thesis that *Sesame Street* improved any aspect of reading readiness among the target population of economically disadvantaged preschoolers.

In this author's analysis it was argued that the differences in home environments might explain much of the positive results attributed to *Sesame Street*. Partial support of this claim is obtained from Cook *et al.* in their analysis of encouraged children. They report that the mothers of encouraged children watched the show more with their children, talked with their children more about the show, and played more games with their children based on *Sesame Street*. Cook *et al.* (1975) conclude, "it was not clear whether the construct causing learning was viewing, the new mother-child interaction pattern attributable to encouragement, or some other correlate of encouragement [p. 146]."

Two broad issues discussed extensively by Cook *et al.* are germane to the general discussion surrounding the advisability of increased educational programming for young children. First, Cook *et al.* argue that *Sesame Street* may be widening the achievement gap between economically advantaged and disadvantaged children (see the discussion of the Coleman Report in Chapter 2). In a relative sense, advantaged children may be getting more benefits than disadvantaged ones. Although disadvantaged children may be helped overall, Cook *et al.* believe that the relative difference between groups is the most important educational issue. It is primarily for this reason that Cook *et al.* question *Sesame Street* as a "public good." Without going into a detailed reply, it seems to this

author that: (1) The Cook *et al.* arguments are premature, since there is considerable doubt, even in the Cook *et al.* evaluation, that *Sesame Street* is making a
meaningful educational difference. (2) Relative gaps may well be important in
the social psychology of group comparison processes. Social psychology and
child development are, however, distinctly different fields of study. The evidence used by the Cook *et al.* group may therefore not apply to the education of
preschoolers, where attainment of a threshold may be more important. (3)
Whether a gap widens or decreases should depend on what is taught. On this last
point, economically disadvantaged preschoolers may require a specifically designed curriculum tailored to their special needs. This issue is discussed in the
remaining portions of this chapter.

One additional point brought up by Cook *et al.* concerns cost–effectiveness.
It is argued by CTW that the unit costs of reaching the individual child with
Sesame Street are extremely low in comparison to more traditional educational
approaches. Cook *et al.* argue that costs will be signficantly higher if encouragement must be applied door-to-door amongst the disadvantaged in order for
Sesame Street to have a meaningful educational impact. They question the
advisability of diverting limited educational resources away from traditional
programs for this purpose.

EDUCATIONAL IMPLICATIONS OF
TELEVISED INSTRUCTION

Sesame Street attempts to teach certain skills in the home that are normally
learned in formal school environments. What is most remarkable about the
conclusions of their research is that their claim to positive results stands in
marked contrast to the reported negative results of almost all formal schooling
efforts for disadvantaged young children (Granger *et al.*, 1969; Jensen, 1969;
McDill *et al.*, 1969; White, 1970). This fact alone should motivate the serious
researcher in this field to reexamine the CTW research efforts to find out what
they did correctly, or conversely, what everyone else did incorrectly.

The Home-Environment Effect

What seems to be a strong likelihood is that CTW stumbled upon a home-
environment effect almost incidental to their educational efforts. In the previous
sections evidence from the ETS report itself was documented. The argument
made for a home-environment effect was quite strong. Of course, further
research is needed to substantiate that conclusion.

Additional support for a home-environment effect comes from other sources.

What has been little recognized until recently is that disadvantaged children's home environments are much more subject to positive influences than was previously thought. To illustrate the point, two references, one recent and the other a bit older, are quoted.

In the research cited by Smith (1968, p. 106), parents in Flint, Michigan were given educational materials (educational toys, children's dictionaries, etc.) and were asked to provide a quiet spot where their child could study and read. Parents were also asked to set aside a time each day to read aloud to their child. Over 90% of the parents responded positively to the requests, and over 90% of the parents wanted the program to continue. "Parents were eager to participate in the program. The contention that these parents were not interested in their children was not, therefore, supported; in fact it was overwhelmingly refuted [Smith, 1968, pp. 106–107]."

In another study, done by Orvis Irwin of the University of Iowa, there are indications that increasing the simulation of the environment of a young child of lower-class background will lead to heightened interest in language and improvements in speech. McCandless (1961) describes Irwin's research as follows:

> Ordinarily, such mothers do little reading to their children at any age, and almost certainly none in the first year or so of their babies' lives. Irwin persuaded 55 mothers to read aloud to their children for at least ten minutes a day from the time that they were little more than babies (one year old). . . .
>
> Irwin measured the youngsters' speech development regularly and found great differences [from controls] in all phases of speech by the time the children were 20 months of age. These differences appear to be highly significant statistically. . . . Irwin reports the experimental mothers' amazement and chagrined amusement: "You asked us to read ten minutes a day," many exclaimed, "but I can't get away from that kid. He wants me to read to him all the time [p. 260]."

There is additional support in the recent research findings confirming that home environments of disadvantaged children are indeed susceptible to outside positive influences. These influences, generally exerted on the mother to alter her behavior toward her child, have proved effective in altering the mother's behavior and in improving the child's intellectual attainments. Table 3.11 presents a brief documentation of a wide range of programs. Indeed, it is hard to find home learning programs that do not claim successful intervention.

Illustrative of the broad purpose of many such home-learning programs, the goals of the Perry Preschool Project are cited:

> The effect of the Ypsilanti program on the mothers of the participating children is intended to be social influence, a gradual but relatively superficial change in the mothers' attitudes and perspectives toward middle-class educational values. . . the process which the children are experiencing by participation in the program is intended to be something more than social influence. It is intended to be a socializa-

TABLE 3.11
Results of Mother–Child Home-Learning Programs

Reference	Comments
Badger, 1968, 1969	Results show gains on Stanford–Binet and ITBA. Mothers' attitudes changed positively in respect to teaching their infants. Concludes that parents must be included in programs for the disadvantaged.
Boger *et al.* 1969	Results show improvement in language performance, self-concept development, and mother–child interaction as a result of a parent-education language program.
Gilmer, 1969	Results show that the two groups that received both sibling and maternal involvement had greater conceptual development. Maximum intervention effects appear to result when mothers are involved in the program, and the younger siblings of these children are also positively affected.
Gordon, 1969	Results show that (1) paraprofessionals can be used to teach mothers; (2) a parent-education program should be part of a comprehensive system of social change; (3) concrete specific stimulation exercises are a sound curriculum approach; (4) how a child is taught may be more important than what he is taught; and (5) standardized techniques for measuring learning and development are needed.
Karnes *et al.*, 1970	Results show gains on the Stanford–Binet and ITBA.
Levenstein, 1971	Program children (the Mother–Child Home Program used specially trained home visitors who visited twice weekly over 7-month periods) made and retained significantly higher gains on intelligence tests than children in contrast groups.
Mann, 1970	Results show that a structured language program (1) produced a significant change in the syntax style of mothers and the pattern of verbal interaction between mothers and children; and (2) effectively changed the syntax of the children.
Micotti, 1970	Results show that children demonstrated marked improvement in concept and language development; mothers showed considerable changes in terms of attitudes, educational materials apparent in the homes, and upkeep of themselves and their homes.
Miller, 1968	Results show that younger siblings whose mothers participated in the early-training program were superior in all comparisons.
Mothers' Training Program, 1970	The participating infants in the mothers' training program show increasing improvement on intelligence tests.

(*continued*)

TABLE 3.11 (Continued)
Results of Mother–Child Home Learning Programs

Reference	Comments
Niedermeyer, 1969	Results show that the Parent-Assisted Learning Program (PAL) and Southwest Regional Laboratory First-Year Communication Skills Program (SWRL) elicited high levels of parent participation and pupil learning.
Orhan and Radin, 1968	Results show that children whose mothers were counseled achieved significantly higher scores on the Metropolitan Readiness Test, and their mothers showed a significantly greater gain on the Cognitive Home Environment Scale.
Rayder et al., 1970	Results show that children whose parents were taught to teach them through the use of educational toys learned a considerable amount.
Schaefer and Aaronson, 1970	Results confirm the success of the program for the home-tutored infants.
Weikart et al., 1970	Results show that children who participated in the program (daily cognitively oriented preschool plus home visits each week to involve mothers in the educative process) obtained significantly higher scores than control-group children on measures of cognitive ability and achievement and received better teacher ratings on academic, emotional, and social development. The significant difference in cognitive ability disappeared by third grade, but other gains were maintained.

tion process, the internalization of values and behavior patterns of the school environment [Perry Preschool Project, 1969].

The positive findings of mother–child home-learning programs seem to be directly related to the positive results reported by CTW researchers. Thus, the thesis that *Sesame Street* is effective needs elaboration in order to fully appreciate its implications. *Sesame Street* might be most effective when the home environment in which it is presented responds favorably to the educational stimulation it provides.

Home environment can create a substantial influence rather early in development. It seems that children can be taught, with sufficient effort, a wide variety of complex perceptual discriminations as early as 6 months (Ling, 1941) or to read before 2 years of age (Mates, 1972). There are, however, two related concerns associated with accelerating these newly found capacities in the human infant. The first is that these abilities must develop in a social context rich enough to support them. An appropriate home environment and the influence of the mother can be decisive. The second concern involves what should and should not be accelerated in the infant. Both concerns are vital to educators involved in child development.

What Does It Mean to Be Disadvantaged?

It is not possible to fully explore at this time what it means to be a disadvantaged child. But briefly, it does not seem to be social class by itself that is the important variable; rather it seems that middle-class parents have different expectations for their children than do disadvantaged parents. Middle-class standards emphasize internalized standards of conduct resulting in self-control, while disadvantaged parents stress qualities that ensure respectability and obedience. Indeed, if the series of studies in recent years from the University of California at Berkeley are to be fully appreciated, it seems that growing up as a well-adjusted middle-class child means having parents who are controlling and demanding but at the same time warm, rational, communicative, and receptive to their children's communications. There is a balance between nurturance and control, high demands and clear communication, along with encouragement of the child's independent explorations. This type of parent has been labeled *authoritative* by Baumrind (1968) and seems most likely to produce children who are very mature, competent, and self-reliant (Baumrind, 1972). Naturally, enough, any child of normal intelligence with such personality characteristics should do well in school.

It is also the case that middle-class children possess more refined learning strategies than do disadvantaged children. These more refined strategies would appear to be taught in the home, most likely as an integral part of the middle-class socialization process. From extensive research in learning experiments with advantaged and disadvantaged children, Rohrer (1971) concludes that differences in learning are not so much due to differences in the ability to learn but to inferior learning strategies of disadvantaged children. Rohrer proposes that the discrepancy in learning ability between middle-class and disadvantaged children exists because successful performance on complex intellectual tasks requires spontaneous, uninstructed conceptual activity, and middle-class children have learned to supply this additional conceptual activity of an elaborative nature without specifically being told to do so, while disadvantaged children have not.

Rohrer's results point toward differences in learning needs between disadvantaged and middle-class children. Disadvantaged children need special training in imaginative conceptual activities, using concrete, explicit, and specific instructional programs.

Another distinguishing characteristic of middle-class children as opposed to disadvantaged ones involves socialization of internalized control over behavior.

There are two extreme patterns of parental discipline that seem applicable to differences between middle-class and disadvantaged homes. The first is characterized as "psychological" or "love oriented" and is labeled by Aronfreed (1968, p. 316) as induction. The basic prototype of the second category is physical punishment, but it may also include "screaming" and "bawling out" and is labeled by Aronfreed (1968, p. 316) as sensitization. Induction-type discipline is predominently used among the upper classes, and sensitization-type discipline is predominently used among the lower classes. The consequences of these different patterns of usage are severe.

> Parents of higher socioeconomic status generally behave in ways which would tend to induce an internal governor in their children. Along with their relatively close control over their children's behavior, they use a verbal medium of discipline and much explicit withdrawal of affection. They also concern themselves with intentions behind their children's actions. Parents of lower socioeconomic status tend to exercise less immediate control over their children's activities, and seem to give them their attention primarily to the visible manifestations of transgression. Their discipline more frequently takes the form of direct attack, with less explanation of their punishment, and is therefore more likely to sensitize their children to the punitive consequences of transgressions. Children from the two major social classes in our society do differ in their evaluative expressions of conscience, and in the orientation of their internalized reactions to transgression, in ways which are predictable from their predominent experience of discipline . . . [Aronfreed, 1968, p. 320].
>
> The children of parents whose disciplinary habits are induction oriented show a more internalized and abstract orientation toward principles of conscience, when they are asked to verbally express and apply their evaluative standards to specific hypothetical actions, than do children of parents whose disciplinary habits are sensitization oriented . . . [Aronfreed, 1968, p. 321].
>
> [In contrast] sensitization discipline tends to subject the child to punishment that is immediate and focused in time. It makes the avoidance or the occurrence of punishment, rather than any act of the child, the event that marks the resolution of a transgression [Aronfreed, 1968, p. 322].

Thus, the comparison of the two forms of discipline yields two different types of children. Induction discipline is found to have positive association with the child's internalized self-corrective reactions to transgressions. Sensitization discipline is found to be associated with the child's tendency to perceive the resolution of a transgression in aversive external consequences that are beyond his control.

What are the educational implications of all this information for the disadvantaged child? As a start toward an answer, the disadvantaged child is typically at a severe handicap in terms of his general socialization. He is not nearly as mature, competent, or self-reliant. His learning strategies are inferior to those of the middle-class child. He does not spontaneously use uninstructed conceptual activities such as verbal mediation ("thinking out") in solving problems. In terms of discipline, he is keyed typically to a moral level that makes prolonged internalization and self-control of behavior infrequent. One could imagine that educating this type of child would present different types of problems than does educating the middle-class child.

What Do We Need to Teach the Disadvantaged?

If the problems of teaching the disadvantaged child are radically different from those of teaching the middle-class child, then this leads quite naturally into a second major problem area—what do we teach the disadvantaged? The most direct approach to this issue is to teach the disadvantaged child those "social attitudes," "learning strategies," and "self-discipline techniques" of a middle-class kind that lead to success in school. This approach, however, is not obvious. *Sesame Street* sees the disadvantaged child as lacking in certain basic skills (such as number and letter recognition, counting, ordering, sorting, etc.) and attempts to teach these skills. CTW's goal seems to be to teach those skills that directly prepare the child for formal schooling. Basically, this approach negates the important socialization distinction previously outlined between middle-class and disadvantaged children. Such an approach would not be ultimately successful in breaking the cycle of disadvantage.

CTW (and ultimately others involved in educational television) should stress socialization of a middle-class kind in their programming. For instance, it might be most instructive to repeat over and over again (with variations) the basic theme of little children misbehaving and their mothers withholding affection until there is a correction of the misdeed by the child. Or, it would be similarly instructive for disadvantaged (and advantaged) children to observe children on TV figuring various problems "out loud" in a variety of different ways. It is important to note that basic learning strategies are hard to acquire and, once acquired, may be infrequently used (especially by the disadvantaged). Observation of others using these learning strategies to solve important problems may instruct the disadvantaged child to use them frequently himself. Finally, the basic attitude that it is desirable to possess internal control over one's behavior, to be able to monitor one's behavior, to introspect and learn to correct one's behavior gradually through this introspection is something within the technical capacity of educational television to teach young children.

Whether or not children socialized within a different framework than middle class can actually acquire the themes of middle-class socialization practices, learn to alter their behavior, and adopt sophisticated learning strategies would be mainly conjecture, since such an approach has not been tried on a mass scale. Observational learning requires environmental support if it is to be sustained in behavior. Therefore, simultaneous to any such socialization efforts through television there must also be parent education that is supportive.

Middle-class parents are already teaching appropriately, and consequently their children readily learn from whatever the source (books, toys, parents, and television). The content of the material learned (be it the alphabet or respect for others) is more readily acquired because of middle-class socialization, which supports such learning. This is not the case for the disadvantaged child, and because of this, other approaches are necessary in order to teach them effectively.

What is perhaps the most important implication of this discussion is that there must be a much greater emphasis on parent education than heretofore attempted. Educational television can be conceived, in most instances, as a "stimulus" for initiating active engagement of the child in the learning process. Television viewing is not generally the learning process itself (although in certain circumstances it can be). The learning process involves an active engagement between learner and material. New material must be integrated in a meaningful way into what is already known by the child. In contrast, television is mostly a passive medium, with little active participation between viewer and screen. Therefore, most of the meaningful learning takes place away from the screen, in real-life situations where actions can be modified, corrected, and repeated; where problems can be studied intensively, reconstructed, and tried out on others. As Kessen (1963) so aptly puts it, there has been a shift in our concept of early development and how the child learns,

> from the child who is a passive receptacle, into which learning and maturation pour knowledge and skills and affects until he is full, to the child who is a complex competent organism who, by acting on the environment and being acted on in turn, develops more elaborated and balanced ways of dealing with discrepancy, conflict and dis-equilibrium [p. 84].

It is for this reason, given the *special* problems of the disadvantaged child, that educational televison must solicit the help of the mother. It has already been documented that mothers of disadvantaged children are generally enthusiastic about receiving such help and that once mothers participate, the home environment generally gets better and children's behavior and cognitive abilities improve.

Another Educational Television Project for Preschool Disadvantaged Children

It is now appropriate to cite research that used educational television with poor whites from Appalachia. In this research, television instruction, when used to do the job of educating preschool disadvantaged children by itself, failed. The possibility of positively influencing the child's environment through a combination of a home-visitor program, mobile instruction, and educational television was explored by Appalachia Educational Laboratory (AEL) Early Childhood

Education Program (Bertram *et al.*, 1971a; Evaluation Report, 1970). The ECE Program was a home-oriented instructional system designed for 3-, 4-, and 5-year-olds, which was used on approximately 25,000 deprived children in Appalachia. The program consisted of a 30-minute daily television lesson, a weekly home visit by a paraprofessional, and group instruction once a week in a mobile classroom. The sample consisted of 450 children, divided into three groups, however, only 30 children were tested for evaluation purposes from each of the three groups. Group 1 received TV instruction and home visits and attended the mobile classroom; Group 2 had home visits; and Group 3 had only TV instruction. It was found (Evaluation Report, 1970) that TV lessons and home visitations (but not the mobile classroom) had a positive effect on children's cognitive development. It was also found (Hines, 1971) that the children who viewed only the television program and were not exposed to the home visitor and mobile van teachers scored significantly lower on the evaluation of cognitive attainments. Results indicate that the home visitor, more than any other part of the program, had a greater potential for influencing the child's behavior, especially if she could produce changes in the child's environment.

The ECE Program is the only other substantially researched educational television effort. Its results are very different from those reported by CTW. Admittedly, there are large difference between the two programs. However, it is still worthwhile to note the ECE conclusion which supports the present contention that changing the home environment creates the most substantial improvement in the child. Educational TV, by itself, produced significantly lower cognitive attainments than those measured in the groups who were additionally exposed to mobile van instruction and home visitors.

There is one last comment that should be included concerning instructional television for preschool children. Specific skills training (letters, numbers, etc.) should be broadened to a much greater extent than, for instance, is represented on *Sesame Street*. The instructional program should include tasks that directly involve middle-class cognitive strategies for their successful solution. Instruction in the traditional skills has little plausibility when applied to disadvantaged children. As Kohlberg (1968) phrases it, after analyzing the problem in detail:

> It is even less possible to use traditional intellectual instruction techniques with disadvantaged preschool children than it is with middle-class preschool children. The notion that academic intellectual instruction can remedy the cognitive—structural retardation of culturally disadvantaged children, then, has little plausibility. Thus, the objectives of preschool programs for the disadvantaged must be phrased in other terms [p. 1039].

These other terms involve a massive influx of general experience from many sources that can serve to structure the world of the child in a more inclusive and abstract way. For instance, there is evidence that the ability to understand the Piaget conservation problems is not improved by specific instruction on them, but only by a general experience from confronting such problems in diverse ways in everyday life. As an example, the child who observes water poured from a short wide glass into a long narrow one and says that there is now more water to drink in the long narrow one fails to understand conservation because the structure of his mental abilities is not yet adequate to deal with the totality of the change simultaneously. His concentration on one specific dimensional change obscures the compensation by another dimension or the possibility of reversal to the original state. Eventually the child learns from an active everyday involvement with such problems—not from specific instruction.

The evidence on Piaget-type conservation tasks indicates that disadvantaged and advantaged children solve them in the same order and rate. However, what differentiates the two classes is that for the advantaged the solutions to these basic problems of everyday experience are seen by their parents and thus by the children themselves as tools to be used on more abstract problems in life. Middle-class parents see their child's solutions of conservation tasks (e.g., substance, weight, volume), classification tasks, ordering tasks, etc., as the beginning in a sequence of abstract accomplishments. In general, this does not seem to be the case for disadvantaged children—their solutions to these basic problems of everyday experience appear mostly as their own ends.

CONCLUSION: THE NEED FOR ALTERNATIVES

Sesame Street, since its inception, has dominated educational television efforts directed at young children. Given the almost total absence of quality offerings prior to *Sesame Street*, it is not difficult to understand how leadership in this field could have been so readily acquired.

The rather impressive display of talent on the production staff, the leading psychologists and editors on the consulting staff, the volumes of research reports, the list of government and private sponsors, the effective advertising on the part of the producers, the international audience, and the apparent popularity of the show itself among both children and parents, have combined to add such an overwhelming positive aura to the production that it seems difficult for anyone else interested in educational television for young children to even contemplate offering alternatives.

But what has been demonstrated in this analysis is that alternatives are vitally needed. It certainly was not the initial intention of the group that founded *Sesame Street* to stifle others in their efforts. (For a delightful personal account of the history and people behind *Sesame Street*, see Mayer, 1972; or for a more recent account, see G. S. Lesser, 1974). They merely did their homework better than anyone else and they provided a much needed service by filling a gap in quality programming for the young child.

Reading through the diverse research reports produced by or for CTW, one frequently gets the impression that *Sesame Street* and its big brother, *The Electric Company*, are not fixed but are constantly evolving. The impression obtained is that any criticism will be labeled as dated or as potentially of use in the next ongoing modification. This impression is misleading, since CTW appears to be open only to criticisms that conform to its basic philosophical position concerning the education of young children. In spite of all the changes in content, the broadening of the kinds of skills taught, the minor changes in format, and the revised emphasis on other techniques of instruction (to name just a few changes), the major philosophical thrust of the producers has remained the same—direct training in the content areas of formal schooling as preparatory to school.

It is hoped that other well-intentioned groups will prepare viable alternatives to *Sesame Street*. To some extent this is already happening (Leifer, Gordon, & Groves, 1974). Sufficiently strong evidence has been presented to justify such proposals.

One proposal is to be found in succeeding chapters of this book. It is based on an extensive survey of the research literature on the cognitive, linguistic, perceptual, and mnemonic development of the child during the preschool years.

4

Cognition and Its Development: Fostering Reasoning Abilities in Young Children

This chapter describes theories and experiments of three different schools of child psychology as they relate to the cognitive development of young children. The purpose of the description is to tie these separate strands together so that an effective instructional strategy and appropriate curriculum content for pre-schoolers can be developed for use on the television medium. The application of this knowledge about young children, much of it recently acquired, to television instruction is the principal goal of this chapter.

The review of the American, Soviet, and Swiss research efforts in child psychology reveal some striking similarities in the descriptions of preschool children offered. In a way, this is remarkable, since the experimental approaches of these groups to children are so dissimilar. The Swiss approach is largely clinical, with little statistical sophistication; the American approach is highly experimental and employs sophisticated experimental designs; and the Soviet approach is strongly influenced by conditioning and is oriented toward practical and pedagogical issues. Such correspondence of results proceeding from dissimilar approaches is highly encouraging, since it suggests an accurate description of children, rather than a product of a particular bias in methodology.

There are, however, some differences between the three schools. The Swiss are considerably more conservative than the Americans and Soviets on the possibility of speeding up development through environmental stimulation. On the other hand, there are some striking similarities between the Soviets and the Swiss in the descriptions of the developmental stages.

Although children seem to pass through fixed sequences of developmental stages in cognition, language, etc., controversy persists over the possibility, or even the desirability, of attempting to accelerate development. Training studies from these three sources are examined to determine whether it is feasible to accelerate development. The tasks taught and the techniques employed are closely scrutinized. This is the issue of instructional strategy, or "how to teach." The applicability of such training to televised instruction is then explored.

Another important issue that warrants extended discussion in this chapter is the question of what to teach. The technology of teaching is advanced enough to teach young children numerous complex skills. The task of psychologists and educators is therefore to discover those skills that are critical to the development of advanced reasoning, particularly those skills that presage future readiness to learn in school. An effort to answer the question of "what to teach" and to apply the answer to televised instruction is another goal of this chapter.

Selecting from the vast array of topics in the literature on early child development was not an easy task. The topics selected were chosen with an eye toward their usefulness for televised instruction. They were also selected because they seemed to illustrate important themes in development that must be achieved by children in order to ensure their readiness for school. Therefore, the topics chosen for review are neither comprehensive in themselves nor representative of the totality of the literature on early child development.

COGNITION

The Theories of Piaget

Sensorimotor Thought

Within Piaget's theory of cognitive development there are four broadly defined periods: the sensorimotor period, from about 0 to 2 years; the preoperational period, from about 2 to 7 years; the concrete operational period, from about 7 to 11 or 12 years; and the formal operational period, which continues into adulthood. The main concern here is with developments within the preoperational period, since this period includes the critical years prior to formal schooling as well as the early school years. However, according to Piaget, the child's accomplishments during the sensorimotor period form the essential base for conceptual thought. Therefore, some understanding of sensorimotor thought should be attained before proceeding to preoperational thought.

There is one topic that stands out above all others in sensorimotor development. That is the development of object concept. According to Bower (1974) Piaget refers to the development of object concept as "the prototype of cognitive development," and the attainment of the object concept is "the most precocious expression of processes that will eventually generate mathematical reasoning and logical thinking in adults [p. 181]."

What is the object concept and what is the course of its development? The usual way in which the object concept is studied is by examining infants' reactions to objects that have vanished or have been hidden. As described by Bower (1974, pp. 183–187), the following is Piaget's (1936/1953, 1937/1954, 1946/1951) account of the six stages in the development of object concept:

Stage 1: 0–2 months. Initially, there is no special behavior toward vanished objects.

Stage 2: 2–4 months. Some tracking with head and eyes occurs after objects have moved out of the field of view.

Stage 3: 4–6 months. Infants reach out and pick up objects that they see. They also reach out and take objects that are partially hidden when presented to them. Infants do not make any attempt to reach out and obtain an object if it is presented to them and then completely covered. According to Piaget and many other observers, "they act as if the object no longer exists [Bower, 1974, p. 183]."

Stage 4: 6–12 months. Infants search for an object that has been hidden in the same place that they have previously found it, even though they have seen it hidden in another place. For instance, an infant finds an object under a cloth several times and then the object is hidden, within the infants view, under another cloth in another place. The infant continues to search for the object under the first cloth in the original place. According to Bower (1974) "This error implies that the infant does not yet really understand that an object which has been covered by a cloth is under that cloth. The infants seem to think that an object that has been hidden will always be found in the same place [p. 183]."

Stage 5: 12–15 months. Infants do not take account of invisible displacements of objects, even when the displacements of the covering object are visible. For instance, two cloths are put on a table. An object is hidden under one of them. The cloths are transposed, entirely in the field of view of the child. The infant searches for the object in the place where it was first placed. According to Bower (1974), "infants seem to believe that an object will be found where it was hidden; they do not take into account invisible displacements of the object even when the displacements of the thing covering the object are fully visible [p. 183]."

Stage 6: 15–18 months. Infants succeed in all of the tasks listed above.

The ages are approximate, and there is considerable individual difference. Bower (1974, p. 180) argues that the changes in infants' behavior toward vanished objects demonstrates that their behavior is being governed by an increasingly complex set of rules, which serve to lessen the dependence of infants upon the immediate stimulus situation and toward rules "that combine perceptual information with information from memory [p. 180]." This development is progressive and, according to Bower, defines cognitive development.

It is possible to trace a similar development of the concepts of space, cause, and time during the sensorimotor period. However, it is sufficient for the present purposes to indicate that children at the close of the sensorimotor period are accomplished participants in the world of objects. Their behavior indicates that they are easily able to follow objects in space, to understand events of a causal nature between objects, and to understand that the duration of an event is independent of personal involvement.

This is a considerable achievement. Consider the following event:

> *A ball is thrown in a very large room along a very complex trajectory—it hits other objects, bounces around, is partially hidden from view during segments of its flight, etc.*

The child at the close of the sensorimotor period has little difficulty in finding the ball at the end of its trajectory. The younger sensorimotor child would not find the ball. Piaget argues that the acquisition of the ability to navigate successfully through the world of objects, places, and events requires the active engagement of children in the world around them. However, this ability develops in the world of action, is constructed in the world of action, and is represented in the world of action. Consequently, the behavioral accomplishments of sensorimotor children are described as preconceptual—that is, they do not require the representation of objects, places, and events either in mental images or in speech. The next development, conceptual thought, requires a leap of a higher order than did previous achievements. The magnitude of the leap is indicated by the length of time it requires children to complete it—approximately 10 years.

The Transition to Conceptual, or Representational, Thought

> Take, for example, a box or some object upon which the child acts. At the end of his sensorimotor evolution he becomes perfectly capable of turning the box over in all directions, of representing to himself its reverse side as well as its visible parts, its content as well as its exterior. But do these representations connected with practical activity ... suffice to constitute a total representation of the box [Piaget, 1937/1954, p. 414]?[1]

Piaget's answer to this question is no. Total representation of the box requires that it be conceived from all sides at once. Children must be capable of locating the box in a system of perspectives in which "one can represent it to oneself

---

[1] Adapted from the conclusion in *The Construction of Reality in the Child*, by Jean Piaget, translated by Margaret Cook, © 1954 by Basic Books, Inc., Publishers, New York.

from any point of view whatever and transfer it from one to the other point of view without recourse to action [Piaget, 1937/1954, p. 414]."

This ability to see the box from all sides at once develops gradually during the preoperational period. Piaget believes that this ability derives from children's gradually adapting themselves to the points of view of others and to the coordination between these different points of view with their own. If children can imagine themselves as simultaneously occupying the positions of several others and also of coordinating the perspective of others with their own perspective, they will solve the problem of the total representation of the box.

However, children at the completion of the sensorimotor period lack these abilities and consequently fail at total representation. For instance, given a model of three mountains, children are incapable of representing to themselves what they would see if they were in the various positions that the doll is placed in. In fact, the children at the earliest stage always see their own point of view as correct. Afterward slightly older children pass through a transitional stage and confuse their perspective with that of the other. Later, older children are able to solve this problem correctly.

Piaget argues that there are two principal limitations of the preoperational stage, which explains why conceptual thought is initially limited and does not advance directly from the fledgling efforts at representing reality already present at the close of the sensorimotor period.

The first limitation of preoperational thought is that reality is represented only for the purpose of exerting an influence upon it. The sole problem for younger preoperational children is to seek success or failure. They do not reflect upon the relations that make an event possible, and do not attempt to discover the underlying operating principles of things in order to discover how they work. Knowledge, as such, is not an aim; success, rather than failure, is the sole desired goal. However, older preoperational children have demands placed upon them by adults that motivate more advanced functioning. Success and failure become dependent upon understanding the operating principles behind the functioning of things. Thus, under the impact of socialization with adults, older preoperational children are motivated by the fact that their actions on things frequently do not produce the desired results. They increasingly seek out the truth behind the appearance or reflect upon the relations that make the result possible. Eventually children generate what are for them relatively sophisticated principles about reality, which they attempt to generalize to other aspects of reality.

The second limitation of preoperational thought is that it is initially ego-centric at the level of social interaction. This is illustrated by two extremes in behavior. At one extreme children take their own point of view, unaware of the point of view of others. At the other extreme, children demonstrate astonishing docility to the statements and demands of others. However, adults require children to see other points of view and incorporate them into their own. They require this of children in increasingly complex situations. Thus, under the tutulage of adults, children are eventually forced to give up both their exclusive awareness of their own point of view and their extreme docility. These two points of view, at first dissociated, eventually merge in such a way that children become more flexible in their social interactions.

The process of development in the sensorimotor stage parallels development in the preoperational stage. Basically, sensorimotor development proceeds from action centered upon the child to a universe existing independently of the child's actions. The initial stages of preoperational thought display a corresponding egocentrism in thought, which only gradually emerges into an objective mental representation of reality. Thus, it is possible to point to similarities in mental processes of babies who believe that objects disappear when they are not in view and preoperational children who believe that the mass of objects change according to their different shapes. In the early stages of conceptual thought processes the object is not conceived in the child's representations as permanent, although it has already achieved this status at the level of action. Similarly, in mental representation the child's concept of space is limited compared with its development at the level of action, where the child can follow an object through a complex trajectory. The preoperational child has difficulty in representing space, particularly when it involves coordinating different perspectives, as the mountain experiment so amply illustrates. Also, causality at the level of mental representation takes on curious aspects, a prime example being transductive reasoning, or reasoning that proceeds from particular case to particular case and does not achieve true generalization without logical contradiction. For instance, younger preoperational children (average age 5 years) explain a shadow produced by an object on a table before their eyes as coming from "under the trees" or other sources of darkness (Piaget, 1966, pp. 181–186). At the early stages of conceptual thought the shadow is a substance emanating from the object and participating with night. Causality at the level of action is, however, more advanced as the child seeks out the contact between objects to explain a result. At the level of mental representation, causality seems to undergo a regression before advancing beyond the capabilities of the sensorimotor period.

The difficulties experienced by children in the preoperational period ultimately herald a much more powerful ability to memorize, organize, retain, and understand reality through mental representations that do not require personal activity. Children eventually reorient themselves away from solving problems exclusively through actions upon objects. They gradually begin to use symbolic representations of reality to solve problems (restating the problem in words or picturing an object and the interrelationship of its parts in mental images). For instance, through the use of speech adults are able to categorize objects and events according to their shared qualities. This facilitates the retention of enormous amounts of complicated information.

The shift from reasoning primarily centered upon the child's own actions to reasoning primarily centered upon language and mental images results in an initial disorientation during the preoperational period. This initial disorientation, however, eventually "pays off" in a much more powerful way of handling reality.

Cognitive Child Psychology in the Soviet Union

The examination of Soviet research efforts in thinking (Zaphorozhets, Zinchenko, & Elkonin, 1964/1971, pp. 186–254) reveals some remarkable correspondences in the descriptions of children by Soviet and Swiss researchers. These findings are encouraging because the research approaches of these two groups differ widely. However, in many instances the Soviets interpret their data differently than do the Swiss. It is this difference in interpretation, supported by additional research efforts, which suggests that it is possible to adapt the research literature on child development to instructional television.

The Soviets make a distinction between visual–motor thinking and discursive thinking. Visual–motor thinking refers to the child's developing ability to solve problems with objects through increasingly sophisticated activities with them. For instance, children initially treat a spoon as an extension of their arm. Consequently, until they discover how to use it as a tool, they drop most of their food. The Soviets point out that the correct use of spoons occurs only after a long training period in which adult instruction plays an important role. According to the Soviets, the highest achievement of visual–motor thinking involves the purely visual inspection of a complex situation (e.g., a lever must be pressed or rotated in order to swing an object into arm's reach) and then, only on the basis of this visual inspection, the performance of the correct practical solution. A closer examination reveals that visual–motor thinking develops through four distinct stages:

1. *Primitive chaotic:* Children do not orient themselves toward the conditions of the problem. They look at the room or the experimenter instead.
2. *Goal directed:* Children focus completely on the goal, try to reach it, but ignore the means to the goal (e.g., lever).
3. *Visual–motor:* Children manually explore both the goal and the means (e.g., the lever connected to the goal).
4. *Visual:* Children explore the problem purely visually; they observe the relationship of the component parts of the lever and its connection to the goal; then they immediately perform the correct practical solution.

Discursive thinking is a later development and involves solving problems exclusively in verbal terms. An experiment by Minskaya (cited by Zaphorozhets *et al.*, 1964/1971, pp. 228–231), gives a clear example of discursive thinking, in addition to illustrating the Soviet position on the stages of thought through which the preschool child passes. The mechanisms responsible for this stage-by-stage transition are also elaborated.

Four groups of children, varying in age from 3 to 7, were asked to solve lever-type problems in the following ways: (a) by operating real levers to obtain real goals; (b) by relying upon their imagination when presented with the real problem; and (c) by narrating the possibilities of solving similar problems whose conditions were described to them verbally. Minskaya's results demonstrate a definite progression in the development of specific forms of thinking during the preschool age—first, (a) visual—motor thinking; then, (b) visual—figurative thinking; and finally, (c) verbal thinking. She proposes that the shift from visual—motor thinking to visual—figurative and verbal thinking depends on the degree of forming higher types of exploratory orientations. For instance, on the same lever-type problems, children were trained to solve them by encouraging verbal interaction between the participating children in addition to visual—motor training. The training influenced a shift to solving the problems using visual—figurative and verbal means. Thus, through orienting children to visual—figurative and verbal means, the number of younger children able to solve problems with these methods increased greatly.

It is also important to note that the Soviets not only emphasize the priority of visual—motor thinking, but also emphasize a two-sided connection between visual—motor and discursive thinking.

> On the one hand, the child's experience of direct actions with objects during the solution of simple practical problems prepares the necessary foundation for the emergence of discursive thinking. On the other hand, the development of discursive thinking changes the nature of objective actions and creates the possibility for a change from the elementary form of visual—motor thinking to the more complex form of an adult's intellectual activity [p. 228].[2]

The Soviets also emphasize that during the preschool period speech itself, as it relates to problem solving, undergoes some important transformations. Zaphorozhets et al. (1964/1971, p. 214) state that speech passes through three developmental stages:

(1) For the youngest preschoolers (3 to 4 years) there seem to be two independent ongoing types of activity: speech activity and intellectual activity that is devoted to the solution of practical problems. Frequent speech patterns at this age include emotional outbursts, echolalia, accidental and purely verbal

---

[2] This and subsequent quotes cited to Zaphorozhets et al., 1964/1971 are from A. V. Zaphorozhets, V. P. Zinchenka, and D. B. Elkonin, Development of thinking. In A. V. Zaphorozhets and D. B. Elkonin (Eds.), The Psychology of Preschool Children. Cambridge, Mass.: MIT Press, 1971. Reprinted by permission of MIT Press.

associations, and appeals to others. This type of speech, isolated from intellectual activity, frequently distracts the younger child from successful problem solving.

(2) In the middle preschool period (5 years), speech becomes the means for reflecting the situation. At this point, speech is a verbal form of activity or a copy of the child's behavior and of the situation. However, analysis reveals that the verbal expression always occurs at the end of the activity. It appears that speech functions at this point to translate the essence of the completed activity involved in performing the task into a verbal form and thus to help the child prepare for variations in the problem.

(3) For the older preschoolers (6 to 7 years), speech now begins to anticipate intellectual activity. At this stage, the child frequently thinks out loud. Furthermore, speech frequently dictates and determines the child's intellectual activity rather than mimicking it. For instance, the important role of speech at this stage is illustrated by an experiment by Levina (cited by Zaphorozhets et al., 1964/1971, p. 214). Children of late preschool age were asked to participate in a game called Silence, in which they were not permitted to talk. Results show that for these children "all attempts to play were paralyzed," that their "behavior became disorganized," and that they "experienced complete failure in the solution of given problems."

The Development of Reasoning

In younger preschoolers there is a general tendency to convert intellectual problems into playful activities (Zaphorozhets et al., 1964/1971, pp. 233–242). Two examples are given:

1. In response to "Which is the 'odd' one among pictures of a cup, glass, saucer, and piece of bread," a 6-year-old child replied, "If I were to have breakfast, I would pour the milk into the cup and would eat the bread. Therefore, the glass is not necessary here. It's extra [p. 235]." Older children and adults are likely to separate the bread from the dishes.
2. In reply to the problem "Six tanks were rolling along, two of them got broken. How many were left?" the younger preschooler responds, "They were fixed and they continued on their way [p. 236]."

The Soviets associate changes in the young ch.d's cognitive activities "with the appearance of new cognitive motives of play and practical activity [Zaphorozhets et al., 1964/1971, p. 236]." For instance, in the solution of puzzles among younger preschoolers playful elements predominate, but among older ones there exists the goal to understand the principle involved in the solution of the puzzle. Thus, the ability to reason emerges in the older preschooler under the pressure to solve problems.

In contrast, for younger preschoolers, to solve a problem means to act. For instance, Zaphorozhets *et al.* (1964/1971, p. 236) cite the case of the 3-year-old who was not able to reach an object placed very high. The experimenter told the child, "Why are you always jumping, it is better that you stop and think how you can reach that!" The child replied assertively, "No need to think, one ought to reach."

An experiment by Zaphorozhets and Likov (cited in Zaphorozhets *et al.*, 1964/1971, pp. 238–244) introduces in a concrete way the major principles involved in the development of reasoning among preschoolers. Children were asked to play a guessing game to determine whether an object would sink or swim if placed in water. After guessing, children could throw the object into the water to test their guess. Among the objects, there were some that were similar in a particular dimension (e.g., size, form, material). Therefore, it was possible to form generalizations that could guide future judgments. In addition, probing questions were asked of the children in order to determine the extent to which they could substantiate their judgments. Four stages of deductive reasoning were found in preschool children:

1. At 3–4 years, children do not employ general propositions; assertions are not supported.
2. At 4–5 years, children employ general propositions, but these propositions reflect reality inadequately. Children attempt to base solutions on generalizations formed on the basis of accidental external cues.
3. At 5–6 years, children employ propositions that approximate the existing aspects of reality but do not encompass all possible cases.
4. At 6–7 years, children employ propositions that correctly reflect reality. Correct deductions are made.

For instance, in solving the syllogism associated with the general proposition that "all wooden objects swim," there is observed the following stage-by-stage progression:

1. Objects will swim "because they want to wade," etc.
2. "Big ones swim and little ones don't," or "Long ones swim and round ones don't," etc.
3. "The heavy ones sink and the light ones swim."
4. "All wooden objects swim."

Venger (cited by Zaphorozhets *et al.*, 1964/1971, pp. 245–251) followed up this line of research by investigating the possibility of training preschoolers in why objects float. In the first series of training experiments the children were given pairs of floating or sinking objects based on material (wooden and metallic) and were allowed to test them in water. On this basis, they were required to form a generalization without help and then to transfer this generalization to new objects. Only half the preschoolers succeeded in forming a generalization using this training method.

In the second series of training experiments the children were allowed to play with the objects as in the first training series and in addition were required to separate the floating from nonfloating objects on the basis of experience and to characterize each group. The experimenter made sure that the child isolated the material of the object as the cause of the floating. This type of training resulted in 40% correct explanations among the younger preschoolers and much higher correct percentages among the older preschoolers. Furthermore, there was correct transfer to new objects, which indicates that the comprehension of the problem was general in nature.

An important conclusion derived from these experiments, and one that will be emphasized later, is that "direct experience in and by itself is . . . insufficient for explaining . . . physical phenomena [Zaphorozhets et al., 1964/1971, p. 250]." In the training of children it is necessary (1) to isolate the problem of generalization; and (2) then to organize the formation of the generalization for the children. The optimal conditions to accomplish these goals for the younger preschoolers are in play situations. However, for the older preschoolers the best progress in teaching them to reason effectively is obtained in exercises where they are guided "by striving for the acquisition of new knowledge about the object [p. 251]." With this type of assistance, the Soviets believe, preschoolers can reach an advanced ability to reason about events occurring around them.

The Soviets furthermore believe that changes in motivation also play a significant role in the solution of intellectual problems in preschoolers. Thus, in addition to the development of intellectual operations, there is a change in motivation in the passage from younger to older preschooler. For younger preschoolers motivation is best aroused by practical problems where they can attempt to fulfill a direct desire, such as reaching a toy. For older preschoolers situations where they can show a competitiveness and display their imagination acquire strong motivational value.

Swiss and Soviet: Similarity and Contrast

Piaget enumerates two principles that distinguish preoperational thought. First, preoperational children are motivated to solve problems by understanding the principles behind their functioning. This motivation is aroused in children through interaction with adults who stress principles of functioning. Thus, children are motivated by the fact that their actions to obtain desired goals frequently fail precisely because they do not consider the principles behind the solution to a problem. As preschoolers get older, they are forced to reflect upon the relations that make success at a given task possible. They learn to order and classify, to discern causal relations, and most important, to generalize these principles to new situations.

Analogously, the Soviets describe a similar development during the preschool years. A characteristic of their research is the demonstration of fixed sequences in the development of reasoning ability in children. At the earliest stages, children's thought is characterized as visual—motor in character. Children's thought proceeds through four stages, with the final development being the ability to explore a problem purely visually, to observe the relationships between the parts to each other and the goal, and then to perform the correct practical solution without trial and error. Later, children develop what the Soviets label as discursive thinking, or the ability to solve problems exclusively in verbal terms. Discursive thinking also undergoes a fixed sequence of development in which speech activity is initially dissociated from intellectual activity, a transition stage where speech activity follows and mimics intellectual activity, and a final stage where speech activity anticipates, and to a large extent determines, intellectual activity.

It is an impressive accomplishment when two independent groups of researchers report close correspondences in research results. The observation of fixed sequences in many different aspects of development in children is an important contribution. The fact that the fixed sequences observed by the Swiss and Soviet groups appear to correspond in most important details hardly seems fortuitous. It means that much greater confidence is possible in estimating the abilities of preschoolers and the paths through which these developments progress. Where there is considerable disagreement is in the interpretation of the meaning of these fixed sequences for the development of the mental life of children.

Piaget's second principle of preoperational thought is that much of its character is explainable as egocentrism in reasoning. According to Piaget, young children are fundamentally egocentric, or look at the world from their own point of view. For instance, children's reasoning is egocentric when they are (1) unable to construct a display from another's point of view; (2) unable to concentrate on two or more aspects of a situation simultaneously, as in the conservation problems; and (3) unable to use language in a way that takes account of the perspective of another. However, the Soviets interpret observations of similar behavior in young children rather differently and criticize Piaget severely:

> Intellectual processes emerge only under specified conditions. A special organization of activity is necessary, providing the child with a realistic acquaintance with those connections and relationships between phenomena that must become the object of his reasoning. . . . An investigation of the child's thinking has to be conducted under conditions such that one can be quite sure that the child is solving an intellectual

problem presented to him, and that he is provided with concrete facts for corresponding generalizations [Zaphorozhets *et al.*, 1964/1971, p. 238].

Thus, the Soviets criticize Piaget for presenting children with problems whose
solutions are not based on children's direct experiences. Rather, the children's
responses that Piaget interprets as demonstrating an inability of the children to
reason from anything but their own point of view are understandable, to the
Soviets' way of thinking in terms of the difficulty of the problems and in terms
of the minimal help provided by Piaget toward the solutions of the problems.

The Soviets take a practical view toward the possibility of accelerating
intellectual development. It is possible provided:

1. A prior analysis of the task is performed that isolates the stages children
   must pass through to arrive at the solution.
2. Children are oriented toward the relationships necessary for an adequate
   understanding of the task, at each succeeding stage of understanding of the
   task.
3. The intensity of training is sufficient for task mastery.

In contrast, Piaget takes a much more conservative position regarding the
possibility of accelerating intellectual development. According to Piaget, the
primary motivational force for intellectual development is conflict. The prototype situation is when a child only partially understands an experience. This
partial understanding induces an internal state of conflict. The effort to resolve
the conflict induces cognitive growth. This suggests that conflict is specific to
the intellectual level of children, since what they understand is determined by
their current level of intellectual development. According to Piaget, resolution of
this conflict requires active engagement by children in problems.

Another very important inference of the cognitive conflict–intellectual
growth model is that children's reasoning abilities are necessarily seen as developing in a gradual manner—conflict, reorganization that resolves conflict and induces cognitive growth, conflict at a higher level, reorganization at a higher level,
etc.

The Piagetians have been adamant in their insistence that cognitive development must occur in a gradual manner. They argue as follows:

1. The growth of reasoning ability corresponds to a growth through reorganization of a hypothesized unified internal structure (Inhelder, Sinclair, &
   Bovet, 1975).
2. A partially understood new experience forces a reorganization of the total
   internal structure so that the internal structure is accommodated to the
   new experience in a larger, more integrated equilibrium of the internal
   structure.

3. The unified internal structure is large and complex because, it is postulated, it is formed from the totality of the person's experience up to that point.

4. In comparison to the internal structure, the partially understood new experience is minute.

5. Since the new experience is small in comparison with the totality of the internal structure, any conflict between the two results in either a small reorganization of the internal structure to include the new experience or a rejection of the new experience until such time as the internal structure is sufficiently developed to be able to integrate the new experience into its structure.

6. Thus, the cognitive conflict—intellectual growth model necessarily sees children's reasoning abilities as developing in a gradual manner. The possibility of accelerating intellectual development is seen as minimal.

If the cognitive conflict—intellectual growth model is correct, then severe limitations are imposed upon all instruction, including televised instruction, which is the main concern of this chapter. According to this model, televised instruction must be specific to the intellectual level of each child viewer and must actively engage the child in order to induce cognitive conflict so that intellectual growth can occur. The resulting intellectual growth is necessarily gradual.

It will be the purpose of the next section to demonstrate that the Piagetian position, as stated above, is untenable. The cognitive conflict—intellectual growth hypothesis will be modified so that it reflects more recent experimental evidence. The modified hypothesis appears applicable to a design for televised instruction that could prove more effective than present efforts.

Training Studies in Cognition

In this section, two successful training studies are examined. The knowledge obtained from them will provide a basis for determining whether intellectual development can be accelerated through televised instruction.

The two studies differ from each other in the training methods used. However, both test the limits of Piaget's cognitive conflict—intellectual growth model by proposing the alternative that massive infusions of correctly directed training can accelerate intellectual development.

Rachel Gelman (1969) trained 5-year-old children on length and number conservation tasks using a discrimination learning set (LS) procedure, to be described in detail later. Gelman assumed that the basic conservation tasks do not direct children's attention to the important quantitative aspects of the task. Consequently, she argues, failure on the conservation tasks may be due to the children's directing their attention to irrelevant features of the task, such as changes in size, shape, and color. The LS training taught children to attend and respond only to quantity cues. Thus, nonconservers were expected to become conservers after LS training.

On the conservation pretest Gelman tested for conservation of length, number, liquid, and mass. Basically, children are nonconservers on the various tasks if they respond as follows:

Length: Given equal sticks with one stick then displaced so that one end protrudes, the child responds that the protruding stick is longer.

Number: Given two identical rows of items, with one then being spread out, the child responds that the longer row has more items.

Liquid: Given two identical beakers of water, with one then being poured into a taller, thinner beaker, the child responds that the taller column has more water.

Mass: Given two equal balls of clay, with one then being rolled into a sausage shape, the child responds that the longer sausage has more to eat.

On the basis of the above tasks, Gelman trained 60 nonconservers, divided into three groups. On the posttest, the same four pretest conservation tasks were administered. In addition, Gelman added two variations on each conservation task. Thus, she was able to test for nonspecific transfer as a result of the LS training on the conservation tasks.

The LS training consisted of 16 length and 16 number problems. Each problem had three objects, two that contained identical and one that contained different quantities (e.g., two rows of five chips versus one row of three chips, or two 6-inch sticks versus one 10-inch stick). Each problem consisted of six trials where the spatial configuration of the two identical and one different quantity was varied. The order of the presentations on the number and length problems was done randomly, rather than in blocks, and there were numerous trials (32 problems X six trials per problem). The children received instantaneous feedback for correct responses. When correct, children were told, "Yes, that is right, and here is a 'prize.' " The prizes were trinkets.

There was also an oddity control (OC) group, in which the children were trained on small toys (e.g., two toy lions and one toy cup). They also received 32 sets of problems with six trials each. The children were alternatively asked to point to the toys that were the "same" or "different." Feedback, as in the LS training, was given.

Another control group had identical training as in the LS group, except that no feedback was given. This group was labeled the stimulus change (SC) condition.

The LS group learned the task very rapidly and reached an asymptotic performance of 95% correct. The SC group was performing slightly better than chance toward the end of the 32 problems. The OC group made virtually no errors in training, indicating that an understanding of "same–different" had most likely been acquired before the training was initiated.

Posttests on the four conservation tasks were administered the day after training and again 2–3 weeks after the first posttest. Since the LS children were not trained on liquid and mass conservation, nonspecific transfer of training could be tested. The results in Table 4.1 show that the LS children were overwhelmingly superior to the OC and SC children on both the immediate and delayed posttests and on both the specific and nonspecific transfer tests.

According to Gelman (1969), the results in Table 4.1 indicate that,

> given appropriate training, one can elicit conservation behavior from children who initially fail to conserve on classical conservation tests. Appropriate training seems to involve two factors: (1) An opportunity to interact with many different instances of quantitative equalities and differences and (2) feedback, which presumably tells S what is and what is not relevant to the definition of quantity [p. 184].

What is most impressive in Gelman's results is the nonspecific transfer effect. Recall that these children did not receive training on liquid and mass conserva-

TABLE 4.1
Overall Proportion Correct in OC, SC, and LS Conditions[a][b]

	Overall proportion correct		
	OC	SC	LS
Specific transfer			
Immediate length test	.075	.27	.95
Delayed length test	.10	.31	.90
. . .			
Immediate number test	.01	.21	.96
Delayed number test	.01	.29	.96
Nonspecific transfer			
Immediate liquid test	.01	.04	.55
Delayed liquid test	.03	.03	.71
. . .			
Immediate mass test	.00	.09	.58
Delayed mass test	.01	.14	.65

[a]Adapted from Gelman, 1969.
[b]Based on number of children who correctly answered zero, one, two, three, or four conservation items correctly on immediate and delayed transfer tests.

tion tests, yet displayed a very high level of success on these tasks at posttest. According to Gelman, these children seemed to be applying a general rule, such as, "it does not matter what you do or pay attention to the way it is at the start [p. 184]." Additionally, acquisition for the LS children was very fast. They were averaging 90% correct responses at the eleventh problem. Gelman (1969) considers it likely that these conservation responses "are present in a child's repertoire, but are dominated by strategies under the control of irrelevant stimuli. If so, training which extinguishes the use of irrelevant cues should also bring out the 'correct' verbal responses [p. 185]."

Kingsley and Hall (1968) successfully used a training procedure that was somewhat different from Gelman's. They argued that most attempts at training on conservation tasks "have ignored the large amount of background knowledge necessary and thus time needed to train children for conservation mastery [p. 1112]." The training procedure they utilized is based on learning-theory principles as developed by Gagné (1965). Gagné analyzes the material to be taught into a hierarchy of subtasks. The sequential accomplishment of the subtasks ultimately leads to success at the criterion task.

They trained 86 5- and 6-year-olds, employing a complex design, with seven different groups of children. The children were trained in conservation of substance, length, and weight. To simplify matters, only the description of the training procedure for conservation of weight will be discussed. Based on a task analysis performed by Kingsley and Hall (1967) the knowledge hypothesized as necessary for conservation of weight (in order of difficulty) is as follows:

1. Know the meaning of appropriate relational terms, i.e., heavier, equal, lighter, more, less, same.
2. Know the meaning of weight independent of amount substance.
3. Know what a scale is and how to determine heavier, lighter, and equal on it.
4. Know the scale is more accurate than kinesthetic cues.
5. Know the effect of adding and subtracting clay on weight.
6. Know the effect of changing shape on weight regardless of other extraneous cues (i.e., labels and appearance) [p. 1114].

The weight conservation test consisted of three parts. In Parts 1 and 3 two clay balls of identical size and weight were used. In Part 2 the balls were equal in size, but one was weighted with a steel ball. In Parts 1 and 2 the children were asked to pick up the balls and judge their relative weights. In Part 3 the children were told that the balls weighed the same. In each part, one of the balls was deformed. After the change the children were asked, "Is the _____ heavier than, or the same weight as, or lighter than the ball?", "Why do you think so?", and "If we weighed them, which would be heavier?"

The training in conservation of weight was conducted for a maximum of nine individual training sessions of 20 minutes each. The training was done in stages, each one more difficult than the next. The training was as follows:

Stage 1.   Children were given two equal size clay balls, but one was heavier because a steel ball was hidden in it. Children were asked the conservation question. Then, balls were dropped into the children's hands to emphasize the weight distinction. It was pointed out that one hand went down farther than the other. It was emphasized to the children that when this happens, one says that this ball is heavier than the other. This was repeated until the children stated this themselves without assistance.

Stage 2.   Those children whose understanding of the weight terms was doubted were given further experience with various sizes and pieces of clay, were asked to compare their weights, were given the ball-dropping experience, were asked the conservation question, and were encouraged to use the term "heavier."

Stage 3.   The children were taught how to transfer their knowledge of weight to the use of a balance scale. They were shown that "the scale reacted the same to the ball-dropping sequence as their hands did." This transfer of training procedure was highly effective. Children learned that the scale could detect finer differences in weight than they could while holding the objects. Children were actively engaged in estimating relative weights of objects varying in size and shape, weighting them, and then evaluating their predictions as "right" and "wrong," etc.

Stage 4.   Children were allowed to "add on" or "take off" clay from objects placed on either end of the balance scale in order to make objects that were unequal in weight the same weight. Active involvement, prediction, forming hypotheses, etc., by the children were encouraged.

Stage 5.   At this point, training in conservation was initiated. The training procedure was extremely varied, with stress placed on a wide range of different types of experience. There was encouragement for active participation and hypothesis testing by the child. Two equal weight balls were removed from the scale: One was deformed (e.g., into a pancake, small pieces, snakes, etc.); sometimes they were labeled (e.g., small ball of dust, big fat rock); sometimes different-colored clay balls were used, etc. The conservation question was asked. The children were also asked to verbalize the relation, "How did they weigh before?, How do they weigh now?"

Stage 6.   The same procedures were employed as in stage 5, except that balls of unequal weight were used. It was discovered that many children thought that any change in physical properties (shape, position of the clay in the room, etc.) also changed weight. After the children admitted their wrong predictions, they were asked, "You said it was heavier (or lighter), but what do you have to do to make things heavier (or lighter)?" "Did you do that?" "Then it could get heavier (lighter)?" "Does the weight change when I move this clay?" (Clay was put on experimenter's head, under chair, etc.). Eventually children were taught that "if you don't add any or take any away, then the weight stays the same as it was before you changed the shape." A related problem was that some children believed that the label given an object determined its weight (rocks are heavy). In such instances, children were forced to recognize that the object "really" was clay.

Kingsley and Hall's results indicate that there is a highly significant increase in conservation responses on both an immediate and a delayed posttest, both for weight and for length conservation. It should be noted that these correct responses occurred well before that age at which conservation of weight (9–10 years) or conservation of length (8 years) normally occurs. Kingsley and Hall (1967) conclude that "there can be little doubt that training brought considerable progress. The task analysis proved to be very effective in defining behaviors which were needed for successful mastery of conservation [p. 1125]."

Contrasting Interpretations

What appears to be demonstrated in the two training studies just cited is the fact that massive infusions of carefully directed training can accelerate cognitive growth. This position is contrary to Piaget's theoretical position, which is that intellectual development must proceed gradually, depends upon experience of a generalized nature, and is unreceptive to massive doses of specific teaching experiences.

Piaget's counterargument is centered around the premise that conservation responses obtained in experiments like the ones just cited are not really what they appear to be, or are pseudoconservation responses. The children, he argues, are responding to covariations in the changing conditions and do not really appreciate the necessary argument that one dimension compensates for another or that the process can be reversed, etc. The fact that 95% correct responses were obtained in Gelman's experiment might be an indication that the responses show a sensitivity to a covariation and, as such, are provisional in nature. A true conservation response, it is argued, would be all or nothing and more unyielding in attempts to disconfirm it. Covariations are obtainable at a very early age (4–5 years) whereas true conservations depend, according to Piaget, on internal modifications and develop around 8–9 years.

Several examples of Piaget's position should clarify the distinctions. Imagine a piece of rope of length A, wrapped around a pulley. As one end is pulled, that part of the rope (B) gets longer, while the far end (C) gets shorter. Children easily discover the covariation involved in the above example (around 4–5 years). If one end gets longer, the other end gets shorter. Also, they just as easily recognize that it is the same rope, which gets shorter and longer in its segments. This does not mean, however, that children have acquired the conservation of length. For the pseudoconserver, longer and shorter are still based on the position of the endpoints of the perceived objects. One stick protruding farther out than another of equal length is still judged as longer.

Another experiment, done by the Van den Bogaerts-Rambouts (cited in Piaget, 1968, pp. 24–25), refines the distinctions. The thinking of preoperational children may be defined as a reasoning in terms of one-way correspondences. Usually, a 5- or 6-year-old will be able to reason in terms of "many-to-one" but not possess the inverse correspondence "one-to-many." Even "one-to-one" correspondence often lacks reciprocity. In the Van den Bogaerts–Rombouts' experiment, a little truck takes a random route through a collection of houses, A,B,C, etc., picking up a colored token in front of each house. The colored token corresponds to the color of the house it is found in front of and to the color of the man who stands in front of each house. At the end of the trip the children are asked why the tokens are in that order. From 5 onward, children have no difficulty in explaining that the tokens correspond to the order in which they were picked up. Only at 7–8 years, however, can the children perform the reciprocal correspondence or retrace the truck's route. According to Piaget, children can seem to possess a concept because they appear to be able to reason effectively in certain situations that involve the concept. However, closer analysis reveals that the concept is not really acquired and is actually reasoning based upon simple correspondence. Possession of the concept requires that children's reasoning be embedded in a system of operations or in a system where children can reverse the process and return to the starting point or compensate a change in one dimension for another. Possession of the concept is only a condition of the stage of intellectual development.

One can stretch the results presented in Gelman's and Kingsley and Hall's experiments to explain them as pseudoconserver responses. Even the nonspecific transfer results obtained in Gelman's experiment can be explained in terms of the children's picking up "many-to-one" and "one-to-one" correspondences without a real appreciation of reversibility and compensation arguments. What, then, do these results and their conflicting interpretations represent in terms of advancing the hopes for more effective televised instruction?

Although Piaget's cognitive conflict–intellectual growth model is hardly disproved by Gelman's and Kingsley and Hall's research, enough evidence has accumulated from other sources (e.g., the Soviet research) to demonstrate that intellectual development can be accelerated when specialized instructional procedures are employed. In the next section, specific illustrations will demonstrate how the specialized instructional procedures previously discussed can be adapted to televised instruction.

IMPLICATIONS FOR TELEVISED INSTRUCTION

The research presented in this chapter suggests certain possibilities for televised instruction. The following formats for cognitive training exercises are presented for illustrative purposes only.

Format 1

Children are taught which objects will sink and which objects will float. The objects used for television presentation are of different materials, different sizes, and different shapes. The televised instructional sequence is as follows:

1. Show a child about to throw a wooden object into a stream or lake.
2. Ask, "Will it float or sink?"
3. Pause, with fanfare, so that the child viewer is encouraged to guess.
4. Child on television throws object into the water.
5. Say, "It floats!" Generate interest through appropriate excitement, etc.
6. Repeat procedures 1–5 with successively larger and heavier objects of the same material and shape.
7. Repeat procedures 1–6, but use another shape of wooden object.
8. Repeat procedures 1–6, but vary shapes of wooden objects on each trial.
9. Show an object used previously. Ask, "What is this object made of?" Pause to allow time for an answer. Then respond, "This object is made of wood." Throw it into the water and exclaim, "Wooden objects float!"
10. Repeat procedure 9 with other wooden objects used previously. Sometimes vary procedure and ask, "Does this object float?"
11. Show a wooden object that is very different in either shape or size from those previously seen by the child. Test the child, as in procedures 1–5, on whether the idea of what makes an object float has been acquired.
12. Repeat procedure 11 with other new wooden objects.
13. Repeat above procedure varying material. Eventually teach child advanced concepts, such as the fact that hollow objects float even when made of heavy materials.

In addition to teaching which objects sink or float, the above training exercise attempts to teach children ways of solving problems that can be used in a wide variety of tasks. The primary objectives of the sink-or-float exercises are the following:

1. To encourage children in the use of speech for formulating strategies to solve problems before problems are actually attempted.
2. To encourage the use of purely visual comparisons between one object and

another rather than immediate experimentation with objects to find a solution. For instance, encourage a purely visual comparison between the wooden object and water rather than exclusive dependence upon actually throwing the object into the water to determine whether it sinks or floats.
3. To encourage forming propositions of a general nature, such as "all wooden objects float." Note: Children may not understand Archimedes' Principle, but the path to its discovery has to come through deriving propositions of this nature.
4. To encourage classifying the objects into material, size, and shape in order to help the children isolate the salient properties of objects that determine whether or not they float; To encourage verbal labeling.

The sink-or-float problem is illustrative of a class of problems that can be used on television to instruct young children. The essential features of such problems are that they encourage (1) an advanced use of speech to solve problems; (2) the use of purely visual means to solve problems rather than exclusive dependency on activity with objects; (3) the formulation of general propositions about an event; and (4) the attitude that events must be explored mentally rather than immediately acted upon to discover correct solutions. For children, developing strategies about "how to learn" and encouraging the motive to learn are important prerequisites for later success in school. Much learning among young children involves self-initiated involvement with objects. However, an important contributor to speeding up this process is through systematic guidance from clear television presentations. Once children have acquired an effective learning strategy, they attempt to generalize it to new problems. Hopefully, the learning strategies acquired through televised instruction will initiate other learning experiences in other aspects of the child viewer's life. It is expected that problems of the type illustrated will eventually teach children how to solve problems through new, creative means that they have figured out for themselves.

Format 2

The following cognitive training exercise illustrates causal relationships in the solution of problems: A child is presented with a series of levers that must be pressed in a fixed sequence in order to obtain a ball. All the connections and workings of each of the levers are exposed to view so that a careful visual inspection reveals what each lever operates. The first lever is connected by a string to a lid at the bottom of a container. When the lever is depressed, the string pulls open the lid at the bottom of the container. The ball falls out and rolls along a trench into another, similar container. There are three more levers (a total of four), which perform the same function as the first lever. If the child presses all the levers in the correct sequence, the ball is obtained in the goal box. The connections on the levers can be changed so that the sequence in which the levers must be depressed in order to obtain the ball are altered. The televised instructional sequence is as follows:

1. Show the entire apparatus.
2. Focus on the ball in container A.
3. Focus on the string attached to the lid at the bottom of container A.
4. Follow the string along to its connection on lever 1.
5. Show a child pressing lever 1.
6. Focus on the ball being released from container A and rolling along the trench into container B.
7. Repeat this procedure with levers 2, 3, and 4.
8. Focus on the ball in the goal box and show the child grabbing the ball and running happily off to play with it.
9. Show another child trying to obtain the ball and not succeeding. Child leaves unhappily.
10. Show a third child concentrating on the levers and their connections. Focus on and trace the connections.
11. Have the child hesitate before pressing the correct lever.
12. Ask, "Is he/she pressing the right button?" Employ suspense to generate tension and encourage guessing by the child viewer.
13. Child presses button and ball rolls to container B.
14. Repeat procedures 10–13 for lever 2; then for lever 3; then for lever 4.
15. Focus on the ball in the goal box and show the child grabbing the ball and running happily off to play with it.
16. Repeat preceding procedures. Use effects that are necessary to maintain interest but do not distract from the task.
17. Change the strings that connect the levers to the containers so that the correct sequence in which the levers must be depressed to obtain the ball is different.
18. Repeat above procedures with new connections. Show some children getting the ball and others failing to get it.

As in the sink-or-float exercise, the lever-pressing exercise attempts to teach children strategies for solving problems that can be used in a variety of tasks. In general, this exercise teaches children the following:

1. It encourages the use of purely visual comparisons. In this problem children are encouraged to visually explore the levers, their connections to the containers, the way in which the ball is released from the containers, and the trenches along which the ball finally reaches the goal box.

2. It encourages the use of speech to record strategies. As various parts of the apparatus are focused upon and traced, children figuring out the operation of the apparatus can be encouraged to label its parts and record the sequence of connections. The child operating the apparatus can say, "This is the lever"; "This is the string"; "This is the lever connected to the container that the ball is in"; "If I push this lever, the ball will go here"; etc.

The lever-pressing exercise, like the sink-or-float exercise, is illustrative of a class of problems that can be used on television to instruct young children. In solving problems of this type, children benefit from making detailed visual comparisons, planning actions in advance, using speech to record plans, and making detailed inspections of moving parts to anticipate the result of a movement. Repeated success on tasks such as the lever-pressing problem requires attitudes of careful attention to detail and repeated going over of connections between moving parts to make sure that they are recorded correctly. Much learning of this type occurs during self-initiated exploratory play with objects. However, this process might be speeded up as a result of intense exposure to training exercises such as the lever-pressing problem. It is hoped that the learning strategies children acquire from the intense exposure to training exercises of this type on television will be used and improved upon by children in other aspects of their lives.

Format 3

The practical consequences of Piaget's discovery that children pass through a stage of nonconservation on various properties of objects have been little explored. One group of child psychologists has used the conservation problems on new intelligence tests that are designed to be relatively "culture-fair." The conservation problems are considered to be a good source for a culture-fair intelligence test because they are solved by children in the same fixed stages in all cultures and also because the age when the conservation problems are solved is for the most part assumed to be independent of specific instruction in the culture. Another group has attempted to disprove Piaget's assertions that the conservation problems cannot be taught through intense sessions of highly specific training. The training experiments conducted by Gelman and by Kingsley and Hall are provocative in that their results can be seen as attempts to contradict a central tenet of Piaget's theory. Even if further analysis of the results of these training studies were to prove that only pseudoconserver responses were produced by the children, this too would be encouraging. Children pass through a stage where they are nonconservers, then a transition stage where they conserve part of the time, and finally a stage where they conserve all of the time. Pseudoconserver responses can account for a large proportion of the transition responses. Therefore, training children in many different types of conservation problems might produce pseudoconserver responses that could eventually form the basis for correct understanding of the concepts underlying the physical transformations that occur in the transformation problems. Based upon this possibility, the following television training exercise has been adapted from Gelman's experiment:

1. Teach conservation of length, present two identical sticks and one stick identical to the other two except that it is longer in length.
2. Ask, "Which is longer?" and present the choices one at a time.
3. Delay. Build suspense. Provide feedback by eventually giving the right answer.
4. Repeat procedures 1–3 at least six times. Vary spatial configuration of presented objects.
5. To teach conservation of number, present two rows of five chips versus one row of three chips.
6. Ask, "Which row has more?" and present the choices one at a time.
7. Delay. Build suspense. Provide feedback by eventually providing the correct answer.
8. Repeat procedures 5–7 at least six times. Vary spatial configuration of presented objects. For instance, compare two rows of five objects 3 inches long to one row of three objects 5 inches long. If children understand the word *more* to mean "number of objects in each row," then their answer is correct. If children understand the word *more* to mean "length of the row," then their answer is incorrect. Through clever use of examples using different spatial configurations children can be taught complex discriminations that result in correct answers.
9. Vary order of presentation of length and number conservation problems randomly.
10. Use different length and number conservation problems. (Gelman used 16 variations of each, with six trials for each problem.)

Format 4

As previously described, Kingsley and Hall trained children on various conservation problems using a task analysis based on Gagné's learning principles. This method requires great discipline in order to teach the various conservation problems, because a hierarchy of subtasks must initially be taught. A brief sketch of how to teach conservation of weight on television, based on Kingsley and Hall's procedures, follows:

1. Two balls, one much heavier, are dropped into a child's hands. One hand goes down much farther.
2. It is emphasized that when this happens, one ball is called "heavier" than the other.
3. Procedures 1–2 are repeated, but objects are varied in size, shape, etc.
4. Vary procedures to define the meaning of the word *heavier*. For instance, show one object as being much harder to lift than another and state, "When this happens, one object is called *heavier* than the other."
5. Present a balance scale and show a child using it. Show the balance reacting to the ball-dropping experience the same way the hands did. An effective television presentation technique could be the use of flashbacks showing balls dropping into the child's hands after showing what happens to the arms of the scale when objects of different weight are dropped into them. Also, the image of the balls dropping into the hands could be lightly superimposed over the scale so that the two balls drop onto the scale and into the child's hands at the same time. Use of slow motion and reverse action for emphasis can also be employed.
6. Repeat procedure 5 but "add on" and "take off" weight from the objects used.
7. Repeat procedures 5–6 but with clay balls equal in weight. Deform one clay ball and repeat procedures 5–6. Vary training procedure. Encourage hypothesis testing by child viewer.
8. Repeat procedures 5–7 but with clay balls unequal in weight. Vary training procedures. Encourage hypothesis testing.

CONCLUSION

What is emphasized in this review of cognitive development is that "learning how to learn" is a real and important aspect of young children's development. Preschoolers require preparation before exposure to school skills. If children's reasoning abilities are sufficiently trained, exposure to school skills will be readily, flexibly, and creatively acquired. Because present efforts at televised instruction for preschoolers are largely restricted to teaching school skills (e.g., letters, numbers, beginning reading) the possibility of television's teaching preschoolers to reason more effectively remains largely untested.

According to Piaget, preoperational children do not attempt to discover the underlying operating principles behind the functioning of things. There is an exclusive concentration on success through hands-on activity. Children must learn, either through their own failures or through instruction from adults, that knowledge of the principles of how devices operate is possible. This knowledge can, in turn, lead to a higher level of success in solving problems.

According to Piaget, there is also a social limitation to preoperational thought. Preoperational children experience difficulty in becoming aware of other points of view and frequently lose their own point of view and, without knowing it, adopt the point of view of others. Eventually, self-initiated experiences and interaction with adults makes children aware of the existence of other possibilities that they then readily adopt.

Also, children passing through what Piaget calls the transition between sensorimotor thought and preoperational thought experience difficulty in representing reality in words and, it can be inferred, in mental images. Children at this age (3—4 years) can much more readily solve problems through direct action on the object(s) of the problem. They have much greater difficulty, and frequently cannot relate to the problem, using words or using pictures of objects and their interrelationships.

The end result is that preschoolers experience difficulties when attempting to reason in words and mental images. They have difficulty stating in words or representing in mental images the transformations and movements of objects in space and time and the interaction of objects with one another. In helping preschoolers develop these advanced reasoning abilities, self-initiated experiences and instruction from adults are necessary and complement each other.

Preschoolers also require instruction that is tuned to their ability to reason and that corresponds to the ways they develop intellectually and socially. Adapting experimental procedures that in some cases have only been tested in preschools for use on television is possible, but hazardous. The only certain way of knowing whether these instructional procedures will work is by trying them out on television. So far, they are untested.

The principles that seem most applicable to televised instruction are the following:

1. It is necessary to analyze the problem and to perform a task analysis.
2. Children must be oriented to the properties of the task necessary for its successful completion.
3. The training must be intense and concentrate on the properties of the task.
4. Children must be given feedback so that they know if they responded correctly.
5. More complex tasks require breaking up the problems into subtasks individually. Afterwards correct subtask solutions must be integrated with each other so that success on the main criterion task is reached.
6. An indirect objective of all the above instructional activity is to teach children how to reason more effectively on their own. Thus, children learn "how to learn" with the expectation that this general increase in level of

reasoning ability will be employed in other tasks that have not been specifically taught.

7. Another indirect objective is to alter children's motivation. In the solution of problems, motivation should initially be directed toward the desire to acquire new information of a general nature that, in turn, can be used on other tasks. Self-initiated activities to acquire new knowledge that can be more generally applied is the goal of all the above teaching but often cannot be taught directly.

A cautious attitude toward teaching children through televised instruction was expressed in earlier chapters. This attitude is still applicable. Television is a one-way communication device. The listener cannot affect the message communicated. This being the case, children are passive recipients of information, except to the extent that they choose to engage themselves with the message. However, the type of active engagement possible through television is particularly limiting given the special nature of preschoolers' reasoning abilities. The importance of active engagement at a physical level with immediate feedback for correct solutions has been isolated as extremely important in the instruction of preschoolers. There seems to be no way of avoiding this unpalatable fact.

However, there are ways of minimizing the absence of two-way communication. Problems vary in the amount and level of feedback necessary to maintain effective instruction. The sink-or-float problem requires successive guesses of either "It will sink" or "It will float." Later in the problem the child viewer is required to determine the material of the object and to classify it with other objects of the same material. Afterward the child is encouraged to fill in the missing link, "Wooden objects float." The feedback necessary for this problem does not appear to be cumbersome for presentation on television, nor does it appear that it will overburden children watching the problem.

The lever-pressing problem requires children to trace causal relations. It is conceivable that even with the encouragement of guessing, anticipation, etc., the attention-maintaining quality of the problem might not be sufficient to keep the concentration of the children watching it. Since feedback and encouragement cannot be individualized to the momentary state of the children watching the problem, then repetition of the problem, with variation where necessary, must substitute. With sufficient repetition it is hoped that each child viewer will receive adequate exposure and devote sufficient attention to the problem to master it. Recall that the children in Gelman's experimental group achiever 90% correct responses on the eleventh problem. Since there were six trials per problem, the children required over 60 repetitions with variation in order to master the task. This seems like an unreasonable amount of repetition in order to teach a concept on television. However, if each different format is recognized as reinforcing the concepts in every other format, then in the totality of the teaching effort this amount of repetition is easily achieved without undue hardship for the children watching.

Gelman's conservation of length training, which uses the learning set training procedure, is easily applied and should not overburden the child viewer. However, Kingsley and Hall's procedure, based on Gagné's learning procedures, is much more complex and may not be practical for televised instruction. Feedback for each subtask and integration of the subtasks with each other to complete the main task successfully is most likely too demanding without individualized instruction. Therefore, complex tasks that must be broken up into smaller teaching segments may prove to be beyond the capability of televised instruction for preschoolers. It remains a task for creative television producers in conjunction with educators and child psychologists to make an effort to teach such complex tasks. The limits of instruction of preschoolers over television will not be determined until such efforts are attempted.

5

Language and Thought:
Relating Language to Experience
in Young Children

In the last 10 years psycholinguistic research on language acquisition has produced a rich body of literature. Possible applications of this literature to instructional television are, unfortunately, too numerous to mention in this brief review. Certain issues will be stressed here, although other issues of equal importance exist.

The following psycholinguistic developments in young children will be examined in this chapter:

1. The process through which children acquire comprehension of the meaning of various important words.
2. The process through which children acquire the ability to describe an event using different sentences that have the same meaning.
3. The effectiveness of training children to solve problems using language as a guide.

Implications for instructional television will be explored following the review of these three topics.

THE ACQUISITION OF LANGUAGE COMPREHENSION

The Semantic Feature Hypothesis

Eve Clark (1973, pp. 65–110) has formulated the following hypothesis to explain the acquisition of word meanings by children:

> When the child first begins to use identifiable words, he does not know their full (adult) meaning. . . . Thus, the child will begin by identifying the meaning of a word with only one or two features rather than with the whole combination of meaning components or features . . . that are used criterially by the adult. . . . The hypothesis therefore assumes that the child's use and interpretation of words may differ considerably from the adult's in the early stages of the language acquisition process, but, over time, will correspond to the adult model [p. 72].

Experiments cited by Clark in support of her hypothesis report results that show developmental progressions in children's acquisition of word meanings. Such progressions include: relational terms (e.g., *more–less, big–small, tall–short, before–after*); dimensional adjectives (e.g., *thick–thin, high–low, fat–thin*); verbs (e.g., *ask* and *tell*); and nouns (e.g., *brother* and *sister*).

The evidence cited on relational terms is representative of much of the experimental results on the acquisition of word meanings. Donaldson and Balfour (1968) were concerned with how 3-year-olds interpreted the relational terms *more* and *less*. Two cardboard apple trees, capable of hanging up to six apples, were presented to children. Each child was asked a variety of questions concerning which tree had more (or less) apples. The most consistent finding was that the majority of the children could not differentiate the word *less* from the word *more*. They treated the word *less* as if it were synonomous with the word *more*. Both words are interpreted as referring to quantity, but the meaning of the word *more* initially dominates the word *less*.

Similar results are reported for the words *same* and *different*. Donaldson and Wales (1970) report that children interpret the word *different* as if it meant the word *same*. On a sorting task children overwhelmingly picked objects that were the same, in response to instructions to choose one that was different. Instructions to pick objects that were the same results in correct choices. Similar results are reported by Webb, Oliveri, and O'Keefe (1974) in a longitudinal study on the meaning of the word *different*.

He. bert Clark (1970, pp. 269–277) notes a characteristic of English usage with regard to comparatives such as *long* and *short*. *Long* is considered the positive term and *short* the negative term. *Long* can be used in the following sentences:

1. The board is 10 feet long.
2. The length of the board is 10 feet in length.
3. The board is long.

Sentences 1 and 2 refer to the "dimension of length" and do not require a standard of comparison. The use of the word *long* in sentences 1 and 2 is referred to by H. Clark as *nominal*. In contrast, the word *long* in sentence 3 is used *contrastively* because it refers implicitly to a standard of comparison. The board is long as applied to some standard or to some average length for boards of this type. The word *short* has a more limited usage. It can be used in sentences of the following type:

1. The board is short.
2. This board is shorter than the other one.

and not:

3. The board is 10 feet short.
4. The short girl is tall.

The word *short* can only be used contrastively. Sentences 1 and 2 require an understanding of "shorter than something else." The word *short* does not refer to the dimension of length in English usage. Thus, the word *long* has both a nominative and a contrastive use. H. Clark refers to *long* as the unmarked term and *short* as the marked of the pair of polar opposites. He also notes (p. 271) that in English, it is always the unmarked term that designates physical extension along a dimension (i.e., *deep–shallow* for depth, *high–low* for height, *distant–close* or *far–near* for distance, *wide–narrow* for width).

The following developmental sequence seems to be followed by young children in their acquisition of polar comparatives:

1. Children use polar comparatives (e.g., *more* and *less*) in the nominal sense only.
2. Since the nominal usage refers to extension and not to its absence, children use both ends of the polar pair (e.g., *more* and *less*) to refer to the extended end of the scale.
3. Lastly, children distinguish the marked from the unmarked term (e.g., *less* from *more*) and apply the marked term (*less*) contrastively only.

For E. V. Clark (1973) this developmental sequence in polar comparative words and comparable developments in other aspects of language use among English-speaking children supports her Semantic Feature Hypothesis. Initially, children use only one or two features to define a word. With the acquisition of semantic knowledge, more features are added to the definition of a word until adult usage is approximated.

For the relational words *after* and *before* (which are not marked and unmarked) E. V. Clark (1971) determined that children initially interpreted *after* as if it meant the same thing as *before*. Only at a later stage do children recognize *after* as being opposite to, rather than synonomous with, *before*.

A similar developmental analysis was applied by E. V. Clark (1973, pp. 96–98) to C. Chomsky's (1969) data on the verbs *ask* and *tell*. Children under the age of 8 years consistently interpret the verb *ask* as if it meant *tell*. For instance, in response to the following instruction:

(1)   Tell X what to feed the doll.

the child answers correctly with,

(1a)   A banana.

But in response to the following:

(2)   Ask X what to feed the doll?

the child answers incorrectly with,

(2a)   A banana.

E. V. Clark interprets C. Chomsky's results as follows:

1. The meaning of *tell* involves learning the request feature.
2. The meaning of *ask* involves learning the request feature.
3. The meaning of *ask* involves learning the allocation of roles.

That is, for the verb *ask* the child must learn the additional feature that the third person supplies the answer.

At this point it is sufficient to recognize that young children possess a different understanding of important English words and use them differently from adults.

A possible explanation of these differences in word use is that there is, in part, a nonlinguistic basis for their acquisition. For instance, consider the acquisition of the locative terms *in, on,* and *under* in young children (E. V. Clark, 1973). *In* is almost always interpreted correctly; *on* is interpreted correctly provided the child does not have the option of placing an object "in" something; *under* is never correct when the child has the option of either placing an object "in" or "on" something. The order of acquisition appears to be *in, on,* and *under*.

In explanation, young children seem to have a linguistic understanding that *in, on,* and *under* refer to location or spatial orientation. Beyond that, however, children appear to employ a nonlinguistic strategy. If possible, place the object "in" something. If this is not possible, place the object "on" something. Finally, if neither is possible, place the object "under" something.

The Dependency of Language on the Stage of Cognitive Development

Another explanation for the development of language comprehension, probably related to the nonlinguistic hypothesis proposed by E. V. Clark, is that differences in word use reflect differences in cognitive abilities. The work of Hermina Sinclair-de-Zwart (1969, 1971a), the principal researcher on language acquisition for the group centered around Jean Piaget in Geneva, supports this position. Sinclair-de-Zwart's approach to this problem parallels Piaget's broader theoretical position on cognitive development.

Sinclair-de-Zwart has provided experimental evidence that supports Piaget's assertion that the stage of cognitive development explains the level of language usage. It follows from this assertion that it is necessary to explore language as a participant in the overall process of cognitive development if we are ever to understand the functioning of adult language. Sinclair-de-Zwart (1971a, pp. 203–214) cites many instances of the child's limited ability to understand spoken language. The following is a list compiled by her of some important limitations of young children's comprehension of spoken language:

(1) *Young children experience difficulty in reflecting upon language itself.* For instance, if a 5-year-old child is asked to make a sentence using the words *coffee* and *salt,* chances are the child will say, "You can't, nobody puts salt in coffee!" Similarly, this child might give as seven the answer to the question "How many words are in the sentence 'Mary has seven dolls'?" In contrast, older children (above 7–8 years) have acquired the ability to dissociate words from their content.

(2) *Young children experience difficulty in keeping the semantic content of a sentence constant while changing its form.* For instance, when 5-year-olds are shown a truck pushing a car and are then asked to describe the event by starting to speak first about the car, a typical response might be "No, I can't; otherwise it would be the wrong way around, the car pushing the truck." However, when younger children (4-year-olds) are asked to perform in the same situation, they generally do not express such perplexities. For instance, they conform by stating, "The car pushes the truck," and then they actually push the car to show what they mean by that sentence. Sinclair-de-Zwart (1971a) speculates that "maybe they expected reality to be adjusted to their description [p. 210]."

(3) *Young children experience difficulty in establishing temporal indicators in their efforts to describe complex events.* For instance, when 5-year-olds are asked to describe complex events such as a girl doll going up a flight of steps and then a boy doll going into a garage, they rigidly adhere to this temporal succession in their description. Either they refuse to start with the boy or do not establish temporal indicators if they are induced to start with the boy. Afterward, however, they indicate it is the wrong way around.

(4) *Young children experience difficulty in understanding passive sentences.* For instance, children are asked to act out with dolls spoken passive sentences such as "The boy was washed by the girl." or "The car was washed by the boy." The first sentence has a reversible agent and patient (the boy can also wash the

girl), whereas the second sentence is not reversible. Before age $6\frac{1}{2}$, these sentences are, in general, not clearly understood. The child frequently takes the first noun as the agent and the second as the patient and, for instance, washes the girl doll with the boy doll. Five-year-olds are frequently in great doubt and seem to eventually compromise by having the dolls wash each other simultaneously. Four-year-olds are perfectly capable of repeating passive sentences such as those described above, but observation indicates that their comprehension is incorrect. By age 5 repetition deteriorates, but comprehension gets better. The child may transform the sentence to its active form ("The girl washes the boy.") and then copy it directly. Only by about the age of 6 is accurate repetition always accompanied by correct comprehension.

Sinclair-de-Zwart suggests that a possible source of the difficulty young children experience in these four examples is due to the fact that language development depends upon the level of cognitive development attained by the child. If these children have not attained a sufficient level of fluency in conceptual thought processes, they will experience difficulty with language problems of the type presented above. An often cited series of experiments by Sinclair-de-Zwart (1969, pp. 322–325) in collaboration with Barbel Inhelder does, in fact, seem to demonstrate the dependency of language upon the child's level of cognitive development. In one experiment a boy doll and a girl doll were given sets of materials such as equal or unequal amounts of clay, equal or unequal amounts of marbles, etc., and the children were asked probing questions such as, "Are both dolls happy?" "Why not?", etc., or they were asked to describe the difference between two pencils (e.g., a short thick pencil and a long thin pencil). The children were also given a comprehension test that consisted of the child's arranging the objects in accordance with verbal instructions. To determine their level of cognitive development the children were given standard Piagetian conservation tasks. There were no differences in comprehension between children who conserved and children who did not. However, the conservers differed from the nonconservers in spontaneous descriptions in three ways:

(1) Children who conserved used more relational terms of the type "The boy has more than the girl" (70% of the time with clay, 100% of the time with marbles). In contrast, 90% of the nonconservers used absolute terms of the type "The boy has a lot, the girl has a little." Of the nonconservers, 20% used comparatives for the discrete units (marbles), and none used comparative terms for the continuous quantities (clay). It is interesting to note that the conservation of quantity with discrete units occurs before the conservation of quantity with continuous quantities.

(2) Children who conserved used more highly differentiated terms. One hundred percent of the conservers used different terms for different dimensions

(e.g., *big–little, fat–thin*), whereas 75% of the nonconservers would use at least one word for two dimensions (e.g., *fat* for *long* and for *thick*).

(3) Children who conserved used coordinated descriptions. Eighty percent of the conservers described two objects differing in two dimensions by coordinating the two dimensions (e.g., "This pencil is longer but thinner, the other is short but thick"). Ninety percent of the nonconservers either described only one dimension or described the objects using four separate sentences ("This pencil is long, the other is short," then all over again, "This pencil is thin, the other is thick").

In a follow-up group of experiments the nonconservers were trained in the expressions used by the conservers. Briefly, the training seemed to involve the experimenter instructing the child and the child instructing the experimenter. The easiest terms to teach were the differentiated terms, next the comparatives, and hardest were the coordinated descriptions. Retest on the conservation tasks revealed that the nonconservers rarely acquired conservation (about 10%). Furthermore, on retest the verbally trained children now frequently noticed the covarying dimensions (e.g., higher level, narrower glass). However, this did not lead them to an argument by compensation and hence to the conclusion that the amount of water in the two glasses was the same. The coordinated descriptions were strongly related to the children who were conservers.

The results of the experiments cited by Sinclair-de-Zwart contribute to the suggestion proposed earlier that language training is incidental to the acquisition of conservation. The results cited on the training exercises suggest that verbal training may direct children's attention to the salient dimensions of the problem, but it rarely results in the acquisition of conservation. The results suggest that language aids in the selection, storage, and retrieval of relevant information but does not appear to produce the cognitive integration and coordination of this information that would be necessary for the solution of conservation-type problems.

However, the manner in which the nonconservers were trained in the expressions used by the conservers is open to the criticism of being too informal and therefore inadequate. Thus, it might not be surprising to many that conservation was not attained on the retest. From the theoretical point of view, the Piagetian's have never believed that specific training could significantly advance cognitive development. The search for optimal environmental conditions and specific types of language training exercises designed to advance cognitive development are best searched out in other quarters.

Language Training

One such source is the Soviet research on the preschool child. Elkonin (1964/1971, pp. 145–150) cites an experiment by Popova where the mastering of agreement of past-tense verbs with nouns according to gender in the Russian language was studied. Two types of training were used. In the first type the experimenter repeated sentences with the noun and the verb in agreement. The child was instructed to repeat the sentences and later to construct them on his own. All errors were corrected. The criteria for success were mastery of the agreement of all nouns and verbs used in the experiment and correct transfer of the principle of agreement to other words. The results of this training method indicate that a substantial effort is required for the child to acquire the principle of agreement between noun and verb (from 180 to 534 repetitions). Although simple repetition of correct word agreements and listening to them in adult's speech eventually lead to moderate success on the task, great effort is required by training method 1.

A second training method, which specifically oriented the child toward the salient elements of the task, was tried (in this case toward the gender-specific endings of nouns in the Russian language). This method achieved considerably greater success. A tower game was devised. Children were to lead animals (three males and three females) into a tower according to gender-specific questions. An incorrect response resulted in the door remaining closed and a correct response resulted in the door opening. If the child immediately and spontaneously corrected a mistake (without help), the door opened. If the child persisted in an incorrect answer, the experimenter corrected the child and the game continued with other words. Of the children who were trained by this second method, 75% achieved complete agreement between noun and verb, with the number of repetitions not exceeding 100.

An important training principle can be extracted from the results obtained by the two training methods. The principle is that "simple exercise and accumulation of experience may not lead to a positive result [Elkonin, 1964/1971, p. 150]." Training method 1 appears to be similar to the training employed by Sinclair-de-Zwart. Consequently, it is not surprising that the results of training in her experiment were unsatisfactory.

However, a method of training that orients the child to the characteristics of the task that are essential for its correct solution yields considerably better results. Specifically, the procedure employed in Popova's second experiment was to organize the child's activity with the words, which in turn oriented the child toward the sound of the words. In general, training should organize a child's activity so that the essential characteristics of the task are focused upon. Repeating the task over and over again with the expectation that the association between one element and another will eventually be attained is not an efficient method of instruction and consequently is frequently unsuccessful.

Determining the correct training procedure for the development of competency in any given task requires a detailed analysis of the task, the levels through which the child must pass to reach the required objective, and how to orient the child's activities to the essential features at each level. Further analysis of this problem will be given citing research in the important area of training in sound analysis among preschoolers. It is generally agreed among psychologists that training in sound analysis is one important precondition for training in literacy.

Children of preschool age encounter difficulty in isolating separate words in a sentence. This difficulty decreases with age. A successful training procedure was devised by Karpova (cited by Elkonin, 1964/1971, pp. 155–157) to aid children in overcoming this difficulty. Karpova applied a methodology that introduced an external action with external supports into the process of isolating words in a sentence. Each word was marked by a plate, and the child was required to remove it each time he encountered a word. Progress was noted for the youngest children (3.5–5 years), middle-aged children (5–6 years), and older children (6–7 years). However, for the younger children the isolation of words in a sentence accomplished with external supports does not transfer to the same task without external supports. Transfer occurred in increasing amounts as the children get older. The general conclusion is that the ability to isolate words develops slowly in the child during the preschool age and that special forms of training can considerably advance this capability.

A more detailed study, this time of the isolation of sounds in words by older preschool children, was performed by Khokhlova (cited by Elkonin, 1964/1971, pp. 172–176). Her initial assumption was that an adequate procedure for training children in sound analysis of words was to have the experimenter pronounce a word and then ask the child to separate it into individual sounds via loud pronunciation. The experimenter helped the child when necessary by asking questions about the order of the sounds in the word. Afterward the child repeated the sound composition of the word, pronouncing each sound sequentially. Words varied in degree of sound-analysis difficulty. Each child was given from 1 hour to 1 hour and 40 minutes of training with 40–45 words. Surprisingly, this training in partitioning words into sounds through loud, separate pronunciation of each sound proved ineffective. The reason proposed for the failure of this training method was that the children were oriented to the articulation of the word, toward a striving to pronounce the word clearly and accurately, and not toward the auditory perception of the word, the crucial element for success in the task.

Testing this assumption involved two more experiments by Khokhlova. In the second experiment each child was given chips of different colors and given the task of isolating each sound by a chip. At the end of each word-sound analysis the child lined up as many chips as there were in the word. The number of words and the duration of training was the same as in the first experiment. Afterward the child was required to perform a word-sound analysis on a series of words without the aid of the chips. Results were superior to those reported in experiment 1, but 75% of the children did not succeed and 25% of the children only partially succeeded (with success equivalent to getting 50–75% correct of all presented words).

In the third experiment a more intense effort at materializing the word sound analysis was attempted. The number of words and duration of training were similar to those of the previous experiments. The child was presented with a graphic scheme in which each little square would represent an individual sound and each chip would be placed within a little square during a word-sound analysis. The child was given a card with a picture of an object on it and below the picture were placed little squares whose number corresponded to the number of sounds in the word. After naming the object, the child performed a word-sound analysis putting into each little square a chip in place of each sound. After mastering word-sound analysis with materialization (stage 1), the child was required to perform the word-sound analysis without the graphic scheme but with the chips (stage 2), and finally without any external aids (stage 3). After completing the three-stage training process only 6% failed completely, 12% were partially successful, and 82% did not make any mistakes, or made only a few, on the word-sound analysis without any aids. In summary, none of the children were successful using the training procedure in experiment 2, and 82% were successful in experiment 3.

Khokhlova's experiments demonstrate that children of older preschool age can be taught to master word sound analysis sufficient for the mastery of literacy prior to familiarity with letters of the alphabet. Of course, the methodology employed was specially developed. A child not exposed to such training would not ordinarily be expected to master the phonological aspect of speech at so early an age.

The three experiments cited from the Soviet literature suggest that a considerable level of creativity is involved in designing training procedures that are not only effective but efficient in producing success on specified tasks. Role repetition of relationships or simple reinforcement of a designated response is frequently unsuccessful or so inefficient that the number of repetitions exceeds practical consideration. This being the case, instructional television requires creative training procedures that are not only applicable to the medium but are also efficient.

Bruner's Position on Language Acquisition

Before discussing the implications of this review to instructional television, research by Jerome Bruner, done at the Center for Cognitive Studies, Harvard University, will be examined. Bruner has produced some provocative research on the development of intellectual abilities in children that has the potential to be applied to instructional television.

Bruner (1964) stresses the importance of the shift from perceptual (or iconic) representation to symbolic (or linguistic) representation during childhood. Bruner states that perceptual representations, in the form of mental images, are essentially static. Bruner believes that it is difficult if not impossible to rearrange mental images into different combinations for the purpose of thought, but views language as a much more powerful tool for thought. Events are translated through language into a rule-bound symbolic system, which is then capable of being altered in ways that may or may not correspond to any possible set of events. This "effective productivity" of language makes it an extremely powerful tool for thinking and problem solving.

Bruner theorizes that iconic representation initially dominates representation through language in the course of cognitive growth. Thus, there are situations in which the perceptual display misleads, or is in conflict with, the verbal representation of a situation. One such instance is in the conservation of quantity test, where water is poured from one container to another of a different shape. Françoise Frank (Bruner, Olver, & Greenfield, 1966, pp. 192–202) placed a screen in front of the pouring so that the children could describe the situation verbally without being confused by the perceptual display. Afterward the screen was removed, and the children were asked again which had more water. None of the 4-year-olds succeeded on the standard conservation task pretest, but 50% of the 4-year-olds passed the test with the screen in place. The change was from 20 to 90% among the 5-year-olds and from 50 to 100% among the 6-year-olds. After the screen was removed, it was only the 4-year-olds who were overwhelmed by the perceptual display and changed their minds. The older children stuck to their decision and typically justified their answer with statements of the type "It looks like more to drink, but it is only the same because it is the same water and it was only poured from there to there." Thus, the children justify their answer that it is the same amount of water by resorting to an "identity" argument, namely, it is the same water and therefore it is the same amount. On a posttest of conservation, thinner beakers or several small beakers were used on the conservation task in contrast to wider beakers on the training task. On this test the 4-year-olds remained nonconservers, 70% of the 5-year-olds showed conservation in contrast to 20% on the pretest, and the older children's conservation responses increased from 50 to 90%. Bruner concludes from this experiment and from others of a similar type conducted under his direction (see Bruner, 1966) that an experience that frees children from "perceptual seduction" and simultaneously encourages verbal representation can alter the course of cognitive growth.

Although there appear to be a number of problems with the training procedures and treatment of data in Frank's experiment, these results, combined with the results from the other experiments directed by Bruner and the Soviet research presented earlier, add considerable credibility to the argument that cognitive growth can be enhanced by employing verbal training techniques that have been tested and found appropriate to the tasks they have been designed to train.

IMPLICATIONS FOR TELEVISED INSTRUCTION

The following examples represent possible applications of the research presented in this chapter to televised instruction. There are innumerable examples of possible teaching formats related to language training. The exercises cited are for illustrative purposes only.

Format 1

From E. V. Clark's research (1971, 1973) it is clear that young children possess only a rudimentary understanding of some very important words, which signify such things as quantity, size, direction, sequence, and command. Apparently, children are able to blunder and bluff their way through adult instructions and commands that use these words until they acquire adult comprehension. It cannot be assumed in television instruction that children have a correct understanding of important words used in communicating various facts and directions to them. The following is a format for the televised teaching to children of the distinction between the meanings of the words *more* and *less*.

1. Show a girl holding a shallow open tray with five candies exposed to view on it.
2. Show a boy holding another, similar tray, but with three candies.
3. Show a hungry child trying to figure out which box of candies to take.
4. Use various instructional techniques to emphasize the manner in which a quantity comparison can be made. For instance, employ a visual counting procedure, such as removing one object at a time from each tray and emphasizing the remainder in the tray that held the greater quantity. Or, start with no objects in each tray and have each child add one candy at a time alternately, with one child adding more candies at the end. Or, present the two trays with different quantities of candy initially and alternatively focus on each piece of candy in each tray in a fixed order so that a matching procedure is encouraged from the children watching on television.
5. Vary the quantity comparison techniques so that the children are encouraged to use all of them.

6. Repeat procedures 1–5 using an incentive for successful choice. For instance, a child must determine which of two sets of identical objects has a greater quantity. The child first selects a reward, then, upon making a correct conservation response, is permitted to carry away the reward.
7. Repeat procedure 6, except vary number, type, and position of objects in each set.
8. Vary question asked on each problem. Sometimes ask, "Who has more to eat—Mary or John?" "Who has less to eat—Mary or John?" The purpose of varying the question is to force a discrimination between the meaning of *more* and the meaning of *less*.
9. Ask question. Pause. Use techniques that develop suspense and anticipation among the children watching at home, so that they are encouraged to guess.
10. Vary presentation so that the attention of the audience is not lost. However, great care must be taken not to use techniques that distract children from concentrating on the activities essential for a correct solution of the task.

The long-range benefits of instructing children in the meanings of various important words, such as *more* and *less* as these apply in physical manipulations transcends the immediate objective of rote training in word definitions. It is important that children be instructed in the adult usage of words for the following reasons:

1. An understanding of the precise meaning of words such as *more–less, big–small, tall–short, ask–tell, before–after, in–on–under*, etc., makes for easier instruction in advanced concepts. If children do not have an adequate understanding of the meaning of words used by adults, the effect of instruction is diminished.
2. Children must be taught to concentrate on a word and reflect upon the specific activity that it represents in the situation in which it is used.
3. Children must learn the value of using words precisely. If E. V. Clark's Semantic Feature Hypothesis is correct (for contrary data, see H. Lesser & Drouin, 1975), children initially acquire a global understanding of the meaning of certain words and in the course of experience acquire a specific understanding. This more specific understanding is discovered in the context of success and failure when following instructions or when children give verbal instructions to themselves. For instance, the failure to distinguish *in, on*, and *under* can lead children into enormous blunders when following instructions. Through such blunders success is ultimately achieved, and children learn to appreciate the power of language to order events, reason about them, and code them in memory for future use.

Format 2

In this exercise children are instructed in the locative terms *in, on,* and *under.* E. V. Clark (1973, pp. 161–182) asked children questions of the form "Put the *x* [in, on, under] the *y.*" The *x* objects were toy animals. There were six *y* reference objects, which provided the following possibilities for placement of the toy animals:

Object	Possibility of placement of toy animal
a box on its side	*in* or *on*
a tunnel through a flat-topped mountain	*in* or *on*
a dump truck	*in* or *under*
a cradle	*in* or *under*
a desk	*on* or *under*
a table	*on* or *under*

Since the hierarchy of responses of young children is *in, on,* and then *under* (E. V. Clark, 1973), they will respond to instructions as follows:

Instruction	Children's response
Put the toy lion *in* the box or *in* the tunnel.	*in*
Put the toy lion *on* the box or *on* the tunnel.	*in*
Put the toy lion *in* the truck or *in* the cradle.	*in*
Put the toy lion *under* the truck or *under* the cradle.	*in*
Put the toy lion *on* the desk or *on* the table.	*on*
Put the toy lion *under* the desk or *under* the table.	*on*

Young children response incorrectly three out of six times. They seem to understand only the general nature of the request. Irrespective of the instruction, whenever possible the first preference is *in*; the second preference is *on*; and the last preference is *under*. Beyond that, young children do not understand the finer distinctions between *in, on,* and *under*.

The following format is designed to teach the distinctions between *in, on,* and *under* on television:

1. Show a box on its side.
2. Show a lion near the box.

3. Show lion tamer commanding, "In."
4. Show lion running into the box.
5. Show lion tamer commanding, "On."
6. Show lion jumping on the box.
7. Repeat procedures 1–6 using different animals and different reference objects.
8. Show lion near cradle and desk.
9. Show lion tamer commanding, "On."
10. Show lion being punished or prevented from jumping into the cradle.
11. Show lion being rewarded for jumping on the desk.
12. Repeat procedures 8–11 with different animals and different reference objects.
13. Use repetition with variation to maintain interest in foregoing procedures.
14. Show six lions in a row corresponding to the six reference objects.
15. Show lion tamer commanding, "Under."
16. Show lions 3, 4, 5, and 6 crawling under the truck, cradle, desk, and table respectively. Lions 1 and 2 do not respond because they cannot go under the box or tunnel.
17. Repeat procedure 16 with *on*.
18. Repeat procedure 16 with *under*.
19. Where appropriate in all the above procedures, provide ample opportunity for the child viewer to anticipate and guess the right answer before it occurs. Encourage guessing using various production techniques that build suspense and generate enthusiasm for the self-discovery of rules that lead to the prediction of the correct response.

It is important that children be exposed to situations that provide the possibility of abstracting rules that define the distinctions between interrelated words that have distinct meanings. The locative words *in, on*, and *under* all refer to the location of an object with respect to a reference object. Adults frequently use these words when making requests of children, and just as frequently fail to clarify what they mean. Usually a loud no or a gesture meaning "put it here" or "It's *on* the desk, not *in* it" suffices to change the child's activity in the correct direction. However, more systematic instruction is desirable and can be provided on television. One possible direction this instruction could follow has just been outlined.

Format 3

Sinclair-de-Zwart (1971a) reports that young children have great difficulty in understanding the meaning of certain basic types of sentence constructions. For instance, it is now generally agreed that the passive construction is difficult for young children to understand. Thus, the correct understanding of the sentence "The boy was washed by the girl" occurs later than its active counterpart "The girl washed the boy." Another instance of difficulty is in understanding and using sentences that establish temporal indicators. Thus, young children have difficulty determining the correct order of activity in a sentence such as "The boy went up the stairs after the girl washed the car." The event described first is generally the one young children consider to occur first in time.

Televised instruction has certain unique characteristics that can be of great benefit when sentence comprehension is taught. The following exercise explores some of these possibilities:

1. Show a truck pushing a car and say, "The truck pushes the car."
2. Show a truck pushing a car and say, "The car is pushed by the truck."
3. Repeat procedures 1–2, except use a car pushing a truck.
4. Repeat procedures 1–3 several times.
5. Blank screen. Say, "The car is pushed by the truck."
6. Build suspense. Encourage guessing as to what children watching will see next. Present alternatives one by one of the car pushing the truck and of the truck pushing the car and ask, "Is this what happens?"
7. Repeat procedures 5–6 for a car pushing a truck.
8. Repeat above procedures for different agents and patients. Children must learn that the passive construction can be applied generally and is not specific to any one situation.
9. Another powerful instructional technique that is easily employed is to create incongruous situations out of incorrect interpretations of the meaning of sentences. For instance, children can be shown what would happen if the sentence "The cat is carried by the elephant" were misunderstood to mean "The cat carries the elephant."

The understanding of various basic types of sentence constructions cannot be assumed when instructing young children on television. Instruction in the understanding of passive-type sentences should teach children that the agent need not always precede the patient when describing an event. The rule for the reversal of the order of presentation of agent and patient constitutes the rule for the construction of the passive sentence. A similar arrangement applies for the description of events where something that happens second is described before something that happens first. A rule is learned for the establishment of temporal indicators. Children learn that language is more flexible in describing events than are the events themselves. Unlike the event itself, certain elements in a description can be stressed, depending upon the needs of the person describing the event.

Encouraging more advanced ways of describing things and events is also possible through televised instruction. Demonstrations describing things and events using relational terms ("The boy has more than the girl"); differentiated terms (different terms for different dimensions); and coordinated descriptions ("This pencil is longer but thinner, the other is short but thick") are easily applied to instruction on television. It may be the case that advanced instruction in ways of describing things and events will not lead to an immediate coordination and integration of these descriptions into the practical activities of children's everyday experience. However, the ability to use relational, differentiated, and coordinated descriptions should eventually promote a conceptual leap whereby advanced descriptions of things and events and the things and events themselves are related to each other in the thoughts of children.

Unlike ordinary discourse between an adult and child, where it is frequently impossible to point to an event that is described, television can readily present the event that is described to the children watching. A direct and immediate comparison between the sentence and a motion picture account of what the sentence represents in terms of an actually transpiring event is always possible. The ability to immediately picture what has been verbally described is a powerful aspect of instruction over television. In this instance, it is used to teach children how to use language more creatively. In other contexts, it is a powerful tool for instruction in general.

Format 4

In this exercise young children are trained in the isolation of words in sentences and in the isolation of sounds in words. The isolation of words in sentences is acquired earlier and is therefore an appropriate beginning exercise for preschoolers. The following is an example of one possibility for training in word discrimination on television:

1. Show a child holding all 10 fingers up.
2. Slowly pronounce a sentence.
3. With each word pronounced, the child puts down one finger.
4. An alternate instructional strategy might be to present a "bouncing ball" that moves from one location to the next with each word pronounced. The child actor can follow the movement of the bouncing ball with corresponding hand movements.
5. Procedures 1–3 or 4 are repeated, except that the child actor pronounces the sentence along with a voice pronouncing it in the background.
6. Children are encouraged to physically participate along with the child actor. That is, children watching are encouraged to put their fingers up and put them down one by one or to bounce along with their hand to each word.

7. A later development is to encourage physical participation, but without an external model. For instance, show a child holding all 10 fingers up, and as the sentence is pronounced, fade out the model so that children watching are encouraged to proceed on their own.

Using a training method that orients children to the essential features of the task is a critical variable for all instruction, and televised instruction is no exception. Every effort should be expended to organize the activities of children watching over television. If this is attained, instruction is likely to produce better results with less repetition. For this reason, obtaining physical participation with a model that orients children to the essential features of the task is, in general, a desirable objective.

The procedure outlined for word–sentence analysis is directly applicable to the harder task of sound–word discrimination. It is hoped that once children acquire a fluency in this type of phonetic analysis of sentences and words, they will be motivated to apply it on their own to sentences produced by themselves and others. Fluency in this type of activity prepares children for literacy, since this ability is one precondition for developing reading skills. However, fluency in word–sentence and sound–word analysis has a more general function. When children are oriented toward the physical characteristics of sounds and toward identifiable larger units of a language, they are oriented toward a property of the language itself in addition to language as spoken for communication purposes. This is a first step toward being able to reflect upon language itself. When children are able to reflect upon language as a system, they acquire the ability to dissociate words from their content and, for instance, no longer say, "Seven," when asked, "How many words in the sentence 'Mary has seven dolls'?" Reflection upon the formal properties of language as distinct from its content is another precondition for literacy.

Format 5

Bruner *et al.* (1966) present experimental evidence that supports the conclusion that iconic representation initially dominates linguistic representation. They believe that young children are easily seduced by appearances. For instance, when verbal reasoning is placed in conflict with an observed transformation of an object (as in the conservation problems), children frequently rely on direct perception and abandon efforts to solve the problem verbally. Bruner *et al.* placed a screen in front of the transformation to shield children from the effects of direct perception and to force them to rely exclusively on verbal reasoning. Afterward the screen was removed, and a conflict between iconic representation and verbal representation was induced. Bruner *et al.* believe that the consequence of inducing conflict in this way produces greater reliance on verbal reasoning. Since greater reliance on verbal reasoning is, for Bruner *et al.*, a more advanced form of reasoning, cognitive development is enhanced.

The following exercise applies their screening technique to televised instruction:

1. Show a child looking at two glasses of water.
2. Pour one into another, wider glass behind a screen.
3. Show the child trying to decide which glass has more water to drink.
4. Alternate close-ups of the unscreened and the screened glasses.
5. Remove the screen.
6. Show a confused child.
7. Show the child pouring the water from the wider glass into the original glass.
8. Show the child pouring the water back and forth, testing the result and exclaiming in surprise, "It's the same water!"
9. Show the pouring in slow motion, reverse action, use visual close-up, with concentration on width compensating height and the reversibility of the pouring activity.
10. Repeat procedures 1–4 and ask, "Does this glass (close-up of screened glass) or does this glass (close-up of unscreened glass) have more to drink, less to drink, or the same to drink?"
11. Delay. Encourage guessing among children watching. Then show two children, both happily drinking the water from the glasses, each starting and finishing at the same time. Exclaim, "They're the same!"
12. Repeat foregiong procedures with variations in size and shape of glasses.

If it is the case that children can be taught to rely more on verbal reasoning than on direct perception by shielding them temporarily from direct perception of a transformation, then television seems to be ideally suited for this type of instruction. There should be no difficulty in illustrating a wide variety of concepts other than conservation of quantity using the screening procedure technique over television. The ensuing conflicts generated in the children watching could induce a greater reliance upon verbal reasoning and thereby reinforce other instructional formats proposed in this chapter and in the chapter on cognition.

CONCLUSION

The topics chosen for review in this chapter question the basic assumption that preschoolers can comprehend and use many of the fundamental words and sentence structures that adults take for granted. Preschoolers have difficulty distinguishing words that signify relationship (e.g., quantity, size, direction, sequence). Part of the difficulty seems to be derived from the imprecise way young children acquire these terms from adults. For many important words, young children initially learn only a general feature of a word (e.g., *big* and *small* refer to size, *more* and *less* refer to quantity, *tall* and *short* refer to height). When this knowledge is combined with gestures and verbal corrections from adults, young children are usually able to zero-in on the precise nature of an adult's commands.

It seems probable that through formal instruction on television, children can be taught to use words more accurately. This training would be part of a more general education in the structure and function of language, of which pre-schoolers are either unaware or only vaguely aware. Awareness of the precise meanings of words, of the specific activity a word demands in a situation in which it is used, and of the value of such instruction is important if children are to acquire the ability to use language precisely, flexibly, and creatively.

Formal instruction logically extends to the comprehension of sentences. For instance, children have difficulty understanding and using sentences with passive constructions as well as sentences that establish temporal indicators for actions. Learning how to describe events accurately in many different ways is part of the general process of discovering the flexibility of language as a communicative medium. Such a discovery by young children can lead to an enormous advance in the ability to reason problems through verbally. Children are no longer restricted to describing the events they observe in the fixed sequence in which they occurred. They can now use language to relate occurrences that are causally connected but spatially and temporally far removed. Language usage attains the flexibility to adjust to the needs of the user instead of rigidly reflecting events directly observed.

Intimately associated with a more precise, flexible, and creative use of language is the ability to describe events using relational terms ("The boy has more than the girl"), differentiated terms (different terms for different dimensions), and coordinated terms ("This pencil is longer but thinner, the other is short but thick"). Preschoolers should learn how to describe events using these advanced forms. Instruction in the use of such forms is not beyond the capability of educational television. However, the mere use of such terms by young children in descriptions need not suggest that they have acquired the full implications of their use. A conceptual leap is required to coordinate and integrate these descriptive forms into the practical activities of children's every-day experience.

Another indicator of an advanced use of language is the ability to reflect upon language itself. Evidence was cited that suggests that young children have difficulty in separating the words in a spoken sentence and the sounds in a spoken word. Special instructional procedures that require children to mark each word or sound with an object seem to be effective in orienting children to the task requirements and consequently to success on the task. Since word–sentence and sound—word analysis are preconditions for training in literacy, instruction should be attempted on television. Such instruction should prove useful.

Another important consideration when training children in the use of language is that they must be taught to rely on verbal reasoning when it is placed in conflict with an observed event. One device for encouraging greater reliance on verbal reasoning is to place a screen in front of the conflictual event (such as a screen in front of the pouring of water from one container to a wider one). In this way, children are forced to rely exclusively on verbal reasoning ("It's the same water"), and are not confused by the different appearance. Formats such as the screening procedure that encourage reliance upon verbal reasoning can easily be fitted to presentation over television.

The previous chapter dealt with preschoolers' cognitive abilities, the present chapter has dealt with their language abilities, and the next two with their perceptual and mnemonic abilities. Obviously, these abilities do not exist in isolation from one another. Making these divisions and considering them in separate chapters for instructional purposes on television has made manageable a very complex presentation. There is no intent to imply that cognition, language, perception, and memory exist in isolation. Each is a different aspect of the overall process of development.

Recall, for instance, from Chapter 3 that preschoolers' speech passes through three stages as it relates to problem solving. For 3- to 4-year-olds speech activity and intellectual activity devoted to the solution of practical problems are entirely divorced from each other. At this age children make no effort to use speech to solve problems. At about 5 years children pass through a transition stage, where speech follows and mimics intellectual activity. At this age speech is a verbal form of activity, a copy of the child's behavior and of the situation. Speech always occurs at the close of the activity and appears to function only as a playback device for the activity. For 6- to 7-year-olds speech begins to anticipate intellectual activity. A two-sided relationship develops between solving problems through manipulating the objects of a problem manually and using speech to anticipate the consequences of physical actions upon objects. With limited experience in solving practical problems through direct action upon objects the development of the use of speech to solve problems would be severely impaired. On the other hand, the development of the ability to solve problems verbally irreversibly changes the course of direct actions upon objects.

The development of language abilities, as described in this chapter, proceeds hand-in-hand with the development of the ability to solve problems verbally. From the perspective of children and of the everyday problems they encounter the two developments are inseparable. If it is the case that language is a higher form of reasoning, as Bruner suggests, then it is desirable to encourage instruction that emphasizes verbal reasoning and at the same time discourages solving problems motorically and through mental imagery. However, if it is the case that verbal reasoning is only one form of reasoning, desirable in certain situations and not in others, then no priority in instruction is suggested. The evidence on the exact relationship of language to reasoning is not yet firmly established. It is this author's opinion that in the absence of a defining statement the best policy to establish for televised instruction is to assume no priority and to encourage children to reason more effectively and creatively in all ways possible. With this in mind, the next chapter discusses visual thinking in young children.

6

Image and Reality:
Refining the Use of Visual Thinking

The most powerful aspect of television is its ability to use visual imagery. Television can present an infinite array of static and kinetic images in controlled formats. These arrays, if correctly designed and tested, offer a unique opportunity to instruct young children in how to reason more effectively.

This chapter starts out with some examples, from American sources, of children's limited abilities in identifying and comparing objects observed under varying conditions of perceptual complexity. Experiments will be cited that demonstrate: (1) the difficulties children experience in trying to locate overlapping and embedded figures in larger displays; (2) the difficulties children experience in the part—whole perception of objects; and (3) the difficulties children experience in recognizing incomplete figures.

Evidence will then be cited from observation of the visual search behavior of children that provides a tentative hypothesis as to why they perform so poorly on tasks such as those listed. Additional documentation from Soviet sources will be cited that supports many of the American findings.

The mere demonstration of developmental differences in perceptual abilities is, however, not sufficient justification for embarking on an ambitious program of televised perceptual training of young children. It is necessary to demonstrate that perceptual growth makes an important contribution to the normal psychological development of children. One requirement is to show that changes in perceptual abilities follow a fixed developmental sequence. That is, it must be shown that all children start out with the same difficulties and overcome them in the same order. This will be done by examining two areas: space perception and mental imagery. It will be shown that perceptual development and intellectual development are intimately intertwined; one cannot occur without the other. Therefore, perceptual training should be a required component of any instructional television program for young children.

The last research topic to be discussed in this chapter is Eleanor Gibson's analysis of how children learn to discriminate letters. Like the other research discussed in this chapter, the growth of children's abilities in the discrimination of letters is a problem in perceptual development. However, Gibson's research is much more applied than the other research because letter discrimination is so obviously a prereading skill. How children learn to discriminate letters will be studied closely because the lessons learned from this research can be readily applied to instruction on television.

In the two previous chapters a review of research was conducted before a separate analysis of the implications of the research to televised instruction was explored. This division has provided a convenient separation of the chapters into discrete areas of emphasis devoted to research and application. This chapter will follow the same design.

OBJECT PERCEPTION

The Untrained Eye

Ghent (1956, 1960) reports on the ability of 4- to 8-year-old children to identify overlapping and embedded figures. She used realistic overlapping figures, geometric overlapping figures, and embedded figures (see Figure 6.1). Children named the objects when the overlapping figures were real objects; they identified the objects from an array when the objects were overlapping geometric objects; and they traced out the hidden object from a sample when the object was an embedded figure. Older children made more identifications than

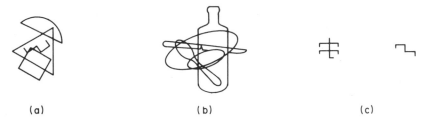

(a)   (b)   (c)

Figure 6.1. Example of (a) overlapping geometric figures; (b) overlapping realistic figures; and (c) embedded geometric figures. [Adapted from L. Ghent, Perception of overlapping and embedded figures by children of different ages. *American Journal of Psychology,* 1956, *69,* 575–587. Copyright © 1956 by The University of Illinois Press and reprinted by permission of The University of Illinois Press.]

younger children. The children found the embedded figures hardest to identify and the overlapping geometric figures easiest to identify. The overlapping realistic figures were of intermediate difficulty.

Ghent (1956) suggests that "the increase with age in ability to unscramble overlapping figures reflects an increase in perceptual span" or "an increase occurs in the number of lines that may be remembered after the eyes have shifted to another spot [p. 583]." With regard to embedded figures Ghent (1956) suggests that "young children have difficulty in perceiving a given boundary as simultaneously belonging to more than one form [p. 585]." An extreme case of contour sharing is the reversible figure, such as the Necker cube.

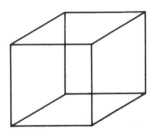

If the reader has difficulty in reversing the Necker cube, it is suggested that he/she try to imagine that the cube is on a glass table and that it is stared at from the underside.

Ghent suggested that the difficulty in identifying overlapping and embedded figures was positively related to the extent that the boundaries of the added forms coincide. Elkind, Koegler, and Go (1964) refined Ghent's hypothesis in a study of part–whole perception. They showed children objects, which, in turn, were combined to form larger objects. For instance, one object was a scooter, the two wheels made of lollipops connected by a lollipop stick, with the handlebars made of candy canes at the end of another lollipop stick. Over an age range of 4–9 years they found a regular decrease in "part" responses from 71% to 21%, a decrease in "whole" responses from 17% to 0%, and an increase in "part and whole" responses from 11% to 79%.

Stages in the Development of Part–Whole Perception

Elkind *et al.* describe four stages in the development of part–whole perception in children:

Stage 1a: (Age 5–6). Most children saw the parts. A few children saw the wholes. No children saw both parts and wholes (e.g., "Some candy suckers and candy canes").

Stage 1b: (Age 6). A few children went through what appears to be a transitional stage. They mentioned the whole and then the parts, then denied seeing the whole (e.g., "A scooter—I mean, candy" and when asked to show the scooter, the child responded, "No").

Stage 2: (Age 7–8). Children mention both wholes and parts but do not integrate them in any way (e.g. "A scooter, candy canes, suckers"). The children seem to be responding as if they "saw the parts and then the whole alternatively and not simultaneously [p. 89]."

Stage 3: (Age 8–9). The part and whole are both perceived and they are attributed to the same form (e.g., "A scooter made of candy").

These stages seem to support Piaget's theory on the development of perceptual processes in children. The ability to decenter, defined as the ability to spontaneously shift focus from one perceptual organization to another is central to Piaget's formulation of the development of perceptual processes. In addition, Piaget states that perceptual development is an aspect of the stage-by-stage cognitive development of children. Therefore, perceptual development is subordinate to intellectual development in the sense that intellectual development predicts perceptual development.

There is also some evidence to suggest a developmental progression in the recognition of incomplete figures. Gollin (1960, 1962, 1964) presented children with line drawings of objects with large portions of their contours omitted. In one experiment five stages of successively more complete pictures were shown to children and adults (see Figure 6.2). Children were required to identify the picture both with and without training. Gollin presents evidence that suggests that training children with intermediate levels of incomplete pictures is more effective than training with complete pictures. Similar work was done by Potter (1966) on figures impoverished by blurring rather than deletion. Adults recognized figures with more blurring than did children. However, young children were hindered less by forming early hypotheses about the pictures than were adults and older children.

The examination of visual search behavior in children as they explore objects is an important way of making inferences about the development of perceptual processes. Pick and Pick (1970, p. 823) cite evidence from work by Mackworth and Bruner (1966), later published (Mackworth & Bruner, 1970), in which 6-year-old children and adults observed a series of photographs that were either

Stage I   Stage II   Stage III   Stage IV   Stage V

Figure 6.2 Succession of stages, from incomplete to complete, in the line drawing of an elephant. [Reprinted with permission of author and publisher from: Gollin, Eugene S., Developmental studies of visual recognition of incomplete objects. *Perceptual and Motor Skills*, 1960, *11*, 289–298.]

progressively blurred or progressively brought into focus. Each successive exposure lasted 10 seconds. Eye movements and eye fixations were recorded using an extremely sensitive recording device. Pick and Pick (1970) report that the children

> tended to focus their fixations on fewer points as the stimulus became more blurred . . . . there was no group trend toward concentration on particular points of the target. Children also scanned less effectively by failing to attend to the most informative aspects of the picture. Furthermore, they were more variable in exploration of repeated presentations of the same picture. Finally, children made many more short eye movements, relative to the number of larger saccades. This last fact is interpreted to mean that they restrict their intake of information when faced with tasks that put a burden on their capacity for information processing—in other words, children develop a kind of tunnel vision [p. 823].

Vurpillot (1968), using the same eye-movement recording device as Mackworth and Bruner, reports on an experiment where children were required to make same—different judgments on the outline drawings of pairs of houses. Each house had three rows of two windows. All the windows may be the same, or one, three, or five windows may be different (see Figure 6.3).

Vurpillot measured the number of correct answers, the number of windows fixated, and inferred the number of paired comparisons the children made while examining the houses. The ideal scanning strategy would be a succession of paired comparisons along a general direction until a difference appears. Children under 6 generally limit their scanning to only a few windows. Consequently, 4- and 5-year-olds made many errors on different pairs, especially when there were few differences between the houses. Children between the ages of 6 to 9 gradually made more systematic use of the ideal scanning strategy.

It is not difficult to notice from Mackworth and Bruner's and from Vurpillot's experiments that children lack direction in their scanning strategies. Apparently, quite a bit of training is required in order to learn how to observe, select, and retain information about objects and events. In addition, all the evidence from the other experiments so far presented in this chapter persuasively supports the position that perception is not a passive receptive process but is, in fact, an active process that requires intellectual activity in order to function effectively. The conclusion from the studies on overlapping figures, part—whole figures, and incomplete figures is that children have a general inability to apply appropriate intellectual activity to direct themselves to the salient aspects of the perceptual tasks and to integrate the incoming perceptual information so that perceptual problems are solved. There are indications from the various experiments that the problems children encounter may not be due to their inability to retain large amounts of information but may be a result of their inability to understand what they have seen. This is a provocative conclusion and it will be considered again later in the chapter.

Figure 6.3. A pair of different houses and a pair of identical houses. [From Vurpillot, 1968.]

The Soviet Position on the Development of Form Perception

The ability of young children to perceive form improves during the preschool age (Yendovitskaya, Zinchenko, & Ruzskaya, 1964/1971, pp. 42–56). Two-year-olds solve the problem of getting three-dimensional objects through corresponding holes in a grid only by means of trial and error. Three-year-olds, on the other hand, use the method of frequent visual comparison and thereby obtain almost entirely errorless results.

Younger preschool children only glance at a new object before trying to use it; older children attempt a relatively detailed visual inspection of a new object before attempting to use it. From a developmental perspective, the perceptual actions of older preschool children borrow from the practical problem-solving method of younger children. Perceptual problem-solving activities only begin to separate from practical problem-solving activities at the ages of 3 to 4 years. Even then, children achieve better results for a long time by practical methods rather than by visual methods.

Tactual manipulation of objects appears to make an important contribution to the development of form perception. Four-year-olds are able to recognize the form of an object that is presented to them tactually better than the form of an object that is presented to them visually. The Soviets maintain that the tactual perception of form occurs ahead of the visual perception of form. They also suggest that the ability to identify forms tactually may be indispensable for the acquisition of the visual perception of form.

Further analysis of the tactual dimension with blindfolded children, asked to familiarize themselves with objects through tactual exploration only, indicates that younger preschoolers merely try to manipulate objects (i.e., to roll, knock, or pull them) as a familiarization procedure; middle preschoolers (4- to 5-year-olds) merely press objects to a motionless hand without making exploratory movements; older preschoolers use the above but add feeling movements of the hand to examine the qualities of objects, such as contour, hardness, texture, etc. Older children's tactual images are richer and correspond more closely to the actual object.

The fact that the tactual perception of form is refined before the visual perception of form does not mean that young children do not visually perceive the different shapes of objects. On the contrary, what is indicated is that form is not distinguished from its object as an abstract entity, but remains inseparably tied to its object. For instance, younger preschoolers invariably refer to various geometric shapes as "balls," "windows," etc.; older preschoolers refer to the same geometric figures with the qualification that "this is like a ball," etc. Thus, older preschoolers begin to abstract forms as properties of objects, which are conceived of separately from the objects themselves.

Visual exploration of objects also changes with age among preschoolers. When eye movements are recorded during the visual inspection of objects, it is observed that 3- to 4-year-olds have many fewer eye movements than older children, that these movements are contained within the figure, and that there are much longer periods of fixation between movements. There is also a complete absence of pattern movement around the contour of the figure, and attention is easily diverted. For these younger preschoolers such primitive methods of visual exploration produce poor results in figure recognition.

As children get older, visual exploration becomes more thorough. Four- and 5-year-olds have many more eye movements that seem to be measuring the dimension and area of the figure. Although measurement of the contour of the figure is still absent at this age, there are noticeable groups of fixations that are directed at the most salient features of the figure.

Eye movements that follow the contour only start to form at about 5 years of age. However, these contour movements frequently stop at a characteristic point on the contour and leave the rest of the contour unexplored. With 6- and 7-year-olds, eye movements simultaneously follow the contour of the figure and also scan across the figure. Children of this age appear to be modeling the form while measuring the area and orienting themselves to the figure. The number of eye movements increases and the duration of fixation decreases greatly in comparison to those of younger children.

With increasing age the perceptual activities of preschoolers become more expansive and successive. This creates the opportunity for solving more complex problems associated with objects presented visually, such as drawing, modeling, constructing, and analyzing the components of objects.

The results of training experiments designed to enhance visual exploration in young children demonstrate some potentially valuable instructional procedures. For instance, children were taught to differentiate between triangles and rectangles. The apparatus consisted of a toy garage with a small screen on top of it. On the screen geometric figures were projected. The children pressed a left key for rectangles. When the children pressed the correct key, a car left the garage. Having developed differentiation on the presented figures, the children were given additional testing using variations of the presented figures in various positions. All preschool children tested on the variations made a large number of errors. According to Yendovitskaya et al. (1964):

> This indicated that the perceptual images formed under these conditions of training are neither adequately stable nor adequately generalized; consequently, they do not contribute to the child's capability for solving complex sensory problems [p. 54].

A much more successful training procedure allowed children to feel and manipulate cardboard geometric figures. The children were taught to follow the contour of each figure sequentially with their fingers, with changes of direction being emphasized through counting. Through such training, children acquired a "system of exploratory actions" that permitted recognition of any variant of a geometric figure.

In summary, it is initially the hand that plays the key role and the eye that serves the auxiliary function in form perception. Later, the eye performs exploratory activity movements without the assistance of hand movements. There is interesting transition phase, when children visually explore the contours of an object with abortive hand movements at a distance. In the last stages of the perceptual process, the exploratory eye movements are considerably shortened and decreased. Children focus directly on the distant, most informative characteristics of the object. They are able to organize a constant internal perceptual model of the object without the necessity of extensive visual exploratory actions. It is important to recognize that this last development is a gradual one that depends upon massive amounts of practical experience and training.

The Soviet research compares favorably with the American research previously described. The eye-movement experiments confirm the findings of Mackworth and Bruner and of Vurpillot. The increase in the adequacy of visual exploration with age appears to be directly associated with improvement in object identification and in comparison of objects. Eye movements simultaneously follow the contour of the figures and scan across it at about the ages of 6 and 7. This development indicates that a higher order of intelligence is directing the exploratory behavior of the older children. What are the intellectual developments that produce this radical change in exploratory eye movements? Whatever they are, the Soviet training experiments indicate that it is possible to instruct children to use these intellectual abilities earlier. The next two sections devote themselves to the nature of these intellectual developments.

The Concept of Space

Monique Laurendeau and Adrian Pinard (1970), at the University of Montreal, have devised a scale for the development of the concept of space in children. The scale is based on five tests originally designed by Jean Piaget and includes: stereognostic (tactual) recognition of objects and forms, construction of a straight line, localization of topographical positions, the concepts of left and right, and coordination of perspectives. The tests were administered to 50 children at each age between the ages of 2 to 12. The tests were given every 6 months up to age 5 and every year thereafter.

The concepts involved in teaching children how to construct a straight line, localize topographical positions, and coordinate perspectives are the most presentable on television. The other two tests are not very amenable to television presentation. Therefore, the following discussion is limited to a detailed analysis of the test, "The Construction of the Straight Line" and a brief description of the tests, "The Localization of Topographical Positions" and "The Coordination of Perspectives."

The test that measures the construction of a projective straight line is divided into two parts, each of which consists of three problems. In the first part, children work on a rectangular board and are required to place eight toy lampposts in a straight line from one toy house to the other toy house. In problem 1, the houses are placed in the upper left and upper right corners; in problem 2, halfway down on the left and right sides of the rectangle; and in problem 3, in the upper left and lower right corner. In the second part a circular board is used, and the required positioning of the lampposts is roughly similar to that required with the rectangular board.

The theory behind the test is derived from Piaget's notion that children develop their concept of space in a topological, projective, and finally Euclidian order. Space, defined topologically, is concerned with order and relations that do not change under certain transformations of objects. It might be nicknamed "rubber sheet" geometry because no matter how much the figures drawn on a rubber sheet are stretched, compressed, or distorted, certain positional relationships, defined as topological relationships, do not change. Space defined in projective terms is concerned with those properties of objects that do not change when the shadow is cast onto a plane surface. The shadow of a line is always a line and the shadow of a circle is always an ellipse. Euclidian space is concerned with the actual lengths and measurements of a figure that remain constant when a figure is moved to or copied in another spot. The perceptual identification of a straight line is attained by children at an early age. However, the ability to construct or reconstruct a straight line is not attained until much later. In particular, this is the case when the child does not have a perceptual guide during the construction (e.g., following the edge of the table). Without a guide children must perform operations of either a projective nature (e.g., sighting along the path) or operations of a Euclidian nature, which implies the construction of a coordinate system (e.g., tracing an imaginary line with the finger, straightening a curved line by pressing it with both hands, using a forearm as a straight edge).

Laurendeau and Pinard (1970) argue that success in lining up the lampposts depends on the level of the child's thought.

> It is not before the age of six or seven years—that is, before the beginning of operational thought—that the child is able to allow the intervention of elements of projective or Euclidian geometry, rudimentary though these may be, into his spatial representations [pp. 112–113].

As soon as the preoperational child is required to construct a straight line through two points, the preoperational nature of the thought processes restricts the child's thought to relations of neighborhood and order—or to topological thinking. Thus, preoperational children commit the following types of errors in trying to fit a straight line between two points:

1. They form special relations between the objects. For instance, a child might make a special effort to place lampposts in pairs so that the bases always touch but fail to orient the pairs in any single direction.
2. Some children can form a straight line only if they can place the elements near the straight edge of a table, etc. Thus, problem 2, where the objects are in the middle of the rectangle, is a more difficult problem for children than problem 1.
3. In constructing the oblique line from the upper left to lower right corner, children make many different kinds of errors. For instance,
   a. Children position the lampposts following the right angle of the table.
   b. Children curve the lampposts in the right direction but then deviate toward the apparently irresistible edge of the table.
   c. Children draw two arcs in the right direction from each house, but the center position drifts toward the edge of the table.

Laurendeau and Pinard classified the children's responses to the six problems into four successively more advanced stages, which form a developmental scale. Stages 2 and 3 are divided into two parts.

Stage 0. Refusal, incomprehension, or inability to construct even a curved or twisting line.

Stage 1. Linear constructions that are of a purely topological nature but are never straight.

Stage 2. Success with straight lines parallel to sides, but failure with obliques. Some children were more affected by the surrounding contour than others. The ones most affected were labeled Stage 2a, and those less affected were labeled Stage 2b.

Stage 3. Mastery of the oblique is obtained. Some children were able to master the oblique construction part of the time. Also, sometimes their lines were not exactly straight. These children were labeled Stage 3a. Other children had completely perfect oblique constructions. These children were labeled Stage 3b.

The results of the distribution of subjects by age and by stage in "The Construction of a Projective Straight Line Test" are presented in Table 6.1. At each age level the stages are distributed in the predicted order of difficulty. Within each stage, as the children get older, a higher percentage of children are successful at that stage. A higher percentage of success at Stage 2 tasks is only achieved at ages 6 and 7.

In conclusion, the results support the contention that the child's spatial representations are topological before being projective or Euclidian. Topological

TABLE 6.1
Distribution of Subjects by Age and by Stage in "The Construction of a Projective Straight Line Test"[a]

				Frequencies							Stage — Cumulated percentages					
Age	N	Unclassified	0	1A	1B	2A	2B	3A	3B	1A	1B	2A	2B	3A	3B
10:0	44	6					3	4	31				100	92	82
9:0	50	8				2	3	12	25			100	95	88	60
8:0	50	3				2	2	17	26			100	96	91	55
7:0	50	8				3	5	12	22			100	93	81	52
6:0	50	10			3	6	11	12	8		100	93	78	50	20
5:0	50	14			6	8	10	10	2		100	83	61	33	6
4:6	50	12	3	4	7	10	6	7	1	92	82	63	37	21	3
4:0	50	3	2	9	18	12	5	1		96	77	38	13	2	
3:6	50	3	1	13	8	17	4	4		98	70	53	17	9	
3:0	50	3	5	9	20	8	3	2		89	70	28	11	4	
2:6	50	1	9	18	16	5	1			82	45	12	2		
2:0	50	1	24	18	5	2				51	14	4			
Totals		72	44	71	83	75	53	81	115						
Median age			2:3	2:10	3:5	4:1	5:3	6:9	8:7						

[a]Reprinted from *The Development of the Concept of Space in the Child* by M. Laurendeau and A. Pinard by permission of International Universities Press, Inc. Copyright 1970 by International Universities Press, Inc.

reasoning is associated with preoperational thought, and projective reasoning with operational thought. Thus, the ability to construct a straight line is related to the child's stage of intellectual development.

In "The Localization of Topographical Positions Test" the children are shown two identical miniature landscapes in which a road, railroad tracks, and several houses of different color appear. In the first part of the test the landscapes are placed side-by-side, and the children are instructed to put a small man "at exactly the same place" as the experimenter's small man. The theory underlying the test is exactly the same as that in "The Construction of the Straight Line Test." The younger children are expected to place their figures using topological relations, and as the children get older, they are expected to employ increasingly sophisticated projective and Euclidian strategies. In the second part of the test the examiner's landscape is rotated 180°. As in the other test the responses of the children are divided into four stages. In the first stage the children refused or did not understand the instructions. In the second stage the children understood the task and applied themselves to it willingly. However, their responses ignored the most elementary projective and Euclidian concepts but respected elementary topological concepts. At this stage children might place the little man between two objects or in, on, or at the edge of an object but never consider spatial relationships of perspective or distance. In the third stage children use some primitive projective concepts in placing their little man. The children in this stage are divided into two levels: children who can place their little man in clearly defined topographical locations (e.g., between a house and a railroad track) but not in more undefined locations (e.g., in an open field with no nearby references). All the children of this stage fail in the correct positioning of their little man when the examiner's landscape is turned 180°. This reveals the primitive basis of the children's projective concepts at this stage. The projective spatial relations established are limited to the child's own body only. At this stage children place objects only according to laterality and depth from their own body.

When the experimenter's landscape is turned 180°, children continue to use this strategy, which, of course, leads to failure. If the child recognizes the failure, a reversion to the more primitive topographical strategy may result. In the fourth stage the children succeed only some of the time when the experimenter's landscape is turned. This means that the children in the last stage are able to free projective and Euclidian concepts from their own point of view. In the last stage children are also defined according to whether they can solve only the easier topographical problems or whether they can solve the harder ones as well. "The Location of Topographical Positions Test" is slightly harder than "The Construction of the Straight Line Test." Both tests produce equally good developmental scales, but the children reach the corresponding stages slightly later in one of them.

In the last test, "The Coordination of Perspectives Test," the data form the same type of developmental scale as the other two tests, but the children reach the corresponding stages at a still later age. Therefore, this test is the hardest of the three tests. There are two parts to this test. In the first part the child is presented with three paper cones (mountains) of different sizes and colors and is required to choose what they look like to a little clay man from various points of view. In the second part the child is shown a picture of the mountains and is asked to determine where the clay man stood when he took the picture. The stage-by-stage development in this test further confirms the position that the child's concept of space develops from an initial topological stage to a projective and Euclidian stage. The data also show a corresponding shift away from an exclusive orientation of children to their own point of view.

The overall analysis of all three of these tests hints at some general principles of perceptual development:

1. At least one aspect of the perceptual process goes through a regular perceptual development. This would be difficult to explain if perception consisted only of a passive recording of observed events.
2. The evidence presented suggests that the correspondences in perception and reasoning ability are not fortuitous. Rather it suggests that perception is an active process that requires direction and integration from intellectual processes.

In the next section another aspect of the perceptual–intellectual relationship will be explored.

MENTAL IMAGERY

This section will present evidence that suggests that important reasoning processes occur in the domain of mental imagery and that these reasoning processes are distinct from other forms of reasoning that may occur through actions themselves, through the use of speech, or through thought. A brief review of some experimental evidence should demonstrate that the distinctions between the various modes of thought are not only real but important.

Since it is impossible to study mental imagery directly, it might be suggested that it should not be studied at all. Piaget and Inhelder (1966/1971) reply to this criticism in the preface to their book *Mental Imagery in the Child*. They state:

> Finally, we should say something about the book's title. Several colleagues have advised us to change it, on the grounds that it might come under the suspicion of "mentalism" and because many writers no longer believe in the existence of images, or at least believe that nothing of import can be said about them. But it must be said that we care little about fashions in psychology, and even less about positivist

prohibitions. . . . As it is our intention next to make a study of memory in the child, we naturally have to begin by examining "images"—even if it is fashionable to pass over the problem in silence [p. xiii].

In spite of intuitions to the contrary from ordinary life, the idea that thought is exclusively identified with language has, until recently, been the dominant view among psychologists.

That thought might be possible without language, does not strike most people as an unreasonable idea. In fact, some artists claim that they cannot express themselves in a purely verbal medium. Even writers, whose life work immerses them in the very task of arranging words and sentences to convey meaning, often complain that their thoughts "will not enter words." It may come as a surprise, then, to find that the predominating view by psychologists over the last half of the century has been precisely the opposite; namely that thought is dependent upon language and not possible without it [Cromer, 1974, p. 184].

A good way to start a demonstration that there are real distinctions between thought in mental imagery and thought that depends upon language is to show that real changes do occur in the reasoning of children prior to their ability to represent these changes in reasoning in language. After a comprehensive review of the experimental evidence that relates the emergence of new concepts in the behavior of children to their efforts to express them in language, Cromer (1974) states that "the evidence is strong that changes in cognition precede the acquisition of new linguistic forms [p. 228]." It follows from an acceptance of this statement that there must be a form of "nonlinguistic" knowledge, which permits children to understand and reason about events prior to being able to represent them linguistically. The two major alternatives to nonlinguistic representation are representation in actions themselves and representation in mental imagery.

The strongest evidence in support of the argument that thought occurs without language comes from consideration of the first 2 years of life. For much of infancy children are prelinguistic. According to Piaget, the dominant form of representation during this period is representation through the child's own actions. Since children are able to solve problems in this stage without language, but with representation in action, Piaget characterizes representation in action as a form of thought that he labels sensorimotor intelligence.

Evidence that changes in thought precede its representation in language come from recent longitudinal research in psycholinguistic development (Bloom, 1970; Brown, 1973; Cromer, 1974; McNeill & McNeill, 1968). For instance, there is strong evidence that some types of negation (nonexistence, rejection, denial) are demonstrated in children's behavior only just before the appropriate linguistic forms appear in the verbalizations of the children themselves. It is suggested that only after the concept emerges "prelinguistically" does the child search for, and find, the correct linguistic form to express it. A similar behavioral development occurs just prior to the linguistic expression of various other advanced concepts. (For the development of time concepts during language acquisition, see Cromer, 1974, pp. 217–229.)

Other evidence for distinct forms of thought comes from Soviet research. Podd'yakov (1974) reviewing the Soviet literature on the development of elementary forms of thinking in preschool children, finds a "polymorphism" to children's thought processes that must be respected. The Soviets distinguish three forms of thinking: visual–action, image-based, and conceptual. These three forms correspond to the previously described thinking in action, in mental imagery, and in words and thoughts respectively. Podd'yakov concludes that visual–action and image-based thinking "contain resources no less powerful than conceptual thinking. . . . These forms of thinking fulfill their specific functions in the overall mental development of the school-age as well as preschool children [p. 43]."

The intent of the discussion to this point has been to distinguish three distinct forms of thought in children with the purpose of justifying the study of the development of mental imagery in children. It should be pointed out that the study of image-based thinking is inferential when compared to the study of thinking based upon action or language. The experimental procedure used by Piaget and Inhelder (1966/1971) to study the development of mental imagery is to present a child with a task that strongly requires image-based thinking for its correct solution. Afterward an analysis of correct solutions and of the types of errors made permits inferences about the process of mental imagery used by the child to mediate a solution to the task. This procedure is repeated on many different types of tasks, which vary in the requirements of mental imagery and vary in their level of difficulty. Different aged children are used in order to trace the developmental progression of mental imagery. In the overall analysis of results inferences about the development of mental imagery and the evolution of its function in the development of the whole person are analyzed.

Another aspect of image-based thinking is that it is inferable from behavior only at the close of the sensorimotor period. Only from about 18 months do behavior observations indicate that children come to the ability to represent reality mentally using visual imagery. At about the same time the child begins to use language. It is for this reason that Piaget characterizes mental imagery and language as manifestations of a general symbolic function, inferable from the behavior of children beginning around 18 months. Other manifestations that appear in the behavior of children at this time are deferred imitation (imitation of the model after it disappears), symbolic play (the game of pretending), and drawing.

Deferred imitation, symbolic play, and drawing are activities that participate, in varying degrees, in the three major forms of thought. Although these activities are not examples of pure forms of image-based thinking, a study of them is instructive because they provide somewhat less inferential hypotheses concerning the structure and function of image-based thinking. Consequently, a study of deferred imitation, symbolic play, and drawing will precede examination of image-based thinking in its purer forms.

Deferred Imitation

Piaget and Inhelder (1969b, p. 53) cite an example of deferred imitation in a 16-month-old girl that should illustrate the concept nicely. She sees a playmate become angry, scream, and stamp her foot. These are new sights to the little girl. An hour or two later the little girl imitates the angry scene while laughing. Although the ability to imitate starts early in infancy, deferred imitation appears only during the second year. The evolution of imitation in children is the following:

1. At about 2–4 months when someone repeats a gesture just made by the child, the child will repeat the gesture.
2. A little later the child will imitate any gesture made by an adult provided the gesture is already in the child's repertoire.
3. Shortly afterward the child tries to imitate a model purely for the pleasure of imitation. No longer is imitation performed automatically. This marks the beginning use of imitation as a desire to represent something intentionally.
4. In the next stage the child begins to copy unfamiliar gestures, but only if the gestures can be performed using visible parts of the body.
5. The next stage involves the imitation of parts of the body that are not visible (e.g., opening and closing of the eyes and mouth). For instance, yawning is not imitated until about the age of one.
6. In the last stage imitation generalizes and is used by children to obtain knowledge about their own bodies and the bodies of others. Imitation becomes deferred and performed for the pleasure involved in representing a model. As such, imitation becomes "a kind of representation in action [p. 56]."

In conclusion, imitation may be considered an early form of representation. It is representation in physical acts that prepares the way for representation in mental images and representation in words and thought. Imitation, when it is used as its own end, is used by children to accommodate themselves to increasingly complex and deferred models.

Symbolic Play

Piaget and Inhelder (1969b, p. 53) cite an example of symbolic play from the same 16-month-old girl just mentioned. The little girl's first "symbolic" game was pretending to sleep. She sat down, smiled broadly, closed her eyes, put her head to one side, put her thumb in her mouth, and used a corner of her tablecloth pretending it was a pillow just as she did when going to sleep. The symbolic games that appeared shortly afterward were putting her stuffed bear to sleep and sliding a shell along a box while saying "meow" just after she saw a cat on a fence.

Piaget considers symbolic play to be the apogee of children's play. Beginning during the first year and continuing into the school years children spend an enormous amount of time in personal make-believe worlds. The emotional, social, and intellectual needs of children are often worked out in make-believe, where they can express themselves in fantasy, far removed from the constraints of actuality. In symbolic play children can tame ferocious dogs and have their dolls finish the food they refused earlier. Because symbolic play is tuned to the highly personal needs of children, it does not generally imitate or accurately copy external reality. The symbols used are frequently understood only by the child (e.g., the shell represents the cat, the cat is made to play in the child's imagination in ways that may never occur in actuality).

Drawing

Drawing rarely appears as an activity of children before 2 to 2½ years. Piaget considers that drawing in its initial stages shares some of the qualities of symbolic play and of the mental image.

Two major positions about children's play exist (Piaget & Inhelder, 1969b, pp. 63–68). The first position is that children's drawings are essentially realistic. The claim is that children attempt to draw actual models and do not attempt drawings from their imagination until after 8 to 9 years. The other position is that efforts at idealization are apparent in children's early drawings. Luquet (cited in Piaget & Inhelder, 1969b, pp. 63–68), in a classic study of children's drawings, determined that "until about eight or nine a child's drawing is essentially realistic in intention, though the subject begins drawing what he *knows* about a person or object long before he can actually draw what he actually *sees* [p. 64]." According to Luquet, the stages of realism that drawing pass through are the following:

1. *Fortuitous realism*: This is the realism of the scribble whose meaning is discovered during the act of construction.

2. *Failed realism*: Children's drawings have a property of synthetic in-capacity. The elements of the drawing are juxtaposed instead of coordi-nated with each other. For instance, hats might appear well above the head and buttons alongside the body.
3. *Intellectual realism*: Children's drawings reflect their knowledge about the object and do not respect visual perspective. For instance, a face in profile might be drawn with two eyes or a man drawn in profile riding a horse will be shown with the visible and invisible leg.
4. *Visual realism*: At about 8 or 9 years drawings begin to respect visual perspective (e.g., a person drawn in profile now is shown with only one eye). Also objects intended as more distant are drawn smaller, according to the receding-lines principle. Finally, the objects in the drawing are now arranged with an overall plan in mind, and the objects themselves now respect geometrical proportions.

Piaget's Analysis of Mental Imagery

Because mental imagery shares in the symbolic activity of children with deferred imitation, symbolic play, and drawing, it is reasonable to anticipate that it also shares many of their properties and functions. The following is a summary of the principles that were derived from the study of deferred imitation, symbolic play, and drawing:

1. The stages in the development of imitation indicate that children can only imitate an act that they can understand. Another observation is that with development imitation moves from being automatically invoked by a model to being selective. That is, the intention to imitate acquires greater importance as children get older. Finally, as children get older, imitation becomes a creative exercise used at their own initiative to obtain knowl-edge of themselves and others.
2. Symbolic play has an imitative component supported by the fantasy life of the child. What is instructive about symbolic play is that it is not con-ducted for purposes of realistic imitation. It can be inferred from chil-dren's activities during symbolic play that the image-based representations that the activities are based upon are creatively applied to meet the needs of the child.
3. The study of the stages of drawing in the child shows that children's drawings are initially realistic in intent and reflect their knowledge about objects. This is a further confirmation of the principle that children's activities are closely bound to their intellectual attainments.

Experimental evidence indicates that during its development mental imagery follows a course that shares some of the attributes of deferred imitation, symbolic play, and drawing. Evidence will be presented that documents the fact that mental imagery becomes more flexible, selective, spontaneous, and creative as children get older. The improvement appears to be related to increases in children's intellectual attainments. Children's ability to analyze perceptual tasks using mental imagery also improves with age. Consequently, the level of sophistication of mental imagery and the purpose to which it can be employed parallel the growth of reasoning ability in children.

Piaget and Inhelder (1966/1971) studied imagery in children between the ages of 4 and 12. There are two basic elements to their classification system:

- *Reproductive images:* Those images that evoke sights that have been perceived previously.
- *Anticipatory images:* Those images that evoke movements, transformations, and their results that have not previously been observed.

In addition, it is possible to subclassify these two categories into images of static configurations, images of movements (changes of position), and images of transformations (changes of form). They found a distinct difference separating mental imagery before 7–8 years and mental imagery afterward. Children below the age of 7–8 have difficulty in reproducing movements or transformations they have observed. They have much less difficulty in reproducing static configurations. A few illustrations of the kinds of difficulties children have in reproducing movements and transformations should be helpful.

Children were presented with a rod, fixed at one end, and were asked to reproduce its rotation from the vertical through 90° to the horizontal. Results show that only at about 7 years are children able to represent reliably the correct movement (Piaget & Inhelder, 1966/1971, pp. 66–84). The children were asked to either draw or copy in gesture or select from prepared drawings the correct movement. The errors they made were rather interesting. Sometimes they drew, copied, or selected only the beginning and end positions, other times only several vertical and several horizontal positions but no oblique positions, other times all the horizontal and vertical positions to form a square, other times varieties of triangular shapes, etc. The errors seem to indicate: (a) a failure to differentiate the extreme static states from the intermediate states; (b) a failure to differentiate the successive positions of the rod from its extremity; and (c) an inability to retain the fixed center of rotation.

In another experiment children were required to anticipate the trajectories of three beads in space (blue, green, red) fixed on a rod rotated 180° about the center bead. The initial position was horizontal. There were four criteria for the evaluation of the trajectory: direction of the paths, circular shape, symmetry in relation to the horizontal axis, and the mere turning on itself of the center bead.

The most remarkable result is that children are able to anticipate the end position of the beads 3 years earlier (about 5 years old) than they can imagine the correct trajectory.

The analysis of errors by age reveals some interesting changes. Four-year-old children generally fail to reverse the order at the end points. Their drawings may not depict trajectories at all (the beads turn on their spots), or the trajectories are vertical or tortuously curved and turn back on themselves. At 5 years crossed trajectories predominate. The end position of the beads may be correct, but the paths may be rectilinear (even for the center bead), square shaped, curved in a variety of ways, or correctly shaped but not symmetrical about the horizontal axis. The children at this age all appear to be concentrating on the final result rather than on the transformation. At 6 years children can better determine the direction of rotation and the shape of the curves. However, it is only at 7 to 8 years that the children attempt to coordinate the relation of the outside beads to each other and attempt to retain the symmetry of the beads in relation to the horizontal axis.

Another experiment was conducted that required children to draw the transformation of a straight wire into an arc or an arc into a straight wire (Piaget & Inhelder, 1966/1971, pp. 161–178). As in the other experiments, children have great difficulty imagining the intermediate positions. Until about the age of 7 children demonstrate a boundary effect in their responses. In imagining the transformation, they draw the straight line so that its ends correspond to the ends of the arc. Thus, at age 5 the children underestimate the straight line resulting from the unbending of the arc by 34%. An overestimation of the arc resulting from the curving of the straight line also occurs at age 5 (29%). It is of interest that a similar underestimation is made when 5-year-olds are asked to make a simple side-by-side copy of a straight line. The children seem more concerned with judging the lengths in an ordinal rather than a metrical fashion. That is, they concern themselves with the points of arrival rather than with the interval between the extremities. Thus, the children try not to go beyond the terminal boundary when copying the line or in anticipating the transformation of the arc into a straight line or vice versa.

The following is the last experiment that will be cited on mental imagery. It is of particular interest because it explores the boundary between mental imagery and memory and also because it has an element of training involved in its design. In this experiment (Piaget & Inhelder, 1966/1971, pp. 242–244) five cardboard squares of different sizes were superimposed on each other. The squares were centered upon each other and in succeeding order, with the largest on the bottom and the smallest on the top. A nail, through the center, staked the squares to a base.

The children had to reconstruct the model using sample squares provided for that purpose. There were two experimental groups. In group 1 the child looked at the stacked squares for 20 seconds. The model was then disassembled, and the child was required to reconstruct it. Two weeks later the child was shown the model again and allowed to make a copy using the assembled model as a guide. Then the model and the child's copy was disassembled, and afterward the child was asked to reconstruct it. In group 2 the order was reversed. The active copy was requested at the first session and the simple perception at the second.

One hundred and twenty children aged 4 to 9 were used, with 20 in each group. In the first session active copying was more successful at all ages than perception only. However, the differences are striking only after 7 years. There is hardly any difference between the groups for active copying in the first and second sessions. This means that a perceptual inspection produces only minimal learning 2 weeks later. However, active copying in the first session leads to considerable improvement at most age levels 2 weeks later. These results are even better than those for active copying in the second session.

Overall, these results are interpreted to mean that active copying serves to organize the memory images so that a subsequent 20-second perception of the model is all that is necessary to analyze it into its constituent relations (ordering by size). This interpretation supports the previously stated principle that children can initiate events only at the level of their ability to organize them. It further suggests that appropriate training techniques can be effective in organizing children's memory. However, the topic will not be pursued now, as it is part of the subject material of the next chapter.

PREREADING SKILLS

For the past several decades educators and psychologists have concerned themselves with questions such as How do children learn to read? What are the tasks that must be mastered in order to become a fluent reader? Why do so many children fail at learning to read at an adult level?

Jeanne Chall, in an impressive review (1967), has analyzed the controversy between the phonetic approach to teaching reading (code-breaking) and the meaning approach (whole-word method). The experimental evidence is far from satisfactory, with virtually no evidence after the fourth grade. However, the existing evidence supports a phonetic approach in most instances. Some of Chall's conclusions are the following:

1. The code-breaking approach produces better overall reading achievement by the beginning of fourth grade.
2. The code-breaking emphasis produces from the beginning greater accuracy in word recognition and oral reading. Reading for meaning may not be better with the phonetic approach in the first grade. However, about the

end of first grade or at the beginning of second grade the child taught phonics catches up to and generally surpasses the child taught by the whole-word method on vocabulary and comprehension scores on silent reading tests. This advantage persists into third grade.

3. The phonetically taught child initially reads slower but with greater accuracy. However, by the third or fourth grade the phonetically taught child catches up to and frequently exceeds the child taught by the whole-word method in reading rate.

4. The child taught by the whole-word method has an initial advantage when reading for meaning. However, the child taught by the whole-word method ultimately falls behind in the second to fourth grades in comprehension and vocabulary test scores, mainly because the child does less well in word recognition.

5. Children of below-average and average intelligence and children from lower socioeconomic classes probably learn better with the phonetic approach, although the results might not show immediately.

6. Children with high mental ability and children from upper socioeconomic classes are less affected by the approach used to teach them to read. They generally learn to read satisfactorily regardless of the approach used.

There is a continuity between Chall's theoretical analysis, which supports the code-breaking approach to teaching reading, and Gibson's experimental evidence that children must be made aware of the distinctive features of letters as a first step to distinguishing them uniquely. Recognizing distinctive features of letters is a prereading skill. However, it is also a form of code-breaking in that it does for graphic forms what phonics does for sound—letter correspondences.

In one experiment (Gibson & Yonas, 1966) children and adults were required to make discriminations between pairs of letters—that is, to make same-or-different judgments. From the results a confusion matrix was constructed, which tells where the errors were made (see Figure 6.4).

With adults, the first split separates the sharp letters with diagonality; the second, the round letters *C* and *G* split off from *EFP* and *R*; the third, the square, right-angular letters (*EF*) split off from the letters differentiated by curvature (*PR*). With children (age 7), the first split is simple curve—straight line; the second, the round letters (*CG*) from *P* and *R*, and the square, right-angular letters (*EF*) split off from the diagonals (*MNW*); third, *MN* splits off from *W*. Gibson (1970) interprets the differences between adult and child processing as:

Children at this stage are doing straightforward sequential processing of features, while adults have progressed to a more Gestaltlike processing, picking up higher orders of structure given by redundancy and tied relations. . . . Adults achieve the highest level of differentiation with the greatest economy of processing [p. 105].

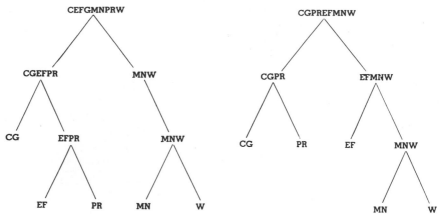

Figure 6.4. Tree structure yielded by confusions in making same–different judgments. The structure on the left was obtained with adult subjects, that on the right with 7-year-old children. [From E. J. Gibson, The development of perception as an adaptive process. *American Scientist*, 1970, *58*, 103–107.]

What are the children learning to respond to when they differentiate graphic forms? Gibson, Gibson, Pick, and Osser (1962) made inferences when they asked children (4 to 8 years) to discriminate letterlike forms from four different types of transformations: (a) three degrees of transformation from line to curve or curve to line; (b) five transformations of rotations or reversal; (c) two perspective transformations (slant left and tilt back); and (d) topological changes (break and close). The children were asked to match the standard with all its variants and to select only the exact copies (see Figure 6.5).

Children of all ages confused the perspective transformations with the standard. Few children made errors with the topological transformations. Rotations and reversals and line-to-curve transformations were confused with the standards by the younger children but not by the older ones. Gibson argues that children learn to distinguish features of graphemes that are invariant and critical for distinguishability within the set. For instance, there are certain distinctive features of the letter *A* that permit its recognition under different writing styles or different typefaces. From the results of this experiment and others (see especially Pick, 1965), Gibson (1963) argues that

there is perceptual learning of the distinctive features of letters in the stage of development before decoding to phonemes begins. This kind of learning is not associative, it is instead a process of isolating and focusing on those features of letters that are both invariant and critical for rendering each one unique.

Teaching is provided the child in this stage of·learning, but it is not the paired associates type. It is rather helping the child "to pay attention to" those features

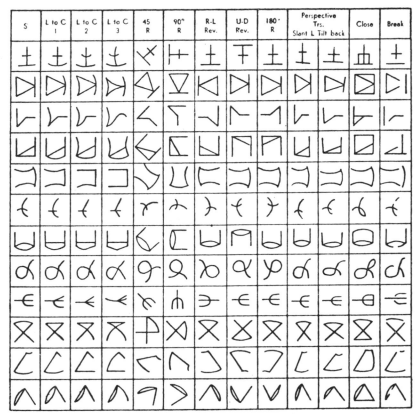

Figure 6.5. Artificial graphic forms and 12 variants. [From E. J. Gibson, Development of perception: Discrimination of depth compared with discrimination of graphic symbols. In J. C. Wright & J. Kagen (Eds.), *Basic Cognitive Processes in Children*. Chicago: University of Chicago Press, 1963. Copyright © 1963, 1973 by The Society for Research in Child Development, Inc. and reprinted by permission of The Society for Research in Child Development.]

which are invariant and distinctive. Learning a name for each letter, on the other hand, is a case of association, but necessarily a secondary stage [p. 21].

According to Gibson, the first stage in learning to read is acquiring the spoken language. The next stage requires learning to decode the written language to speech. There are several substages to this last stage. The first is learning to distinguish the different letters. As the previous experiments demonstrate, this involves a growing awareness of and sensitivity to the distinctive features of letters. This is a preliminary and necessary step before learning letter names. A later development is learning to decode the letters into sounds of speech. The last development, acquired only by the skilled reader, is to use all the "rules" in the language, such as spelling regularities and grammatical structure, so that processing written material occurs in larger and more complex "chunks."

All of the perceptual developments that Gibson describes as stages in learning to read are paralleled in the perceptual developments described in other sections of this chapter. It is likely that the perceptual and intellectual activities that are necessary to identify overlapping, part–whole, and incomplete figures represent processes similar to those activities necessary to investigate the differences between letters. The discrimination may be more fine-grained when sorting different letters from each other, but the process of picking out distinctive features is, in principle, the same as determining the differences between two objects. The previously cited experiments by Mackworth and Bruner (1966) and by Vurpillot (1968) indicate that children lack sophistication in their scanning strategies. This is probably also the case when children scan different letters. Children have to be taught scanning strategies that distinguish the important from the unimportant features of letters and to apply this knowledge toward effective letter recognition.

There are indications that children already possess many of the strategies required to distinguish letters before ever having been asked to do so (Gibson, 1974). It seems that the opportunities children have for visually exploring and solving problems benefits them when confronted with the problem of distinguishing letters from each other. This observation supports the inference that children who are more effectively trained in the solution of problems presented to them visually will also be better prepared to discriminate letters.

The above argument does not support the contention that the most effective approach to teaching letter recognition is to teach it by associative training, or by showing the letter and then saying it. Associative training might be effective in the long run, but it is not likely to be sufficiently wide in scope. Each different variation of a letter (and there are numerous variations) would have to be taught associatively. Therefore, associative training in letter recognition would be inefficient.

The most effective way to train letter recognition would seem to involve the direct training of children in distinctive features and their particular combinations into letters. The exact mechanism for such training on television will be explored in the next section in Format 5. The training would not be a passive presentation of the letters and their associated names, but would actively engage the children to the limit of their intellectual capacity. As such, it would be one more aspect of perceptual problem solving, outlined in this chapter. Learning how letters are distinguished shares a common property with other perceptual problems, such as the problems involved in the perception of space or in image-based thought. If children are previously trained to a high level of competency in the solution of problems presented to them visually, then the fine-grain discriminations involved in letter recognition will be readily and flexibly acquired.

IMPLICATIONS FOR TELEVISED INSTRUCTION

Television's primary emphasis on the visual makes it an ideal medium for teaching children how to solve problems presented to them visually. The formats that follow are designed to illustrate the possibilities of the television medium for teaching advanced perceptual skills and will awaken, I hope, the interest of large numbers of child viewers to the delights of successfully solving problems presented to them directly from a television set. What is taught in each format is justified by the preceding theoretical analysis. It should be recognized that each format is meant as a guide, the bare skeleton of the finished product.

Format 1

The methods employed in teaching children how to recognize overlapping, embedded, part–whole, blurred, or impoverished figures should overlap. With the understanding that the methods employed to teach identification of overlapping realistic figures can be transferred to other types of figures, this format will only examine instruction in the identification of realistic overlapping figures.

1. Present the spoon in Figure 6.1 alone.
2. Overlap it with the plate (see Figure 6.1).
3. Overlap it with the knife (see Figure 6.1).
4. Overlap it with the bottle (see Figure 6.1).
5. Use various techniques to make the spoon catch the eye or stand out:
   a. The spoon starts to glimmer, glitter, glow, or flash on and off in comparison to the other figures with which it is overlapped.
   b. The spoon moves (rotates, etc.) while the other figures remain stationary. The spoon eventually returns to its original position. Alternatively, the background moves while the spoon remains stationary.
   c. The spoon grows in size while the other figures remain the same size.
   d. The other figures diminish in size while the spoon remains constant.
   e. The other figures blur or vanish and then become distinct again while the spoon remains well defined in a stationary and conspicuous position.
   f. The plate, knife, and bottle are shown without the spoon. The spoon is slowly drawn, in bold relief, overlapping the other figures.
   g. A centipede crawls around the contour of the figure. A roadrunner

races around the contour. A frog hops from one place on the contour of the figure to another, sometimes following the contour, sometimes jumping across it. A butterfly flits from one spot to another on the figure. A flock of birds lands on the figure in a way that makes it stand out.

6. Play the game of "find the hidden object." At various stages children are asked, "Find the spoon?"
7. Delay to allow children time to find the overlapping object. Ask, "Have you found the spoon?"
8. "Here's a hint." Employ one of the techniques in procedure 5.
9. Delay long enough for continued search for the spoon.
10. Repeat procedures 6–9 but vary the hint (see procedure 5). More than one hint may be given (e.g., the spoon may glow and the background may simultaneously diminish in size).
11. Repeat the game of "find the hidden object" with a different object from the array.
12. Repeat the game of "find the hidden object" with a different array of objects.

The procedures employed in this format derive from experimental evidence presented earlier in this chapter. The training should respect the developmental progressions confirmed by the experimental evidence. Overlapping realistic figures are easiest to identify, whereas overlapping geometric figures are hardest for children between 4 and 8 years (see Figure 6.1). Since the proposed televised training is for children below 6 years, most of the training should be with realistic overlapping figures. Embedded figures present special problems. Apparently, they get harder as the extent of the shared boundaries increases. Therefore, in order to provide meaningful training in the identification of embedded figures for the largest possible audience of preschoolers, a greater concentration on the identification of embedded figures with a small percentage of shared contours is preferable. Research on the stages children pass through in the identification of part–whole figures (see Elkind et al., 1964) is also informative as to the level of difficulty children can tolerate if instructed on the identification of these figures on television. The research performed by Gollin on incomplete figures (see Figure 6.2) and by Potter (1966) using impoverished figures adds some striking insights into the possible effectiveness of training procedures on television. The results of these experimenters show that young children are less affected by forming previous hypotheses when attempting to identify incomplete and impoverished figures. One possible explanation is that children are more flexible and adaptable than adults. However, evidence from this chapter and from Chapters 4 and 5 indicates another possibility. Children are more likely to perform better on the above task because they fail at integrating and organizing their previous guesses with their current opinion. Other research by this author (H. Lesser, 1974) confirms the inability of children to adequately organize their own hypotheses sequentially. Guessing games with incomplete and blurred figures, using procedures similar to those employed in Format 1 with overlapping figures, is another way television can be used to instruct children. Children can play a guessing game as incomplete figures become more distinct. Experience at tasks such as these may help them to better organize their deductions.

Format 2

A slightly different aspect of the perceptual process relates to the development of children's scanning strategies. The previously cited work by Mackworth and Bruner, by Vurpillot, and by the Soviets shows that with increasing age exploratory eye movements become more expansive and successive. The increased efficiency in exploratory eye movements with age creates a greater opportunity for children to solve problems presented to them visually. Several techniques that can enhance the development of exploratory eye movements in children are particularly applicable to television presentation. The following format, which employs Vurpillot's experimental procedure (see Figure 6.3), explores several of these techniques:

1. Present the pair of identical houses in Figure 6.3.
2. Ask, "Are the houses the same?"
3. Delay so that child viewer can compare the windows and decide.
4. Turn the lights "off" in all the windows except for the upper left pair.
5. Encourage eye movements between the two windows by flashing the light on in one window while flashing it off in the other window, and back again, etc.
6. Ask, "Are these windows the same?"
7. Delay to give children an opportunity to decide.
8. Repeat procedures 4–7 for the upper right pair of windows, the middle pair, and the lower pairs of windows, respectively.
9. Repeat procedures 4–7 but this time start with all the lights out. Light different pairs of windows in a planned order. Leave the lights on in each comparison pair so that at the end of the comparisons both houses are completely lit.
10. When both houses are completely lit, ask, "Are these houses the same?"
11. Delay giving children a chance to decide.
12. Answer, "These houses are the same because all the windows are the same." Simultaneously emphasize sameness by close-ups of the pairs of identical windows.

13. Repeat procedures 4–7 but scan the windows in different planned sequences: right to left, left to right, up to down, and down to up.
14. Repeat procedures 4–7 for houses that have different pairs of windows.

A unique feature of television presentation is the precise level of control that is possible over the visual display. Through adroit manipulation of the visual display, children's fixations can be shifted from one spot to another on the screen. In Format 2 this is accomplished by back and forth flashing of the lights in the windows. If attentive, children will switch their focus from the window that disappears to the window that appears. On their own, young children do not scan effectively. Precise control over the perceptual display can force a desired scanning strategy. However, there are important distinctions between an efficient but forced scanning strategy and a voluntary one. Enough evidence exists to conclude that scanning strategies improve as children get older. There is evidence that suggests that certain training procedures can be effective in improving scanning strategies and that this improvement translates into better identification of figures. The Soviet research, which requires children to feel and manipulate around the contours of cardboard figures and to count the changes in direction, shows that children can be taught to use, at their own initiative, a general system of exploratory actions that can be successfully used to identify most types of figures. The next question is, "Can forced scanning teach children a system of exploratory actions equivalent to that obtained by training in manipulation?" The similarities between forced scanning and tactual following of contours are obvious, except that in the one instance the scanning is performed with the finger and in the other with the eye. However, up until now it has not been possible to control scanning activity in any practical manner. Consequently, little attention has been devoted to attempting to teach through the use of this method. Since television is an ideal medium upon which to employ teaching by forced scanning, some defining research is needed in this area.

The evidence presented thus far indicates that intellectual devleopment is characterized by a search for "rules" through which behavior may effectively be guided. If a perceived event is beyond the capacity of young children to organize, they frequently do not attempt to organize it. Instead, they restrict the inflow of information. This is observed in the "tunnel vision" effect discovered by Mackworth and Bruner, where it is observed that children "restrict their intake of information when faced with tasks that put a burden on their capacity for information processing." Similar results were reported by psychologists in the Soviet Union. However, the behavioral characteristics of tunnel vision can be forcefully altered on television through a carefully controlled manipulation of the visual display.

a. *Children fail to attend to the most important aspects of a picture.* They can be forced to attend to the salient features if the less important features are blurred or blacked out.

b. *Children are variable in exploring repeated presentations of the same picture.* Again, children can be forced to attend to the same features on repeated television presentations.

c. *Children do not follow contours.* Various techniques unique to television have been described that can force contour following or make it extremely likely to occur.

d. *Children do not scan across figures, measuring their dimensions.* This activity can also be forced or easily encouraged on television.

e. *Children fixate too long on particular spots. Brief exposures are more desirable for efficient scanning.* Exposure time to each element of a figure can be easily controlled on television.

Earlier in this chapter it was argued that the activities children engage in when observing objects and events are directed by intelligence. As intelligence develops, the perceptual activities engaged in become more sophisticated. The central issue is whether intelligence can be accelerated by forcefully guiding perceptual activities along the dimensions necessary for successful problem solving. This is a difficult question to untangle, since it is undoubtedly the case that sophisticated perceptual activity could not occur without adequate intelligence to guide it. It is equally the case, however, that intelligence would be retarded if sophisticated perceptual activities, capable of abstracting complex information, did not develop. A position strongly supported is that intellectual development and the development of advanced perceptual activities are interrelated.

If advanced scanning strategies are encouraged, intellectual growth is obtained. If intellectual growth occurs, advanced scanning strategies emerge. This issue was raised in other contexts in Chapters 4 and 5. Then, as now, the conclusion is that massive infusions of carefully directed training can accelerate intellectual growth. Children have to "learn how to learn." Carefully directed observations and comparisons can orchestrate the development of intellectual growth.

However, active engagement by the child is a necessary prerequisite for effective teaching. Children must become engrossed in the flux of perceptions presented to them, motivated by a desire to find the correct solution. With effective guidance, children will more readily "discover" the rules and principles that are most likely to lead to success on specified problems. It is hoped that learning strategies acquired from television will eventually transfer to activities in other aspects of the child's life.

Television is a medium with unique visual possibilities. The limits of these possibilities for instruction of young children have hardly been determined.

Format 3

Conceptions of space take many forms. Maturation in space perception can be seen as the development of the ability to construct a straight line, or as the ability to position objects accurately in situations with few landmarks, or as the ability to coordinate perspectives. When children draw, they are confronted with each of these issues—and many more. Therefore, drawing exercises presented over television are ideal as a means for illustrating to children the problems involved in spatial representation.

1. Present a magic drawing board on which line drawings of objects and events appear.
2. Slowly draw a little girl, but with details uncoordinated. The buttons are drawn in the wrong place; the ears are incorrectly positioned; the hat is above the head, etc.
3. Point out the incongruities. For instance, make the buttons more conspicuous (e.g., make them glitter, etc.)
4. Ask, "What's wrong with the buttons?"
5. Delay. Build suspense.
6. Move the buttons or erase them and redraw the buttons correctly placed.
7. Repeat with other incorrectly coordinated details.
8. Draw a man riding a horse in profile. Show both legs.
9. Ask, "What's wrong?"
10. Delay. Build suspense.
11. Say, "This leg can't be seen. It's behind the horse."
12. Say, "Now it's right."
13. Have the rider slowly turn the horse so that the leg that is not visible is now visible. However, do not allow the other leg (now behind the horse) to disappear.
14. Say, "What's wrong?"
15. Delay. Build suspense.
16. Say, "This leg can't be seen. It's behind the horse." Erase the leg.
17. Repeat procedures 8–16 several times with minor variations.
18. Repeat procedures 8–17 with different drawings. Emphasis must be placed on the general rule that objects or parts of objects that are hidden behind other objects are not drawn if the intent is to achieve visual realism.

Size–distance relationships can be taught using similar procedures as those employed in Format 3. Objects that are farther away should be drawn smaller according to the receding-lines principle. For instance, two dogs can be drawn in a field (with receding lines drawn in). The dog farther away is drawn much smaller. The dog in the distance approaches the closeup dog, then both dogs walk into the distance (and objectively decrease in size), etc. Drawings emphasizing spatial relationships can be highly instructive to young children. For instance, how to plan space *in advance* by blocking out space for each object before drawing it is an effective way of teaching children how to anticipate many of the properties of space (e.g., distance, order, relations, perspective, dimensions, movement). A magic drawing board exercise would have the additional feature of encouraging children to anticipate or try to guess at what is being drawn.

Format 4

The visual characteristics of television are ideal for presenting movements and transformations of objects. The research reviewed earlier demonstrates that young children have difficulty in representing to themselves, in mental images, the trajectories and transformations of objects. The following format outlines a procedure for enhancing the ability of children to represent trajectories and transformations of objects in mental images:

1. Present a rod in the vertical position fixed by a nail at the bottom.
2. Allow it to fall in the clockwise direction 90° to the horizontal position.
3. Repeat several times. Use slow motion and stop action to emphasize the intermediary positions.
4. Put a ball at the end of the rod, and as the rod falls, outline the end of the trajectory on the background.
5. Show a child trying to catch the ball in flight at the end of the rod. Emphasize errors, such as trying to catch the ball in (a) the upper right corner; (b) the lower left corner; etc. Also have the child succeed in catching the ball at various correct intermediary positions.
6. Ask, "Will the child catch the ball?"
7. Delay. Build suspense. Show the child either failing or succeeding at catching the ball.
8. Repeat with variations.
9. Repeat with different trajectories (e.g., somersaults, rod with three different size beads on it rotated 180° in space through the center bead).

The precise control of the presentation of moving visual displays provides a unique opportunity to emphasize in close-up and in slow motion the precise details of movements and transformations of objects. Apparently, children devote scant attention to the details of the movement itself. Instructional techniques ideally suited to television can entice children into noticing the details of movement. Slow-motion and stop-action exercises that require guessing about the position of an object at any intermediary point in its trajectory are only some of the possibilities available for television presentation.

Format 5

At the end of the section on prereading skills it was promised that attention would be given to methods of teaching letter identification based on training in distinctive features of letters. The following is an outline of a procedure for training children to identify letters based on their distinctive features:

1. Show the letter C and the letter E side-by-side. The letter C represents a class of letters dominated by the distinctive feature of curvature. The letter E represents a class of letters dominated by the distinctive feature of straight line. According to Gibson, the curve—straight line distinction is the first discrimination children make when identifying letters.
2. Ask, "Are these letters the same?"
3. Delay. Build suspense. Use close-up, etc., to emphasize critical differences between letters. Give answer.
4. Repeat procedures 1—3 with other curve—straight line comparisons. Also present for comparison letters that are identical.
5. Repeat procedures 1—4 with more difficult, higher level comparisons. Compare round letters (e.g., C, G) with letters that emphasize roundness and straight lines (e.g., P, R) and compare square letters (e.g., E, F) with those that possess diagonality (e.g., M, N, W).
6. Repeat procedures 1—5 with higher level comparisons. Compare round letters (e.g., C with G) or compare round and straight letters (e.g., P with R).
7. Repeat procedures 1—6 with transformation comparisons of letters. The hardest comparison is to compare a letter with the transformation of itself and to then make a "same—different" judgment (see Figure 6.5 for possible transformations). Size transformations do not change the identity of the letter (e.g., a lower-case letter a is compared with an upper-case letter A), neither do fat—thin transformations (e.g., a fat letter P is compared with a thin letter P). On the other hand, an upside-down transformation changes a letter M into a letter W. Children must be taught to identify all the transformation rules that do not affect the identity of a

letter and to discriminate them from the transformations that do affect letter identity.

Being able to identify letters according to their distinctive features is only one aspect of prereading training. Children must not only be accurate, they must also be efficient and rapid in their identifications. To accomplish this end, children can be given televised exercises that require them to scan an array of letters (under varying time restrictions) and to pick out all the examples of a specified letter.

It should be emphasized that distinctive-feature training teaches rules for letter identification and is not associative training. A corresponding, but secondary stage, is learning the names of the letters. Phonetic analysis is another prereading skill. Procedures for training children in word–sentence and sound–word analysis on television were presented in Chapter 5 (see Format 4). If children reach school age having acquired the broadly based strategies of distinctive-feature analysis and word–sentence and sound–word phonetic analysis, transfer of these skills to actual reading should be rapid and complete.

CONCLUSION

The overpowering visual aspect of television is both its greatest advantage and greatest problem when considered from the perspective of educating young children. The issue is how to control the visual presentation for instructional purposes while retaining its appeal to young children.

The approach adopted in this chapter was to determine the natural course of perceptual development in children and then to apply it directly to television instruction. Thus, the difficulties children have in the following perceptual problems were examined: (1) locating overlapping and embedded figures in larger displays; (2) locating parts and wholes in figures, both separately and simultaneously; (3) recognizing incomplete figures and figures impoverished by blurring; (4) organizing and ordering objects and events in space; (5) mentally representing in images the paths and transformations of objects; and (6) the problem of identifying letters.

Being able to achieve success on these tasks is important because of the general utility of each task. Each of the tasks examined involves elements of such general skills as: systematic search, attention to details, ordered scanning and comparison, short- and long-term memory, simultaneous consideration of different aspects of figures, sequential testing of hypotheses, self-initiated discovery of rules, and the construction and reconstruction in space of objects and their relations.

It should be noted that the learning strategies taught in this chapter are basically the same as those in Chapters 4 and 5. Only the content upon which they are taught differs. It is important to recognize that a skill learned in one area (e.g., language) does not automatically transfer to another area (e.g., visual problem solving). Therefore, it is necessary to teach similar skills in different domains and, at the same time, to encourage cross-modal integration of these skills. Eventually, children should discover that what they have accomplished in one domain is related to their accomplishments in another. At this point, rules of functioning learned in one domain will be applied without direct instruction in other domains. "Learning how to learn" becomes a generalized and unified activity of children. This stage of development provides a firm base for the more complex, more abstract learning acquired in school.

7

Past, Present, Future:
The Structure and Function
of Memory

Memory is the essential ingredient that binds together most of the different aspects of human thought and activity. Unfortunately, the study of how memory develops has only recently become a concern among child psychologists in the United States. Two reviews by established researchers in the field (Flavell, 1970; Hagen, Jongeward, & Kail, in press) offer interesting comments on memory development. Flavell devotes considerable attention in his review to research conducted under his direction. As an established Piagetian scholar, Flavell is aware of Piaget's extensive contribution to the field. The review of Hagen *et al.* has the advantage of 5 years of awakened interest among American psychologists in how children's memory develops. Consequently, the research Hagen reviews is more broadly based. Neither the review of Hagen *et al.* nor the research conducted under Hagen's direction appear to have been influenced by Piaget. Also, the research conducted by both investigators was done independently of Soviet efforts. Neither investigator had been aware of already existing Soviet research. Flavell (Appel, Cooper, McCarrell, Sims-Knight, Yussen, & Flavell, 1972) specifically acknowledged "clear scientific priority to Russian investigators [p. 1380]."

In recent years Piaget and his collaborators in Geneva have conducted a lengthy series of experiments on the development of memory and its relationship to the development of intelligence. Over 20 experiments and theoretical conclusions are reported in their book *Memory and Intelligence* (Piaget & Inhelder, 1973; in French, 1968). Briefer reviews can be found in Inhelder (1969, pp. 337–364), Piaget and Inhelder (1969b, pp. 80–83), and Sinclair-de-

Zwart (1971b, pp. 125–135). These experiments contain the largest body of systematically collected evidence concerning the development of memory.

American research efforts have been considerably more scattered. One exception is the work of John Flavell and his associates at the University of Minnesota. In a series of experiments they have demonstrated developmental changes in the use of verbal mediation to facilitate recall and the use of various behaviors that facilitate memory, such as clustering of information, spontaneous rehearsal, self-testing, cueing, etc. In contrast, the earlier work on children's memory was mostly concerned with changes in memory capacity. Because of the regularity of these changes with age, norms were readily established and incorporated into standardized tests of mental ability (see Hagen *et al.*, in press). Only recently, however, has there been concern with what happens in the "black box" or with an explanation of why and in what ways memory changes as children get older.

As was indicated earlier, Soviet research is considerably more advanced than American efforts. The Soviets distinguish between voluntary, intentional memorizing and involuntary, unintentional memorizing. A regular developmental sequence is noted whereby only older preschoolers employ intentional measures to facilitate later recall. In addition, specific pedagogical techniques have been devised by the Soviets to enhance the development of advanced memorization strategies in children.

Although research in the three groups has been characterized by different methods and emphasis on different features of memory development, significant convergence on numerous important issues occurs. The first task in this chapter is therefore to review the literature on memory development. Afterward, as was the practice in Chapters 4, 5, and 6, implications for televised instruction will be explored.

RESEARCH ON MEMORY DEVELOPMENT

American Research

Current American research has been heavily influenced by the information-processing approach to psychology. This approach is mentalistic in the sense that it attempts to specify the mental processes that intervene between stimulation and response. Parallel questions deriving from this approach are: How is the organism programmed? How is information transformed when it is received? How is information retrieved from the system? In this section experiments have been selected with a two-fold purpose: (1) to illustrate the principal conclusions of the American researchers; and (2) to apply the illustrations to televised instruction.

An extensive literature testifies to the mediational role played by verbalizations in facilitating performance by older children and adults on a wide variety of tasks (Stevenson, 1972a). However, young children are reported to have a deficiency in verbally mediated performance. In the process of examining this deficiency Flavell, Beach, and Chinsky (1966) distinguished between what they called a production deficiency and a mediational deficiency. The following are their definitions:

- *Mediational deficiency:* The young child's verbalizations are deficient in mediational power. The child spontaneously produces potential verbal mediators, but unlike the older child, these verbalizations fail to affect performance.
- *Production deficiency:* The young child's difficulty is that the verbal response tends not to be made. If the verbal responses are induced, they have mediational power.

To determine the basis for the observed deficiency, Flavell *et al.* (1966) presented seven pictures in a circular display to groups of 5-, 7-, and 10-year-olds. The experimenter pointed to three pictures to be remembered on that trial. Measurement of verbalizations during a 15-second delay period before recall was attained by putting a space helmet on the children and pulling the visor down over their eyes so they could not see. The experimenter was proficient in lip reading. Two of the 20 5-year-olds, 12 of 20 7-year-olds, and 17 of 20 10-year-olds showed detectable verbal activity. Those children who verbalized showed more recall than those who did not.

In a related experiment (Keeney, Cannizzo, & Flavell, 1967) first-grade children were given the same task as the one just reported, and those who did not verbalize were instructed to whisper the names of the pictures to be remembered. Before inducement the children who spontaneously rehearsed had better recall than those who did not. After inducement recall improved among those who did not verbalize spontaneously, so that there were no important differences between the two groups. However, in a subsequent task without inducement, 10 of 17 nonverbalizers reverted to their previous silence, and recall declined. The children were not given feedback on the effects of rehearsal on recall. This may be a reason why rehearsal did not persist.

The above results support the production-deficiency hypothesis. Younger children have the verbal skill but do not spontaneously use it to mediate performance. When induced to do so, however, they can use these verbal skills to improve their performance.

The basis for the production deficiency was further explored by Flavell and his associates. They entertained the following two explanations for the production deficiency of younger preschoolers:

1. *Linguistic hypothesis:* Five-year-olds can translate linguistic competence into verbal utterance in only a limited number of contexts where it would be appropriate for improved performance. Accordingly, language in its broadest sense entails a progressive ability to structure situations linguistically in ever more diverse and complex situations.

2. *Cognitive-immaturity hypothesis:* The four parts of this hypothesis have been nicely phrased by Flavell *et al.* (1966):

> An S who codes and rehearses is, first of all, responding to the task in an intellectually active fashion. . . . He "goes beyond the information given" . . . in accordance with what looks like a self-generated cognitive strategy. Second, in continuously rehearsing . . . S is demonstrating a capacity for sustained attentional focusing in the absence of both perceptual and social . . . supports for doing so. Third, coding and rehearsal represents a time-binding, goal directive effort. He codes for the future . . . and he also keeps the past alive by carrying that code forward. Viewed in this way, our kindergarten Ss may have failed to talk to themselves for reasons having nothing whatever to do with their level of linguistic development. That is, they may simply have been too young to engage in the kinds of intellectual activities . . . of verbal coding and rehearsal [pp. 297–298].

The cognitive-immaturity hypothesis is consistent with Piaget's thesis that the development of advanced forms of memorizing is tied to the child's level of understanding, which, in turn, is tied to the child's level of intellectual development. In another article (Keeney *et al.*, 1967, p. 965) the authors support the more broadly based cognitive-immaturity hypothesis as being more consistent with their own data and with evidence presented by other researchers.

John W. Hagen (Hagen & Kingsley, 1968; Kingsley & Hagen, 1969; Hagen, Hargrave, & Ross, 1973) has confirmed many of Flavell's findings using a serial recall task. The task consists of presenting eight pictures, each depicting a familiar animal, to a child. Each card is shown briefly, one at a time, and turned face down in a row in front of the child. The order is varied on each trial so that learning particular locations for each card is not possible. In the Hagen, Hargrave, and Ross experiment half the children were prompted or induced to rehearse the names of the cards, while the others were not. The children were 5- and 7-year-olds. Rehearsal facilitated recall at both age levels. However, on a posttest 1 week later improved recall due to induced rehearsal the week before disappeared. Since younger children do not spontaneously employ rehearsal without promptings by another person, reduced recall was expected. Hagen *et al.* (1973) offer the following interpretation of their results:

> One is left with the question of why, then, do children of this age not use rehearsal spontaneously? . . . We have already considered the possibility that the ability to use self-prompting and self-correction is now well developed at this age. Investigators might do well to devise training programs to improve these skills in young children. As demands increase, new ways of remembering must be devised. Finally, we must

acknowledge that memory is but one component of cognition. A vast number of changes occur in cognitive processes during this time of development ... and no doubt memory abilities depend upon, as well as influence, the course of development of many of these [p. 204].

Flavell, Friedrichs, and Hoyt (1970) confirm many the conclusions of Hagen *et al.* (1973). In an exhaustive experiment devoted to the study of acquisition strategies in young children length of study time and number of exposures to black and white drawings were recorded. The drawings were mounted in windows that could be illuminated by pressing a button. The task was to learn which picture was located in each window. The children were told that they could expose each picture as long and as often as they wished. During preparation for recall the experimenter left the room. The frequency and duration of exposure were recorded and the verbal and nonverbal activities of the child were also recorded through a one-way mirror. The children tested were in nursery school, kindergarten, and second and fourth grades.

Four different task strategies are reported:

1. *Overt naming of the pictures:* This was done frequently by the fourth-grade children and infrequently by the younger groups.
2. *Rehearsal:* This increased over the duration of the study for the two older groups (especially for the fourth-graders). There was no reported increase for the younger groups.
3. *Anticipation:* This consisted of self-testing prior to illuminating a drawing. This technique was used primarily by the fourth-graders and to a less extent by the second-graders.
4. *Pointing to the actual location of the stimuli:* This was used increasingly over trials by the fourth graders only.

Only the fourth-graders consistently used task-appropriate strategies to aid in recall, and only these children changed their strategies during their study time to enable them to more regularly employ these strategies. This suggests that only the older children were monitoring their performance and correcting their strategies as they progressed in task mastery.

What happens when children are induced to cluster pictures of items into categories in a recall task? Moely, Olson, Halwes, and Flavell (1969) presented a circular arrangement of objects from four different categories (animals, furniture, vehicles, clothing) to children from 5 to 9 years of age. In the control condition the children named each picture and were given 2 minutes to rearrange them if they wished. The children in the naming condition labeled each picture, and the experimenter named the four categories of pictures. In the teaching condition the children named each picture, after which the experimenter asked the children to sort the pictures into groups "that go together or are alike," helped where necessary, and asked the children to label the resulting items in each category. The experimenter left the room during a 2-minute study period before recall. The children were observed through a one-way mirror. Their manual manipulations of the pictures and verbalizations during the study period were recorded.

In the study period the 5- and 6-year-olds in the teaching condition manually organized the pictures into categories to a much greater extent than did the 5- and 6-year-olds in the control and naming condition. Naming was ineffective in obtaining a manual reorganization of the pictures into categories for the 5-year-olds, and the results did not differ from the control condition. Manual reorganization of the pictures was slightly better for the 6- to 7-year-olds, with the pattern of results between the three conditions approximately the same as with the 5- to 6-year-olds. For the 8- to 9-year-olds naming and teaching were both effective and approximately equal, and the control condition was ineffective in producing manual organizing of the pictures into categories. At all ages subsequent recall was higher for those children who used manual groupings.

Moely *et al.* (1969, pp. 32–33) also note a consistent spontaneous developmental progression in the use of strategies employed when gathering information for subsequent recall in the task:

1. Verbalization of the stimulus names during the study period (frequent even at the kindergarten level).
2. Verbal rehearsal of the stimulus names after the stimuli have been removed prior to the recall testing (infrequent prior to grades 1 and 2).
3. Self-testing (infrequent prior to grade 3).
4. Manual clustering during study periods (infrequent prior to grade 5).

Both self-testing and manual clustering of items reflect active learning by children. They deliberately control and modify the stimulus input rather than passively accept it. Thus, the teaching condition taught 5- and 6-year-olds active learning strategies that significantly improved their recall performance. Although not tested, previous results indicate that 5- to 6-year-olds will not spontaneously transfer the strategies learned from others in the teaching condition to other recall tasks without help or considerably more experience.

In an associated experiment (Ritter, Kaprove, Fitch, & Flavell, 1973), children between 3 and 5 years were tested on their ability to use retrieval cues to facilitate recall. In the first stage of the experiment children were asked to place six pictures of men with six toys closely associated with their occupations (e.g., football player—football). Each man was placed inside one of six houses, and the toys were visibly placed in a box outside of each house. Then the children were required to match a duplicate picture of each man by visibly placing it on the roof of the "friend's" house. Essentially, the children were required to use a visible cue (toy) to locate an invisible object (man in the house). In the second stage of the experiment the cueing procedure was reversed. The toys were removed and the children were required to remember them using the visible drawings of the men on the rooves as cues. There were no developmental differences in recall on the first task, but developmental differences in recall did appear on the second task. On the second task only the older children were markedly successful in using the men as retrieval cues for the toys. About 75% of the older children were able to retrieve the toys using the men as cues without prompting or with only minimal prompting. In contrast, almost half the 3- to $4\frac{1}{2}$-year-old children required the strongest form of prompting before using the men as retrieval cues. About one-third of the younger children completely failed at using the men as retrieval cues, even when induced to do so with the strongest promptings.

The experiments reviewed here clearly demonstrate that young children do not very often deliberately store information with a plan for later retrieval. If not instructed, young children do not rehearse, verbalize relations, manually cluster items, self-test, etc. It is as if young children have not yet developed "intelligent structuring and storage of input, intelligent search and retrieval operations, and . . . intelligent monitoring and knowledge of their storage and retrieval operations. . . [Flavell, 1971, p. 277]."

The following quote summarizes Flavell's (1971) interpretation of American research on memory development. It also prepares the reader for Piaget's ideas on memory development, which are elaborated in the next section.

> There is rather good agreement among us as to what memory development is the development of: it is largely the development of the mind itself, but the mind as viewed from a certain angle, or with respect to one of its numerous adaptational tasks. Part of the mind's job description is to store and retrieve data, and the mind does this particular job with the same equipment and in much the same way that it does all of its other cognitive jobs. This review of memory development suggests a useful strategy for studying it empirically. The strategy is to identify some of the more important, memory-relevant things that adults seem to do and then try to figure out what developmental level of black box could or would do such things. The strategy, in other words, is to try to translate interesting memory phenomena into cognitive—developmental phenomena—to view them through a cognitive—developmental lens, so to speak—and then to try to imagine the developmental course of these memory phenomena by trading in our general knowledge of cognitive growth [p. 275].[1]

Swiss Research—Piaget

Piaget believes that how well children remember something depends on their stage of cognitive development. An extremely simple example from Sinclair-de-Zwart (1971b) illustrates this point:

---

[1] From J. H. Flavell, What is memory development the development of? *Human Development*, 1971, *14*, 272–278. Reprinted by permission of S. Karger AG, Basel.

If I am shown a bottle held obliquely with wine running out if it, I do not have to "remember" that the bottle was not corked and sealed. Knowing what happens to open bottles when one turns them upside down makes the information of the absence of the cork redundant. If it is true that intelligence changes the code according to which memory encodes and decodes, the same situation presented to children at different levels will carry a different information load and will be encoded in a different way [p. 128].

Unlike the American research reviewed, Piaget does not concentrate on problems that demand a strong verbal element for successful performance. Piaget and his associates have been more concerned with the errors children make when trying to interpret and remember an object or event presented visually. The types of errors children do make when asked to remember some relatively simple event are nothing short of spectacular. For example, children were presented with four glasses: a tall thin glass filled with yellow liquid; a short wide one filled with red liquid; and two empty glasses of the same dimensions as the filled ones, respectively. The yellow and red liquids were poured into the empty glasses of the same dimensions. Then the liquids were poured back again, but interchanged so that the yellow liquid ended up in the short wide glass and the red liquid ended up in the tall thin glass. When 4- and 5-year-olds were asked what they had seen, they maintained that the yellow liquid was poured into the glass with the red liquid and vice versa. When asked to demonstrate, Piaget (Sinclair-de-Zwart, 1971b) found:

To our own surprise, the children actually took up the two glasses that were filled with liquid and tried to pour, simultaneously, the yellow liquid into the glass with the red liquid and the red into the glass with the yellow. Questioned as to whether they really thought this could be done, they maintained their answer: "Yes, if you're clever enough." "Won't the red and the yellow get all mixed up?" was our next question. Many hesitated or simply said "no." One child said, "Yes, maybe, but it will unmix itself in the end [pp. 130–131]."

This error in memory could not have been based upon experience, since it is an impossible event. However, errors of this type may be based upon children's incomplete understanding of objects and events that are, in turn, based upon their stage of cognitive development. With this idea in mind, a more formal analysis of experiments conducted by Piaget and his associates will be examined.

Sixty-two children from $3\frac{1}{2}$ to $8\frac{1}{2}$ years were asked to remember a serial configuration (Piaget & Inhelder, 1973, pp. 29–49; Piaget, 1968, pp. 1–16; Inhelder, 1969, pp. 337–364). The task consisted of asking children to look carefully at 10 sticks (9–15 cm) arranged in a series from smallest to largest and to remember them later. A week later the children were asked to indicate by gesture and then by line drawing what they remembered. The children were not shown the model again. Another drawing was requested 6–8 months later.

Children pass through a fixed developmental continuum in their ability to order sticks into a series. The following is a brief description of the stages:

Stage 1: No attempt at ordering the sticks.

Stage 2: Failure to construct the overall series. Rods are combined into (a) big and small elements; (b) pairs of large and small elements; (c) tops correctly aligned but without a horizontal base; (d) roof-shaped configurations; and (e) correct seriations of three to six rods by trial and error.

Stage 3: Complete success by trial and error. If intermediate-size elements are introduced, children reconstruct the entire series rather than inserting them directly in their correct place.

Stage 4: Planned ordering. Children proceed systematically from longest to shortest or from shortest to longest (e.g., any element E is treated as if E is less than F, G and greater than D, C). Intermediate elements are immediately inserted into the complete series. Children understand transitivity and use it in constructing the series (A is less than C if A is less than B and B is less than C).

These four stages correspond to different levels in children's thought processes: Stage 1 is preoperational, Stage 2 is transitional, Stage 3 is empirical seriation, and Stage 4 is operational.

The memory drawings produced by the children fall into three distinct categories (see Figure 7.1). They also form a developmental progression, with

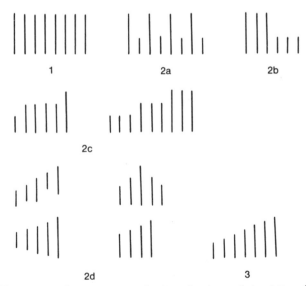

Figure 7.1. Three types of memory reproduction of a size-graded seriation. [From *Studies in Cognitive Development: Essays in Honor of Jean Piaget* edited by David Elkind and John H. Flavell. Copyright © 1969 Oxford University Press, Inc. Reprinted by permission.]

the youngest children producing category 1, intermediate-aged children producing various mixtures of the four types of category 2, and the oldest children producing category 3.

Clear relationships exist between the stage of cognitive development of children and the level of memory in their drawings. After 1 week 83% of the preoperational children produced drawings of memory type 1; and 17%, of memory type 2 (a–d). Of the transitional children 65% produced drawings of memory type 2 (a–d); and 35%, of memory type 3. Of the empirical seriation children 27% produced drawings of memory type 2 (a–d); and 23%, of memory type 3.

However, the most remarkable result was an improvement in memory 6–8 months later. Inhelder (1969, p. 343) reports that 74% of all the children and 90% of the children between 5 and 8 years of age improved in their drawing of the sticks from memory. The progress was gradual. If children produced a memory drawing of type 1 at 1 week, they were likely to produce a memory drawing of type 2 at 6–8 months. Similarly, a type 2 drawing at 1 week was likely to improve to a type 3 drawing at 6 months.

Piaget (1968) interprets the improvement in memory over time to mean that

> in six months, in the case of seriation or ordering, . . . the child has continued to compare objects of different sizes, etc., outside and well beyond the experiment which we presented to him. . . . the new scheme [the way the model is understood] of the next level serves as the code for decoding the original memory. The final memory . . . is . . . a decoding, but it is the decoding of a code which has changed, which is better structured than it was before . . . and not what it was at the time when the decoding was done [p. 5].

According to Piaget and Inhelder, what is remembered depends on how well children understand what they observed. Observation, however, depends upon cognitive development. In certain simple cases, such as in the cited example, therefore, memory should improve over time.

Another example that illustrates the principle that memory depends on how well children understand what has been observed is the water level problem. All children have observed water levels of many different shapes and materials. If experience were the deciding factor, children should be able to indicate by gesture or by drawing that the water level in a container is always horizontal regardless of the shape or slant of the container. However, Piaget and Inhelder (1973, pp. 295–308) and Inhelder (1969) determined that the ability to predict the inclination of the surface of a liquid in a bottle about to be tilted in a specified way is not acquired by children before 9 to 10 years.

In a memory experiment Piaget and Inhelder presented a drawing of a partially filled bottle at a slant for children to remember. Children were shown a drawing of the bottle inclined at 45° and one-fourth filled with colored water.

Figure 7.2. Figure used as standard for memory reproduction of water-level orientation. [From *Studies in Cognitive Development: Essays in Honor of Jean Piaget* edited by David Elkind and John H. Flavell. Copyright © 1969 Oxford University Press, Inc. Reprinted by permission.]

The bottle rests on a table, which provides an external line of reference (see Figure 7.2). The children were asked to draw what they remembered after 1 hour, after 1 week, and after 6 months, respectively. Sample children's drawings are presented in Figure 7.3.

The drawing of the inclined bottle was shown to 66 children between 5 and 9 years of age, divided into two groups: (1) memory tested after 1 hour and after 1 week, respectively; and (2) memory tested after 1 week. Memory was divided into six types (see Figure 7.4). The correct-memory drawings (type 6) are produced by about one-third of the 8-year-olds. Nine-year-olds do only slightly better. Mistakes (types 1–4) are produced by 75% of all 5- to 7-year-olds. Type 5 rarely occurred and seems to represent a suppression of the problem. Similar results are obtained when children are shown an empty bottle and are asked to imagine or deduce the angle of the liquid.

Fifty-five of the original children were retested after 6 months. All the children remembered the partially filled bottle, and their responses fitted into the six categories previously described. Correct responses (type 6) decreased

Figure 7.3. Memory reproductions of water-orientation standard. [From *Studies in Cognitive Development: Essays in Honor of Jean Piaget* edited by David Elkind and John H. Flavell. Copyright © 1969 Oxford University Press, Inc. Reprinted by permission.]

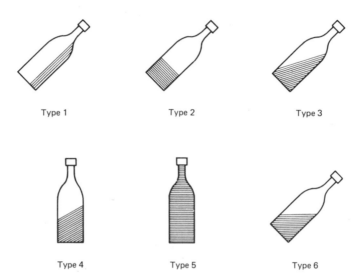

Figure 7.4. Memory of the water level according to developmental stages. [Adapted from Piaget & Inhelder, 1973.]

among the 5- to 6-year-olds, but increased from 10 out of 37 to 16 out of 33 among the 7- to 9-year-olds.

The results on the memory of horizontal levels partially reproduce the results obtained in ordering sticks into a series. The same effect, the improvement of memory over a relatively long period of time, occurs in both experiments.

In the horizontal level of water experiment "the memory played the part of the interpreter and not simply the recorder [Piaget & Inhelder, 1973, p. 302]." As the children get older, the interpretation changes, and consequently the memory changes. The experiments on spatial representation presented in Chapter 5 (see Laurendeau & Pinard, 1970) demonstrate that children are not able to construct and use an external spatial reference system until about 8 or 9 years of age. In order to do this, children must attain the operational stage of development. This fact explains the gradual appearance of correct memories between 7 and 9 years. Only at this age do children acquire the capability to overcome the distracting influence of the sides of a bottle and construct a horizontal water level based upon an external system of reference. The regression in memory of the younger children is also instructive. Piaget and Inhelder (1973) interpret this to mean that "the excellent initial memories of these subjects do not go hand in hand with operational understanding [pp. 303–304]." Their initial understanding was inadequate to support longer term memory.

In the last to be cited of Piaget and Inhelder's experiments on memory (Piaget & Inhelder, 1973, pp. 74–97; Inhelder, 1969, pp. 349–353) children were given problems to remember that were designed to create conflict between

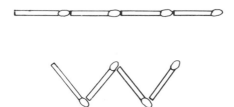

Figure 7.5. Figures used as standards for memory reproduction of length and number. [From *Studies in Cognitive Development: Essays in Honor of Jean Piaget* edited by David Elkind and John H. Flavell. Copyright © 1969 Oxford University Press, Inc. Reprinted by permission.]

two or more possible ways an event could be understood. The distortions in memory produced by the children add some additional insights into the memory process. Children were presented with four matches placed in a horizontal line and another four matches presented directly underneath in a flattened zigzag (see Figure 7.5). Previous research shows that a comparison of this kind causes a conflict in young children between their understanding of numerical equality and equality of length. It was previously demonstrated in Chapter 5 (see the transformation of the arc into a straight line and vice versa) that children initially understand length ordinally or by correspondence of the end points. This means that young children will judge the zigzag as shorter because its end points do not coincide with the straight line. However, this creates a conflict in young children, since the zigzag should have fewer elements. The experimental results show the progressive resolution with increasing age of the memory of this conflict in young children.

Seventy-eight children between the ages of 5 and 8 were shown the matches in Figure 7.5. The children were divided into two groups and given memory tests exactly as in the horizontal-level-of-liquid experiment. There were five discernible types of memory drawings produced by the children (see Figure 7.6). Type 1 shows no numerical or figural correspondence. Type 2 shows the dominance of coincidence of extremities over numerical correspondence. Type 3 respects the numerical correspondence and false coincidence of the extremities. In type 4 the zigzag is drawn correctly but the numerical correspondence is violated. Finally, in type 5 the correct drawing is attained.

As in the other memory experiments the type of children's memory is related directly to age. Type 1 memory is produced by the younger children. They do not understand the conflicting elements, and their memory drawings do not reflect a conflict. Type 2 represents what Piaget calls a figurative solution to the conflict and is gradually replaced by type 3 and type 4 (called semifigurative and seminumerical solutions) at around 6 or 7 years of age. The correct solution does not predominate until about the age of 8 years.

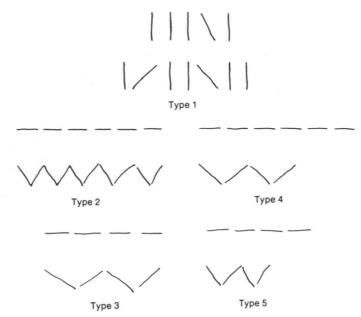

Figure 7.6. Types of memory reproductions of length and number. [From *Studies in Cognitive Development: Essays in Honor of Jean Piaget* edited by David Elkind and John H. Flavell. Copyright © 1969 Oxford University Press, Inc. Reprinted by permission.]

As in the previous experiments the results are explained on the basis of the development of operative thinking by the child.

> It seems that children of a preoperational level apprehend the numerical correspondence. But they do not yet possess the scheme of the spatial conservation that would enable them to understand that a line twisted into a zigzag remains of the same metrical length as it was before transformation. It was as if the children made a memory preinference as follows: If the two lines are equal by numerical correspondence of their elements their extremities must coincide [Inhelder, 1969, p. 352].

It should be noted that the conflict between the numerical correspondence and the noncoincidence of the end points can be eliminated by changing the figures from being formed by discontinuous elements (matches) to continuous lines. Memory drawings based on continuous lines produce hardly any deformations, and then only with the youngest children.

This concludes the review of experiments conducted by Piaget and his associates. A review of the Soviet literature on memory development will be presented in the next section. The Soviet experiments strongly support the results obtained by the American researchers. They are not nearly as supportive of Piaget's results, partly because their emphasis is different. They are more directly concerned than Piaget with the application of their results to preschool education. It should be noted that if temporal priority were being honored, the review of the Soviet research would have occurred first. The Soviet research was initiated about 10–20 years before the American and Genevan efforts.

Soviet Research

The following discussion comes from Yendovitskaya (1964/1971b, pp. 89–110). Memory as a psychological process is constructed and modified during development. Before 2 years of age memory is described as exclusively unintentional and involuntary. Memory is unintentional if it depends upon chance encounters with objects and involuntary if no specific goal to remember occurs. For example, the seeing of one object may invoke the memory of another object in children because the two objects were experienced together in the past. The recollection of the other object is not intentional, because the object is not sought out, nor is it voluntary, because there is no specific attempt to remember the object. However, if the original experience is repeated, it is not uncommon for children below 2 years of age to remember minute details that occurred even a year earlier (such as an accident on a trip to a doctor). During the return visit children may experience associations that result in both the recall of events previously seen on the original trip and, curiously, the expectation that these events will invariably occur again (such as the accident).

Another characteristic of 3- to 4-year-old children is that they cannot yet set a goal to memorize or recall. However, they can memorize connections that are constantly repeated, either spatially or by temporal contiguity. Only rarely does reproduction and recall of specified, assigned material occur as its own goal among younger preschoolers. Basically, reproduction and recall occur for younger children within narrow limits specified by assigned tasks that require reproduction and recall for the attainment of a concrete goal.

In the middle preschool period (5 years), intentional memorizing–recalling gradually appear in the behavior of children. The earliest sign is the appearance of simple repetition, which indicates an understanding that certain facts must sometimes be memorized for successful attainment of goals. Simple repetition does not mean that children direct themselves toward special strategies for memorizing. Only toward the end of the middle preschool period do children attempt strategies intended to better retain facts in memory. Such strategies include elementary systematization and logical analysis. Also, in the middle preschool period there is an improvement in the content of the material to be remembered. Younger preschoolers retell a fairy tale citing only the main events; older preschoolers not only cite the main events but also attempt to cite the details and the same verbal expressions in the original text.

Certain conditions are important for the memorization and reproduction of texts, such as poems by younger preschoolers. The text should have an emotional content to which young children can easily relate. The text should present clear images that stimulate imagination and encourage mental and physical activity. Sonority of the textual material is important, as it helps children develop a good verbal—motor image, important for memorizing. That is, when the text is read, the sounds convey clearly the movements described in the story. There should also be a clear correspondence of the rhythm of the textual material with the rhythm of body movements. All these conditions are helpful to young children when memorizing textual material. Incidentally, these facts support the proposition that young children's memory is mainly of a motoric and visual—graphic type.

Older preschool children (6 years) frequently intend the memorization and recall of information and employ various intentional strategies to improve this end. They use words to analyze the material to be remembered, group material in predetermined categories of objects or phenomena, and establish logical connections. For the most part, however, memory during the entire preschool age is involuntary and unintentional. That is, young children remember situations, words, or objects and their interrelationships while working at tasks and only as they need the required information to accomplish their goal.

One important factor that determines the increase in effectiveness of memory during the preschool years is the level of activity directed toward objects being memorized. For instance, children who actively construct an identical copy of a display of toys are more likely to remember the display than other children who passively observe the display but do not reconstruct it.

Another important positive influence on memory during the preschool period is the formation of the development of effective strategies for memorizing. One such strategy is to relate objects to a definite category and to group objects by meaning. Children's earliest categorizations are formed during the process of direct practical activity with objects. Thus, the plate, the knife, the fork, the spoon, etc. are unified into one category because the child associates them with eating.

Toward the end of the second half of the preschool period children become less dependent upon practical activities with objects for their categorizations and begin to form categories on the basis of semantic groups. For instance, Yendovitskaya (1964/1971b, pp. 101–102) investigated the influence of verbal mediation on building semantic connections. Preschool children were asked to memorize words presented to them. As an aid to memory, the children were given pictures and asked to match a picture to each word so that the meanings corresponded. They were also asked to verbally justify their reasons for selection. Afterward each picture was presented, and the children were asked to remember the words they had previously matched to the pictures. Children remembered the correct word only when they gave verbal justification for their selection of the picture. Younger children (3–5 years) were more likely than older children (5–7 years) to make a selection and not give a reason. Thus, younger children did less well in remembering the words.

Children's activities can be organized in such a way that their abilities in recalling and memorizing are improved. When children are given tasks with clearly defined goals, they are more likely to experience a need to analyze and isolate objects, events, and situations and their interrelationships for the purpose of achieving the defined goal. Initially, it may be adults who point out what is important, what must be remembered, and how best to remember it. Later, children learn to perform the same activities on their own initiative.

Yendovitskaya (1964/1971b) concludes that:

> cultivating at this age elements of purposeful memory, forming the ability to present oneself consciously with a goal to remember, and forming the ability to recall and to utilize the methods and means necessary to accomplish this goal are the essential preconditions for the successful training of the child in school [p. 105].

IMPLICATIONS FOR TELEVISED INSTRUCTION

Memory exercises should be included in any effort to instruct young children through television. The following formats have been devised from the experiments reviewed in this chapter and are intended for illustrative purposes only.

Format 1

Young children require instruction in the use of rehearsal strategies on recall tasks. The serial recall procedure employed by Hagen et al. (1973) is an ideal task for teaching verbal rehearsal strategies on television to young children. Two principal rehearsal strategies are possible using the serial recall task. The first strategy consists of naming each card as it appears. The second strategy is called cumulative rehearsal and consists of naming all of the preceding pictures and the present picture in their order of appearance. For preschoolers, naming seems to improve recall best for the later items on the list, and cumulative rehearsal seems to improve recall best on the earlier items. The following format will employ cumulative rehearsal in its design:

1. Say, "Repeat after me."
2. Show a picture of a fish on a card.
3. Say, "Fish."
4. Turn over the card.

5. Show a picture of a cow on a card.
6. Say, "Repeat after me—fish, cow," pointing to first the fish and then the cow.
7. Repeat procedures 2–6 for a total of five pictures (fish, cow, bear, tiger, cat).
8. Ask, "Find the bear." Show all the cards lined up in a row and face down.
9. Delay. Build suspense.
10. Recite the list, "Fish . . . cow . . . bear . . . tiger . . . cat." Allow time to make a selection.
11. Silently scan each card. Allow time for selection.
12. Point to each card and enumerate, "fish, cow, bear. . . ." Stop and turn over bear.
13. Repeat memory game with same pictures. Vary order of cards and vary position of cards to be recalled.
14. Make memory game more difficult. Difficulty is increased by adding more cards to the recall task.

This is a memory game that can be conducted in rapid sequence on television. With sufficient embellishments it can delight young children and at the same time help them become aware of strategies for remembering that are at their disposal. An important characteristic of the above task is that it provides feedback on the children's answers. Whenever possible, feedback should be provided.

Format 2

The Ritter et al. (1973) experiment demonstrates that young children do not spontaneously use retrieval cues to facilitate memory. This experiment used a row of six house—toybox units and required children to recall a person using a closely associated toy as a retrieval cue. It then reversed the procedure and used the person to retrieve the name of the associated toy. The following format duplicates the Ritter et al. experiment for television presentation:

1. Present a row of six house—toybox units.
2. Place a football player in the first house and a football, clearly visible, in the toybox.
3. Repeat with other occupations until all the house—toybox combinations are filled. Stress the relation between the toy and the occupation of the person in the house. For instance, the football player might use the football before entering the house.
4. Show a duplicate football player.

5. Ask, "Where is the other football player? The two football players are friends and want to be together. Can you find his friend?"
6. Show searching behavior (e.g., the football player searches all the toy-boxes).
7. Ask, "Did you get it right? Did you find the other football player?"
8. Repeat procedures 2–9 for other occupations.
9. Change procedures so that the various occupations serve as retrieval cues for the occupation-related toys.

The previously cited experiment by Yendovitskaya (1964/1971b, pp. 101–102) also requires children to use retrieval cues. Her results replicate Ritter et al. in that she demonstrates a deficit in the spontaneous use of retrieval cues by 3- to 5-year-old children. However, Yendovitskaya's procedures present additional data on the conditions that facilitate the use of retrieval cues on recall tasks. Those children that gave verbal justification of the match they made between word and picture were better able to recall the word when presented with the picture. Active engagement in creating a story that connects the item to be remembered to a retrieval cue facilitates recall. Spontaneous use of active engagement is infrequent among preschoolers and should be encouraged.

Format 3

The types of problems Piaget uses in his experiments are commonly encountered by children in the course of their everyday activities. Therefore, Piaget-type problems, presented as memory exercises, can be particularly useful for television presentation because they relate to the problems children encounter in their daily lives. The following format illustrates a teaching exercise on the water-level problem suitable for television presentation:

1. Present a glass pitcher, in the upright position, partially filled with water.
2. Emphasize the horizontal level of the water by any of the following methods:
   a. Make the surface of the water glow, shimmer, etc.
   b. Blur the pitcher while the water level remains well defined.
   c. Tilt the pitcher to either side while emphasizing the horizontal level of the water.
   d. Construct an obtrusive external reference system that extends beyond the water level on either side of the pitcher. For instance, place the pitcher on a table, and on both sides place two piles of books the same height as the water level. Emphasize this point by placing a ruler across the books in front of the water level. Tilt the pitcher and point out that the water always remains horizontal and parallel to the line extending between the two piles of books.

e. Float objects on the surface of the water to emphasize the upright position on the invariant horizontal surface.

3. Pour the water in the pitcher into various-shaped containers, such as the following:

a. Pour into a glass container with a spout halfway up. Emphasize the water dripping out when it reaches the spout. Also, vary the slant of the container from the upright.

b. Pour water into many different, irregularly shaped containers. Place them side-by-side to facilitate comparison.

c. Place a smaller glass inside a larger one. Pour water into the smaller container until full. Continue pouring until the water level in the larger glass reaches the water level in the smaller glass. Then continue pouring until the larger glass overflows. At all times emphasize the parallel nature of the two water levels.

4. Employ various guessing games in which the object is to anticipate the height and orientation of the water level before the water is poured or before the container is tilted. Whenever possible provide feedback with the correct solution.

This exercise, though simple in conception, teaches an advanced concept. It instructs in the important notion of relativity of frames of reference. The container forms one external reference system, but the water surface conforms to another, broader reference system defined by gravity. Relativity in frame of reference is an idea that evolves developmentally through the preschool and school years. In the cognitive domain, being able to concentrate simultaneously on more than one aspect of a problem involves simultaneous mental manipulation of more than one frame of reference. This ability is essential for many tasks. In the social domain, being able to take and integrate other points of view with one's own is essential for effective interaction with others. This format instructs children in only one situation on the relativity of frame of reference. Exercises that involve the same concept in different situations have been presented in other chapters. The hope is that televised instruction can provide sufficient understanding so that children will attempt (1) to apply these concepts to their everyday experience; and (2) to integrate the concept acquired from specialized instruction on distinctive problems into a unified whole.

Format 4

Young children do not very effectively remember the elements of pictures presented to them. They do not seem to apply a sufficiently active strategy or logical analysis to the task of finding efficient ways of organizing a picture into classifications that would make the task of remembering easier. The following is a memory game designed to impress upon children the importance of organizing a picture into interrelated elements for later recall:

1. Present a picture.
2. Remove it.
3. Present interrelated parts of the picture that are meaningfully connected to each other (e.g., a girl throwing a ball to a boy).
4. Relate the objects in the picture to each other so that they are essential to the total understanding of the picture. For instance, subparts of a picture (a boy eating, a boy drawing, etc.) are isolated, and a simple story is told that connects the diverse subparts to each other.
5. Repeat the same picture several times. It is also desirable occasionally to construct a different story line to connect the elements into a totality with a different meaning. Children must not believe that for each picture there is only one important set of interrelationships and only one possible story that connects the events displayed in the picture. It is the versatility of the process of organizing pictures, irrespective of their content, that must be emphasized. Hopefully, with sufficient instruction, children will be able to initiate the process and complete it successfully on their own.
6. As a final exercise children should be induced to remember the picture by reconstructing the story line.

Format 5

Since verbal mediation exerts a strong positive influence on memory, exercises that teach the child its value should be adapted to television instruction. For instance, the previously described experiment by Yendovitskaya (1971b) that investigated the influence of verbal mediation on building semantic connections is easily applied to television presentation as a memory game:

1. Present a word verbally, but without a picture (e.g., *ball*).
2. Associate the word with a visually presented event (e.g., show a picture of a child playing with a ball).
3. During presentation of the picture verbally describe the association (e.g., say, "The child plays with the ball.").
4. Repeat the procedure with different words.
5. Show the part of each picture that was associated with the spoken word but omit the visual presentation that represents the word (e.g., show the child but do not show the child playing with the ball).
6. Say one of the words.
7. Show all the picture parts associated with the words (e.g., show the child, etc., on a split screen).

8. Delay to give children time to decide which picture goes with the verbally presented word. Encourage guessing.
9. Fade out all choices but the correct one and have the picture of the correct choice grow in size to cover the entire screen.
10. Repeat the word, the picture with its visual association, and say the association (e.g., say, "Ball," show the picture of the child playing with the ball, and say, "The child plays with the ball.").
11. Repeat the procedure with different words until all the words in the list have been used.
12. Use the same format repeatedly. Occasionally repeat a word but use a different association (e.g., "The ball rolls down the hill."). The children must be discouraged from associating a word with only one situation. The importance of verbal mediation as a general strategy is being taught and not the rote memorization of particular (and arbitrary) associations.

CONCLUSION

American research on memory has concentrated on children's deficiencies in verbal skills that facilitate recall. The research reviewed documents the fact that preschoolers do not spontaneously use verbal mediators and when induced to use verbal mediators, they do not persist after inducement has ceased. Rehearsal and anticipation, or self-testing, both verbal and nonverbal, is also infrequently observed among preschoolers on memory tasks. A deficiency in clustering items into categories (both verbal and manual) was also observed among preschoolers. Finally, preschoolers demonstrated a deficiency in the use of retrieval cues to facilitate recall.

Explanations proposed to explain the above deficiencies include:

- *Linguistic deficiency:* Preschoolers have only a limited ability to structure situations in words.
- *Cognitive immaturity:* Coding and rehearsing are intellectual active strategies that represent a plan for coping effectively. They require intellectual maturity for their utilization.

Flavell favors the cognitive-immaturity hypothesis. He argues that children fail to talk to themselves because they are too young to engage in the intellectual activities implied in coding and rehearsing. It is argued by him that linguistic development has little to do with the deficiency in coding and rehearsing. Consequently, deficiencies in recall resulting from a lack of verbal mediators are most likely attributable to inadequate cognitive maturity. This supports the idea, presented on numerous occasions in other chapters, that children's achievements in diverse areas (e.g., thinking, language, perception, memory) are dependent upon the general level of the child's intellect.

Piaget, in an extended series of simple but clever experiments, demonstrates the dependence of memory on the level of children's understanding. Three of Piaget's experiments were extensively reviewed in this chapter: (1) memory for an ordered series of sticks; (2) memory for the surface of a liquid in a container; and (3) memory for a horizontal line made of four matches in comparison to a zigzag line made of four matches directly underneath. Piaget notes an improvement in memory on the first two tasks after 6–8 months. He attributes the improvement to an increase in understanding of the observed situation over time. The memory changes because the code that the child uses to record the event changes. In the last experiment Piaget argues that a conflict exists in the child between the concept of number and the concept of length. This is induced by the two different rows of matches. This conflict produces predictable distortions in memory. Memory improves after 6–8 months as the child's intellectual level advances.

Soviet research on memory has direct instructional objectives. Soviet researchers describe memory at the preschool age as primarily unintentional or involuntary, because any specific goal to remember in the behavior of children at this age is infrequently observed. Only toward the sixth year does intentional memorizing begin to be noticed. Later various strategies form to enable better retention of facts in memory. These strategies include verbal and nonverbal elementary systematization, logical analysis of material, and greater concentration on the form of the material to be remembered. The amount of active engagement by the child in the event being memorized has been singled out as important in determining the effectiveness of memory during the preschool period. Categorizations based upon a clearly defined group of physical activities with objects (e.g., all the items used in eating) are within the grasp of younger preschoolers. The Soviets stress the fact that children's abilities in memorizing and recall can be improved if they are given tasks with clearly defined goals where they experience a need to analyze and isolate objects, events, situations, and their interrelationships.

This chapter is the last of four chapters dealing with specific aspects of children's functioning. Many qualities, specific to young children's thought, have been reviewed in these four chapters. Consistent and related developmental progressions have been observed, and television exercises specific to these progressions have been designed. In the concluding chapter likely future developments are reviewed and a specific proposal, designed to transform the theoretical analysis performed in this book into televised productions, is offered.

8

A Proposal:
Effective Instructional Television
for the Preschool Child

This chapter will be devoted to the as yet unrealized potential of instructional television aimed at young children.

From the preceding chapters it should be clear that televised instruction for preschoolers has certain inherent limitations:

1. Normal broadcast television is one-way communication. Televised presentations do not provide individualized responses to the reactions of the viewer.
2. Preschoolers require specialized instruction attuned to their cognitive abilities. Curriculum and instructional techniques cannot be watered-down presentations for adults. They must be designed specifically to meet the distinct qualities of preschoolers' processes of thought.
3. Preschoolers from disadvantaged backgrounds who are "at risk" educationally may require specific instructional techniques designed to meet their cognitive needs.

There are two alternatives currently available that could, in part, overcome these restrictions. The first is improving normal broadcast television, and the second is utilizing the relatively recent development of computer-assisted instruction (CAI).

Normal broadcast television is restricted by the distinct qualities of children's thought. Preschoolers ordinarily learn best by "hands on" physical activity with objects. According to Piaget, as objects are manipulated and goals fail to be attained, the ensuing conflict produces a restructuring and growth in thought processes. Other research, principally American and Soviet, indicates that by careful attention to the requirements of the task and to the capabilities of the child, learning does occur with visually presented material. Whatever the resolution of this conflict of opinions, it is obvious that a successful effort to teach children via television will require superior planning and a thorough understanding of child development.

Normal broadcast instruction must be superior instruction if it is to overcome the inherent limitations of one-way communication. Designing superior instructional techniques and applying them to appropriate age-related tasks for television presentation has been a goal of this book. The television exercises contained herein are carefully grounded in theory and empirical research. Consequently, it is expected that they will provide effective instructional television for preschoolers.

The *Sesame Street* approach, closely examined in Chapters 2 and 3, combines entertainment with instruction. That *Sesame Street* entertains is certainly attested to by its popularity. That *Sesame Street* teaches effectively has been seriously questioned. The exercises presented in this book are, like *Sesame Street*, designed to entertain children by intriguing them, by capturing their imagination, by provoking their thought through interesting problems, and by motivating them to test out on real-life objects what they have observed on television. The major difference is that the instruction and curriculum herein proposed are tied more tightly to what child psychologists know about children's thought and how it develops. It is for this reason that this proposal might be much more effective than the instruction employed on *Sesame Street*. These are the limits: Competition between television stations requires material that attracts preschoolers, but the need to attract preschoolers may deter serious instructional objectives.

When independent commercial television provided the first direct competition to the BBC in England, massive dial-shifting away from the more informative, higher cultural and educational standards of the BBC occurred. The effect that severely lowered the BBC's popularity might be called a "lowest common denominator" phenomenon. Large segments of the audience shifted away from "demanding" television, which requires concentrated effort to be fully appreciated, to less demanding situation comedies, Westerns, etc., many of which were imported from the United States. If the lowest common denominator proves to be the overriding influence determining the popularity of children's programming, then cooperation between television stations to provide a regular "instructional children's hour" might be necessary to ensure accessibility of instructional television to all segments of the population of preschoolers. This is only a possibility and is subject to further exploration. It is not a proposal. It has already been noted, however, that children from impoverished backgrounds watch virtually no educational television but restrict their watching to cartoons and similar less demanding fare. These are the children most in need of help, and the evidence indicates that, with rare exceptions, they are not getting it.

At some point, society will have to wrestle with its values and determine what role(s) television will play vis-à-vis children. As previously indicated, educational television appears to have a much greater potential than is presently realized. Public policy will utlimately determine the extent and nature of any societal commitment to instructional television.

The most obvious alternative to normal broadcast televised instruction is the as yet experimental computer-assisted instruction(Cleary, Mayes, & Packham, 1976; Hammond, 1972). Under a $9 million grant from the National Science Foundation, two different approaches are being developed. The Ticcit (time-shared interactive, computer-controlled information) system is decentralized, is built around small computers, and has a self-contained package of hardware, operating programs, and course material for each participating school. The principal display device is a color television set. The Plato (programmed logic for automatic teaching operations) system is centralized, features a large centralized computer servicing many schools, and uses a new type of visual display—a plasma panel—especially developed for CAI. Each system uses a different approach to the development of course material. Ticcit utilizes a formal approach, employing teams of programmers, educational psychologists, and specialists in the subject matter. The Plato program, in contrast, is informal, letting teachers design their own courses, with Plato staff available when necessary.

In the Ticcit system the terminals are either directly connected to two mini-computers or are remotely connected through cable-television channels. One computer services the terminal while the other does most of the actual processing of student answers. Each dual-computer setup is capable of handling at least 100 terminals. The television sets display computer-generated graphical or printed material or short video-tape films. Random-access record players, controlled by the computer, provide audio information. Initial cost for the Ticcit system with 128 terminals is $400,000, exclusive of course-material expenditure. This translates to about 35¢ per student hour, considerably less than current junior college instructional expenses. Currently the Ticcit system is undergoing trials at junior colleges, teaching remedial and freshman English and mathematics. The Ticcit system is applicable to home use via closed-circuit cable systems.

The Plato system is much more elaborate. It is designed around four central processors, and services 4000 student terminals within 800 miles of the computer. Plato is the most ambitious time-sharing system yet attempted. The terminal consists of a visual display device—the plasma panel—a telephone line to the computer, a keyboard, a random-access audio device that both plays and records, and an infrared sensor system that responds to the touch of a finger on any part of the visual display. The plasma panel is a simple device of two sheets of glass between which are embedded two fine-wire grids. A gas between the sheets is ionized by applying a voltage at selected points on the grid. This produces a display. The display is maintained by a weaker alternating voltage applied to the entire grid. The grid is extremely fine (512×512) and thus produces extremely sharp images of any type. Since the panel is transparent, color slides and motion pictures can be superimposed upon the grid. Plato is remarkable in that the terminals are linked to the computer over ordinary telephone lines, produce sharp and elaborate displays, write 180 characters per second, and respond to the student within 0.1 second (Ticcit requires 0.5 second). Furthermore, a single educational television channel will service as many as 1000 remote terminals. A new programming language has been developed, based upon English grammar and syntax, for use by teachers with no knowledge of computers who are designing courses. The Plato system is reported to have taught a Latin course at the college level at a much higher level of efficiency than traditional instruction. In another experiment with grade school children Plato taught the principle of balance by allowing children to explore by trial and error "the motions of a man balancing a stick, eventually discovering the effects of overcorrection and the principles of dynamic balance [Hammond, 1972, p. 1112]."

Computer-assisted instruction is not a new educational development. In the early 1960s Omar Khayyam Moore (1966, pp. 169–216) was teaching extremely young children reading and writing skills using the then innovative "talking typewriter." Although the device is primitive by current standards, the curriculum and instructional strategy he designed was a remarkable achievement considering the dominent influences in psychology at that time. Moore designed what he considered an optimal environment, called the autotelic responsive environment, for the development of learning skills. An autotelic activity is one that is engaged in for its own sake and not for obtaining rewards or avoiding punishments that have no inherent connection to the activity. In practice, lab assistants never reward or punish children or provide assistance in using the talking typewriter. Learning is generated with the aid of the child's natural curiosity. The responsive environment has the following characteristics: free exploration, immediate consequences of actions, self-pacing, optimal opportunity to discover relations of various kinds, and structure so that series of discoveries about the physical, cultural, and social world are likely to be made.

Phase 1 is free exploration. Each child's fingernails are color-coded, and the keyboard is also color-coded to encourage correct fingering. In this phase, the talking typewriter is set so that the child can explore the keyboard freely. Whenever a key is depressed, the typewriter types the character in large type and pronounces its name. When the child begins to lose interest, phase 2, search and match, begins. Without warning, every character on the keyboard except the match locks to a character illustrated on a special display. The typewriter pronounces the character, waits for a correct match from the child, and then pronounces the character again after the match is successfully made. Variations of search and match, each successively more challenging, are provided until the child masters the keyboard. When interest wanes, phase 3, word construction, begins. There are two forms of phase 3, word construction—reading and word construction—writing. Both activities are alternated. In phase 3, type 1, the typewriter exposes a word; the child types the word; the typewriter pronounces each letter before and after it is struck; after the word is struck, the typewriter calls for a space; then the typewriter pronounces each letter and the word. In phase 3, type 2, words are presented word-by-word on tape for typing. Word lists are generated from observations of the children's own conversation. In an alternative version children take their own dictation. In phase 4 the child learns to read and write by copying visually presented sentences and stories, by typing them from tapes, or by writing original material.

Moore reports spectacular results using the autotelic responsive environment approach. The children demonstrate their individually acquired skills in a social situation by participating in the writing of a newspaper. Several rather impressive stories in the newspaper, written by first-grade and kindergarten children, are illustrated by Moore (1966, pp. 181—182). It is not unusual for 3-year-olds to demonstrate competence in reading and writing. On entering first grade some children demonstrate reading and writing abilities at the sixth-grade level.

More recently, similar results have been demonstrated in the field of music instruction. The Suzuki method teaches young children, starting at 2 years of age, to play the violin. Suzuki's teaching method appears to be structured along the general guidelines established by Moore. In both instances, the required skills are learned at the child's initiative, for their intrinsic merit.

The principles and specific techniques of the autotelic responsive environment provide an example of the potential usefulness of the latest generation of computer-assisted instruction hardware. The new generation equipment is considerably more flexible. Many different skills can be programmed for instruction onto the new terminals, including all of the cognitive, language, perceptual, and mnemonic exercises illustrated in this book. The future of computer-assisted instruction, it seems, lies in what is taught and the methods used to teach it. More will be known about this new technology after December 1976, when an evaluation report is scheduled for release by Educational Testing Service, Princeton, New Jersey.

This chapter closes with a specific proposal. In order to use instructional television optimally, including the new technology of computer-assisted instruction, concentrated efforts by diligent teams of professionals are required. The complexity of the differences between the thought processes of children and adults has only recently come under investigation. Because of these differences and the subtleties involved in applying this knowledge to the fullest, more harmonious and more frequent contacts between researchers, networks, independent television stations, and producers of children's programs must be initiated. It may take years to translate new knowledge to practical purposes. My proposal, specifically designed for instructional television, is to set up a research clearinghouse, jointly staffed by academic researchers and those experienced in the actual production of television programs. New research would be screened for its potential applicability. The more promising research findings, along with suggestions for applying them, would be made available, as a public service, to all involved in the production of children's programs.

The complexities of the qualitative differences of the thought and perceptual processes of young children are such that television presentations that prove both educational and entertaining to older children and adults may often be simply entertaining to the younger audience. It is therefore essential that research into the instructional effectiveness of televised programs shift primary focus from the popularity of presentations and instead focus primarily on the type and amount of learning that has occurred among its preschool viewers. The most satisfactory mechanism for meeting this critical evaluation would be the establishment of interdisciplinary teams of experts to test specific concrete goals for children's television programs. Only when the planning and evaluation of children's viewing material becomes rigorously controlled by achieved results will the true limits of instructional television be approached.

References

Appel, L. F., Cooper, R. G., McCarrell, N., Sims-Knight, J., Yussen, S. R., & Flavell, J. H. The development of the distinction between perceiving and memorizing. *Child Development*, 1972, *43*, 1365–1381.

Aronfreed, J. *Conduct and conscience.* New York: Academic Press, 1968.

Badger, E. Mothers' training program: The group process. Urbana, Ill., 1969. (ERIC Document Reproduction Service No. ED 032 926).

Ball, S., & Bogatz, G. A. *The first year of Sesame Street: An evaluation.* Princeton, N.J.: Educational Testing Service, 1970. (Distributed by Teachers College Press, New York.) (a)

Ball, S., & Bogatz, G. A. *A summary of the major findings in "The first year of Sesame Street: An evaluation."* Princeton, N.J.: Educational Testing Service, 1970. (b)

Ball, S., & Bogatz, G. A. Some thoughts on this secondary evaluation. In T. D. Cook, H. Appleton, R. F. Conner, A. Sheffer, G. Tamkin, & S. J. Weber, (Eds.), *"Sesame Street" Revisited.* New York: Russell Sage Foundation, 1975.

Bandura, A. Influence of models' reinforcement contingencies on the acquisition of imitative responses. *Journal of Personality and Social Psychology*, 1965, *1*, 589–595.

Bandura, A. Social learning theory of identificatory processes. In D. A. Goslin (Ed.), *Handbook of socialization theory and research.* Chicago: Rand McNally, 1969.

Bandura, A. (Ed.). *Psychological modeling.* Chicago: Aldine-Atherton, 1971.

Bandura, A. *Aggression: A social learning analysis.* Englewood Cliffs, N.J.: Prentice-Hall, 1973.

Bandura, A., Grusec, J. E., & Menlove, F. L. Observational learning as a function of symbolization and incentive set. *Child Development*, 1966, *37*, 499–506.

Bandura, A., Ross, D., & Ross, S. A. Imitation of film-mediated aggressive models. *Journal of Abnormal and Social Psychology*, 1963, *66*, 3–11. (a)

Bandura, A., Ross, D., & Ross, S. A. Vicarious reinforcement and imitative learning. *Journal of Abnormal and Social Psychology*, 1963, *67*, 601–607. (b)

Barcus, F. E. *Saturday children's television.* Newtonville, Mass.: Action for Children's Television, 1971.

243

Barcus, F. E. *Television in the afternoon hours.* Newtonville, Mass.: Action for Children's Television, 1975. (a)

Barcus, F. E. *Weekend commercial children's television.* Newtonville, Mass.: Action for Children's Television, 1975. (b)

Baumrind, D. Authoritarian versus authoritative parent control. *Adolescence,* 1968, *3,* 255–272.

Baumrind, D. Socialization and instrumental competence in young children. In W. W. Hartup (Ed.), *The young child: Reviews of research* (Vol. 2). Washington, D.C.: National Association for the Education of Young Children, 1972.

Bechtel, R. B., Achelpohl, C., & Akers, R. Correlates between observed behavior and questionnaire responses on television viewing. In G. A. Comstock, E. A. Rubinstein, & J. P. Murray (Eds.), *Television and social behavior* (Vol. 4). Washington, D.C.: U.S. Government Printing Office, 1972.

Berkowitz, L. Control of aggression. In B. M. Caldwell & H. R. Ricciuti (Eds.), *Review of child development research* (Vol. 3). Chicago: University of Chicago Press, 1973.

Berkowitz, L., & Geen, R. G. Stimulus qualities of the target of aggression. A further study. *Journal of Personality and Social Psychology,* 1967, *5,* 364–368.

Bernbaum, M. Educational television for preschool and kindergarten children: An abstract bibliography. Urbana, Ill.: ERIC Clearinghouse on Early Childhood Education, 1972.

Bertram, C. L., Pena, D., & Hines, B. W. *Home-oriented preschool education program: Summative evaluation report.* Charleston, W. Va.: Appalachia Educational Laboratory, 1971. (a)

Bertram, C. L., Pena, D., & Hines, B. W. Evaluation report: Early childhood education program, 1969–1970 field test. Summary report. Urbana, Ill., 1971. (ERIC Document Reproduction Service No. ED 052 837) (b)

Biblow, E. Imaginative play and the control of aggressive behavior. In J. L. Singer (Ed.), *The child's world of make-believe.* New York: Academic Press, 1973.

Bloom, L. *Language development: Form and function in emerging grammars.* Cambridge, Mass.: M.I.T. Press, 1970.

Bogart, L. Warning: The Surgeon General has determined that TV violence is moderately dangerous to your child's mental health. *The Public Opinion Quarterly.* 1972–1973, *36,* 491–521.

Bogatz, G. A., & Ball, S. *The second year of Sesame Street: A continuing evaluation.* Princeton, N.J.: Educational Testing Service, 1971.

Boger, R. P. *et al.,* Parents as primary change agents in an experimental Head Start Program of language intervention. Experimental program report. Urbana, Ill., 1969. (ERIC Document Reproduction Service No. ED 044 168)

Borton, T. Dual audio television. *Harvard Educational Review,* 1971, *41*(1), 64–78.

Bower, T. G. R. *Development in infancy.* San Francisco: W. H. Freeman, 1974.

Bronfenbrenner, U. Who lives on *Sesame Street? Psychology Today,* 1970, *4,* 14–20.

Brown, R. *A first language.* Cambridge, Mass.: Harvard University Press, 1973.

Bruner, J. S. The course of cognitive growth. *American Psychologist,* 1964, *19,* 1–15.

Bruner, J. S., Olver, R. R., & Greenfield, P. M. *Studies in cognitive growth.* New York: Wiley, 1966.

Cater, D., & Strickland, S. *A first hard look at The Surgeon General's Report on Television and Violence.* Palo Alto, Calif.: Aspen Program on Communication and Society, 1972.

Cater, D., & Strickland, S. *TV violence and the child.* New York: Russell Sage Foundation, 1975.

Cazden, C. B. Subcultural differences in child language: An interdisciplinary review. *Merrill-Palmer Quarterly,* 1966, *12*(3).

Chall, J. *Learning to read: The great debate.* New York: McGraw-Hill, 1967.

The Children's Television Workshop (pamphlet). *The New Yorker,* 1970.

Chittendon, G. E. An experimental study in measuring and modifying assertive behavior in young children. *Monographs of the Society for Research in Child Development,* 1942, *7,* (1, Serial No. 31).

Chomsky, C. S. *The acquisition of syntax in children from 5 to 10.* Cambridge, Mass.: MIT Press, 1969.

Clark, E. V. On the acquisition of the meaning of "before" and "after." *Journal of Verbal Learning and Verbal Behavior,* 1971, *10,* 266–275.

Clark, E. V. What's in a word? On the child's acquisition of semantics in his first language. In T. E. Moore (Ed.), *Cognitive development and the acquisition of language.* New York: Academic Press, 1973.

Clark, H. The primitive nature of children's relational concepts. In J. R. Hayes (Ed.), *Cognition and the development of language.* New York: Wiley, 1970.

Cleary, A., Mayes, T., & Packham, D. *Educational technology.* New York: Wiley, 1976.

Coates, B., & Hartup, W. Age and verbalization in observational learning. *Developmental Psychology,* 1969, *1,* 556–562.

Coleman, J. *Equality of educational opportunity.* Washington, D.C.: U.S. Department of Health, Education, & Welfare, 1966.

Collins, W. A. Developmental aspects of understanding and evaluating television content. Symposium on television and young children's behavior, Society for Research in Child Development, 1973.

Comstock, G. *Television and human behavior: The key studies.* Santa Monica, Calif.: Rand Corporation, 1975.

Cook, T. D., Appleton, H., Conner, R. F., Shaffer, A., Tamkin, G., and Weber, S. J. *"Sesame Street" revisited.* New York: Russell Sage Foundation, 1975.

Cooney, J. G. *Sesame Street. PTA Magazine,* 1970, *64,* 25–26.

Cromer, R. F. The development of language and cognition: The cognition hypothesis. In B. Foss (Ed.), *New perspectives in child development.* Baltimore, Md.: Penguin Books, 1974.

Culhane, J. Report card on *Sesame Street. The New York Times Magazine,* May 24, 1970.

Dann, M. The "Street" that runs around the world. *New York Times,* August 6, 1972.

Donaldson, M., & Balfour, G. Less is more: A study of language comprehension in children. *British Journal of Psychology,* 1968, *59,* 461–472.

Donaldson, M., & Wales, R. J. On the acquisition of some relational terms. In J. R. Hayes (Ed.), *Cognition and the development of language.* New York: Wiley, 1970.

Duckworth, E. Piaget rediscovered. In R. E. Ripple & V. N. Rockcastle (Eds.), *Piaget rediscovered.* Ithaca, N.Y.: Cornell University Press, 1964.

Eckman, P., Liebert, R. M., Friesen, W. V., Harrison, R., Zlatchin, C., Malmstrom, E. J., & Baron, R. A. Facial expressions of emotion while watching televised violence as predictors of subsequent aggression. In G. A. Comstock, E. A. Rubinstein, & J. P. Murray (Eds.), *Television and social behavior* (Vol. 5). Washington, D.C.: U.S. Government Printing Office, 1972.

Efron, E. Shoot-out on *Sesame Street. TV Guide,* March 11, 1972.

Eisner, M. TV Kidtime entering its "prime," but writers are key to upgrading. *Variety,* Sept. 15, 1971, p. 34.

Elkind, D., Koegler, R. R., & Go, E. Studies in perceptual development: II. Part–whole perception. *Child Development,* 1964, *35,* 81–90.

Elkonin, D. B. Development of speech. In A. V. Zaphorozhets & D. B. Elkonin (Eds.), *The psychology of preschool children.* Cambridge, Mass.: M.I.T. Press, 1971. (Originally published, 1964.)

Evaluation Report: Early Childhood evaluation program, 1969, field test. Urbana, Ill., 1970. (ERIC Document Reproduction Service No. ED 041 625).

Feshbach, S. Aggression. In P. H. Mussen (Ed.), *Carmichael's manual of child psychology* (Vol. 2) (3d ed.). New York: Wiley, 1970.

Feshbach, S., & Singer, R. D. *Television and aggression.* San Francisco: Jossey-Bass, 1971.

Feshbach, S., & Singer R. D. Television and aggression: A reply to Liebert, Sobol, and Davidson. In G. A. Comstock, E. A. Rubinstein, & J. P. Murray (Eds.), *Television and social behavior* (Vol. 5). Washington, D.C.: U.S. Government Printing Office, 1972. (a)

Feshbach, S., & Singer, R. D. Television and aggression: Some reactions to the Liebert, Sobol, and Davidson review and response. In G. A. Comstock, E. A. Rubinstein, & J. P. Murray (Eds.), *Television and social behavior* (Vol. 5). Washington, D.C.: U.S. Government Printing Office, 1972. (b)

Flapan, D. P. *Children's understanding of social interaction.* Unpublished doctoral dissertation, Columbia University, 1965.

Flavell, J. H. Developmental studies of mediated memory. In H. W. Reese & L. P. Lipsitt (Eds.), *Advances in child development and behavior* (Vol. 5). New York: Academic Press, 1970.

Flavell, J. H. What is memory development the development of? *Human Development,* 1971, *14,* 272–278.

Flavell, J. H., Beach, D. R., & Chinsky, J. M. Spontaneous verbal rehearsal in a memory task as a function of age. *Child Development,* 1966, *37,* 283–299.

Flavell, J. H., Friedrichs, A. G., & Hoyt, J. D. Developmental changes in memorization processes. *Cognitive Psychology,* 1970, *1,* 324–340.

Fowles, B. M. *A pilot study of verbal report in formative research in television.* Unpublished doctoral dissertation, Ferkauf Graduate School, Yeshiva University, 1973.

Fowles, B., & Voyat, G. Piaget meets Big Bird: Is TV a passive teacher? *Urban Review,* 1974, *7*(1), 69–80.

Franck, G. J. *Über Geschehensgestaltungen in der Auffassung von Filmen durch Kinder.* Leipzig: J. A. Barth, 1955.

Freyberg, J. T. Increasing the imaginative play of urban disadvantaged kindergarten children through systematic training. In J. L. Singer (Ed.), *The child's world of make-believe.* New York: Academic Press, 1973.

Friedlander, B. Z., Wetstone, H. S., & Scott, C. S. Suburban preschool children's comprehension of an age-appropriate informational television program. *Child Development,* 1974, *45,* 561–565.

Friedrich, L. K., & Stein, A. H. Aggressive and prosocial television programs and the natural behavior of preschool children. *Monographs of the Society for Research in Child Development,* 1973, *38*(4) (Serial No. 151).

Gagné, R. M. *The conditions of learning.* New York: Holt, Rinehart & Winston, 1965.

Geen, R. G., & Berkowitz, L. Name-mediating aggressive cue properties. *Journal of Personality,* 1966, *34,* 456–465.

Geen, R. G. & Berkowitz, L. Some conditions facilitating the occurrence of aggression after the observation of violence. *Journal of Personality,* 1967, *38,* 666–676.

Gelman, R. Conservatism acquisition: A problem of learning to attend to relevant attributes. *Journal of Experimental Child Psychology,* 1969, *7,* 167–187.

Gerbner, G. Violence in television drama: Trends and symbolic functions. In G. A. Comstock, E. A. Rubinstein, & J. P. Murray (Eds.), *Television and social behavior* (Vol. 1). Washington, D.C.: U.S. Government Printing Office, 1972.

Ghent, L. Perception of overlapping and embedded figures by children of different ages. *American Journal of Psychology,* 1956, *69,* 575–587.

Ghent, L. Recognition by children of realistic figures presented in various orientations. *Canadian Journal of Psychology*, 1960, *14*, 249–256.

Gibbons, S. Y., & Palmer, E. L. *Pre-Reading on Sesame Street*. New York: Children's Television Workshop, 1970.

Gibson, E. J. Development of perception: Discrimination of depth compared with discrimination of graphic symbols. In J. C. Wright & J. Kagan (Eds.), *Basic cognitive processes in children*. Chicago: University of Chicago Press, 1963.

Gibson, E. J. The development of perception as an adaptive process. *American Scientist*, 1970, *58*, 103–107.

Gibson, E. J. Trends in perceptual development: Implications for the reading process. In A. D. Pick (Ed.), *Minnesota symposia on child psychology* (Vol. 8). Minneapolis: University of Minnesota Press, 1974.

Gibson, E. J., Gibson, J. J., Pick, A. D., & Osser, H. A developmental study of the discrimination of letter-like forms. *Journal of Comparative Physiological Psychology*, 1962, *55*, 897–906.

Gibson, E. J., & Yonas, A. A developmental study of visual search behavior. *Perception and Psychophysics*, 1966, *1*, 169–171.

Gilmer, B. R. Intra-family diffusion of selected cognitive skills as a function of educational stimulation. Urbana, Ill., 1969. (ERIC Document Reproduction Service No. ED 037 233).

Gollin, E. S. Developmental studies of visual recognition of incomplete objects. *Perceptual Motor Skills*, 1960, *11*, 289–298.

Gollin, E. S. Factors affecting the visual recognition of incomplete objects: A comparative investigation of children and adults. *Perceptual Motor Skills*, 1962, *15*, 583–590.

Gollin, E. S. Perceptual learning of incomplete pictures. *Perceptual Motor Skills*, 1964, *21*, 439–445.

Gomberg, A. W. *The four-year-old child and television: The effects on his play at school*. Unpublished doctoral dissertation, Teachers College, Columbia University, 1961.

Goranson, R. E. Media violence and aggressive behavior: A review of experimental research. In L. Berkowitz (Ed.), *Advances in experimental social psychology* (Vol. 5). New York: Academic Press, 1970.

Gordon, I. J. Early child stimulation through parent education. Urbana, Ill., 1969. (ERIC Document Reproduction Service No. ED 038 166).

Gouin-Décarie, T. A study of the mental and emotional development of the Thalidomide child. In B. M. Foss (Ed.), *Determinants of infant behavior* (Vol. 4). London: Methuen, 1969.

Granger, R. L. *et al*. *The impact of Head Start: An evaluation of the effects of Head Start on children's cognitive and affective development* (Vol. 1). Athens, Ohio: U.S. Office of Economic Opportunity, Westinghouse Learning Corp. & Ohio University, 1969.

Guillaume, P. *Imitation in children*. Chicago: University of Chicago Press, 1971. (Originally published, 1926.)

Hagen, J. W., Hargrave, S., & Ross, W. Prompting and rehearsal in short-term memory. *Child Development*, 1973, *44*, 201–204.

Hagen, J. W., Jongeward, R. H., & Kail, R. V. Cognitive perspectives on the development of memory. In H. Reese (Ed.), *Advances in child development and behavior* (Vol. 10). New York: Academic Press, in press.

Hagen, J. W., & Kingsley, P. R. Labeling effects in short-term memory. *Child Development*, 1968, *39*, 113–121.

Halloran, J. D. *Findings and cognition on the television perception of children and young people*. Munich: Internationales Zentralinstitut für das Jugend- und Bildungsfernsehen, 1969.

Hammond, A. L. Computer-assisted instruction: Two major demonstrations. *Science*, 1972, *176*, 1110–1112.

Hanratty, M. A., Liebert, R. M., Morris, L. W., & Fernandez, L. E. Imitation of film-mediated aggression against live and inanimate victims. *Proceedings of the 77th Annual Convention of the American Psychological Association*, 1969, *4*, 457–458.

Helitzer, M. & Heyel, C. *The youth market: Its dimensions, influence and opportunities for you.* New York: Media Books, 1970.

Hentoff, M. *Sesame Street—Hypnotic.* Vogue, February 1, 1970.

Hicks, D. J. Imitation and retention of film-mediated aggressive peer and adult models. *Journal of Personality and Social Psychology*, 1965, *2*, 97–100.

Hicks, D. J. Effects of co-observer's sanctions and adult presence on imitative aggression. *Child Development*, 1968, *39*, 303–309. (a)

Hicks, D. J. Short- and long-term retention of affectively varied modeled behavior. *Psychonomic Science*, 1968, *11*, 369–370. (b)

Himmelweit, H. T., Oppenheim, A. N., & Vince, P. *Television and the child.* London: Oxford University Press, 1958.

Hines, B. Attainment of cognitive objectives. Technical report no. 3. Urbana, Ill., 1970. (ERIC Document Reproduction Service No. ED 052 833).

Hines, B. Unpublished manuscript. Charleston, W. Va.: Appalachia Educational Laboratory, in press.

Hoffman, M. L. Moral development. In P. Mussen (Ed.), *Carmichael's manual of child psychology* (Vol. 2). (3d ed.) New York: Wiley, 1970.

Holt, J. Big Bird, meet Dick and Jane. *Atlantic Monthly*, 1971, *227*, 72–74.

Inhelder, B. Memory and intelligence in the child. In D. Elking & J. H. Flavell (Eds.), *Studies in cognitive development: Essays in honor of Jean Piaget.* New York: Oxford University Press, 1969.

Inhelder, B., Sinclair, H., & Bovet, M. *Learning and the development of cognition.* Cambridge, Mass.: Harvard University Press, 1975.

Jensen, A. How much can we boost I.Q. and scholastic achievement? *Harvard Educational Review*, 1969, *39*(1), 1–123.

Johnson, N. Beyond *Sesame Street. National Elementary Principal*, 1971, *50*, 7–13.

Karnes, M. B., *et al.*, Educational intervention at home by mothers of disadvantaged infants. Urbana, Ill., 1970. (ERIC Document Reproduction Service No. ED 139 944).

Keeney, T. J., Canizzo, S. R., & Flavell, J. H. Spontaneous and induced verbal rehearsal in a recall task. *Child Development*, 1967, *38*, 953–966.

Keilhacker, M. The German report. In J. D. Halloran (Ed.), *Findings and cognition on the television perception of children and young people.* Munich: Internationales Zentralinstitut für das Jugend- und Bildungsfernsehen, 1969.

Kessen, W. Research on the psychological developments of the infant: An overview. *Merrill-Palmer Quarterly*, 1963, *9*, 83–84.

Kingsley, P. R., & Hagen, J. W. Induced versus spontaneous rehearsal in short-term memory in nursery school children. *Developmental Psychology*, 1969, *1*, 40–46.

Kingsley, R. C., & Hall, V. C. Training conservation through the use of learning sets. *Child Development*, 1968, *38*, 11–26.

Kliger, S. Fog over *Sesame Street. Teachers College Record*, 1971, *72*(1), 41–56.

Kohlberg, L. Early education: A cognitive-developmental view. *Child Development*, 1968, *39*(4), 1013–1062.

Laurendeau, M., & Pinard, A. *The development of the concept of space in the child.* New York: International Universities Press, 1970.

Lefkowitz, M. M., Eron, L. D., Walder, L. O., & Huesman, L. R. Television violence and child aggression: A follow-up study. In G. A. Comstock, E. A. Rubinstein, & J. P. Murray (Eds.), *Television and social behavior* (Vol. 3). Washington, D.C.: U.S. Government Printing Office, 1972.

Leifer, A. D., Collins, W. A., Gross, B. M., Taylor, P. H., Andrews, L., & Blackmer, E. R. Developmental aspects of variables relevant to observational learning. *Child Development*, 1970, *42*, 1509–1516.

Leifer, A. D., Gordon, N. J., Groves, S. B. Children's television, more than mere entertainment. *Harvard Educational Review*, 1974, *44*(2), 213–245.

Leifer, A. D., & Roberts, D. Children's responses to television violence. In G. A. Comstock, E. A. Rubinstein, & J. P. Murray (Eds.), *Television and social behavior* (Vol. 2). Washington, D.C.: U.S. Government Printing Office, 1972.

Lesser, G. S. Designing a program for broadcast television. In F. Korten, S. Cook, & J. Lacey (Eds.), *Psychology and the problems of society*. Washington, D.C.: American Psychological Association, 1970.

Lesser, G. S. Learning, teaching, and television production for children: The experience of *Sesame Street. Harvard Educational Review*, 1972, *42*(2), 232–272.

Lesser, G. S. *Children and television: Lessons from Sesame Street*. New York: Vintage Books, 1974.

Lesser, H. Children's unusual responses to observed movement. *Journal of Genetic Psychology*, 1974, *125*, 201–206.

Lesser, H. The growth of perceived causality in children. *Journal of Genetic Psychology*, in press.

Lesser, H., & Drouin, C. Training in the use of double-function terms. *Journal of Psycholinguistic Research*, 1975, *4*, 285–302.

Levenstein, P. Verbal interaction project: Aiding cognitive growth in disadvantaged preschoolers through the Mother–Child Home Program. July 1, 1967–August 31, 1970. Urbana, Ill., 1971. (ERIC Document Reproduction Service No. ED 059 791).

Liebert, R. M., & Baron, R. A. Short-term effects of televised aggressive behavior. In J. P. Murray, E. A. Rubinstein, & G. A. Comstock (Eds.), *Television and social behavior* (Vol. 2). Washington, D.C.: U.S. Government Printing Office, 1972.

Liebert, R. M., Davidson, E. S., & Sobol, M. P. Catharsis of aggression among institutionalized boys: Further discussion. In G. A. Comstock, E. A. Rubinstein, & J. P. Murray (Eds.), *Television and social behavior* (Vol. 5). Washington, D.C.: U.S. Government Printing Office, 1972.

Liebert, R. M., Neale, J. M., & Davidson, E. S. *The early window: Effects of television on children and youth*. New York: Pergaman Press, 1973.

Liebert, R. M., Sobol, M. D., & Davidson, E. S. Catharsis of aggression among institutionalized boys: Fact or artifact? In G. A. Comstock, E. A. Rubinstein, & J. P. Murray (Eds.), *Television and social behavior* (Vol. 5). Washington, D.C.: U.S. Government Printing Office, 1972.

Ling, B. C. Form discrimination as a learning cue in infants. *Comparative Psychological Monograph*, 1941, *17*(86).

Little, S. Children's Television Workshop. *Saturday Review*, 1969, *52*, 60–62.

Little, S. From A to Z on Sesame Street. *Saturday Review*, 1970, *53*, 62–64.

Lyle, J., & Hoffman, H. R. Children's use of television and other media. In G. A. Comstock, E. A. Rubenstein, & J. P. Murray (Eds.). *Television and social behavior* (Vol. 4). Washington, D.C.: U.S. Government Printing Office, 1972. (a)

Lyle, J., & Hoffman, H. R. Explorations in patterns of television viewing by preschool-age children. In E. A. Rubenstein, G. A. Comstock, & J. P. Murray (Eds.), *Television and social behavior* (Vol. 4). Washington, D.C.: Government Printing Office, 1972. (b)

Maccoby, E. E. Selective auditory attention in children. In L. P. Lipsett & C. C. Spiker (Eds.), *Advances in child development and behavior* (Vol. 3). New York: Academic Press, 1967.

Maccoby, E. E. Early stimulation and cognitive development. In J. P. Hill (Ed.), *Minnesota symposia on child psychology* (Vol. 4). Minneapolis: University of Minnesota Press, 1969.

Maccoby, E. E., & Konrad, K. W. The effect of preparatory set on selective listening: Developmental trends. *Monographs of the Society for Research in Child Development, 32,* 1967 (4, Serial No. 112).

Mackworth, N. H., & Bruner, J. S. Selecting visual information during recognition by adults and children. Unpublished manuscript, Harvard Center for Cognitive Studies, 1966.

Mackworth, N. H., & Bruner, J. S. How adults and children search and recognize pictures. *Human Development,* 1970, *13,* 149–177.

Madsen, C. H., Jr. Nurturance and modeling in preschoolers. *Child Development,* 1968, *39,* 221–236.

Malcolm, A. H. "Sesame Street" rated excellent: 2-year study finds it helps children of the poor learn. *New York Times,* November 5, 1970.

Mann, M. The effects of a preschool language program on two-year old children and their mothers. Final report. Urbana, Ill., 1970. (ERIC Document Reproduction Serivce No. ED 045 224).

Mates, B. Early reading: A developmental psycholinguistic approach. *Early Child Development and Care,* 1972, *1*(3), 285–296.

Mayer, M. *About television.* New York: Harper & Row, 1972.

McCandless, B. R. *Children and adolescents—Behavior and development.* New York: Holt, Rinehart & Winston, 1961.

McDill, E. L., McDill, M. S., & Sprehe, J. T. *Strategies for success in compensatory education: An appraisal of evaluation research.* Baltimore, Md.: The John Hopkins Press, 1969.

McNeill, D., & McNeill, N. B. What does a child mean when he says "no"? In E. M. Zale (Ed.), *Proceedings of the conference on language and language behavior.* New York: Appleton-Century-Crofts, 1968.

Meichenbaum, D. H., & Turk, L. Implications of research on disadvantaged children and cognitive training programs for educational television: Ways of improving "Sesame Street." *The Journal of Special Education,* 1972, *6*(1), 27–42.

Melody, W. *Children's TV: The economics of exploitation.* New Haven, Conn.: Yale University Press, 1973.

Micotti, A. R. Dame school project (bi-lingual preschool project), Santa Clara County Office of Education. Final report. Urbana, Ill., 1970. (ERIC Document Reproduction Service No. ED 046 514).

Milgram, S., & Shotland, R. L. *Television and antisocial behavior: Field experiments.* New York: Academic Press, 1973.

Miller, J. O. Diffusion of intervention effects in disadvantaged families. Urbana, Ill., 1968. (ERIC Document Reproduction Service No. ED 126 127).

Minton, J. H. The impact of "Sesame Street" on reading readiness of kindergarten children, Ph.D. diss., Fordham University, 1972.

Moely, B. E., Olson, F. A., Halwes, T. G., & Flavell, J. H. Production deficiency in young children's clustered recall. *Developmental Psychology,* 1969, *1,* 26–34.

Moore, O. K. Autotelic responsive environments and exceptional children. In O. J. Harvey (Ed.), *Experience, structure, and adaptability.* New York: Springer Publishing, 1966.

Morris, N. S. *Television's child.* Boston: Little, Brown, 1971.

Mothers' training program, Urbana, Illinois: Model programs. Childhood education. Urbana, Ill., 1970. (ERIC Document Reproduction Service No. ED 045 781).

Murray, J. P. Television in inner-city homes: Viewing behavior of young boys. In G. A. Comstock, E. A. Rubinstein, & J. P. Murray (Eds.), *Television and social behavior* (Vol. 4). Washington, D.C.: U.S. Government Printing Office, 1972.

Niedermeyer, F. C. Parent-assisted learning. Urbana, Ill., 1969. (ERIC Document Reproduction Service No. ED 042 588).

Noble, G. The English report. In J. D. Halloran (Ed.), *Findings and cognition on the television perception of children and young people.* Munich: Internationales Zentral-institut für das Jugend- und Bildungsfernsehen, 1969.

Noble, G. Effects of different forms of filmed aggression on children's constructive and destructive play. *Journal of Personality and Social Psychology*, 1973, *26*, 54–59.

Noble, G. *Children in front of the small screen.* Beverly Hills, Calif.: Sage Publications, 1975.

Noble, G., & Martin, C. Sport outcomes and subsequent aggression among aggressive and non-aggressive viewers. Dublin, 1974.

Noble, G., & Mulcahy, J. An experimental attempt to isolate a cathartic response to televised aggression. *Bulletin of the British Psychological Society*, 1974, *27*, 175.

Open *Sesame:* Close schools? *About Education—The Philadelphia Journal*, 1971, *3*, 1.

Opie, I., & Opie, P. *Children's games in street and playground.* Oxford, England: The Clarendon Press, 1969.

Orhan, S., & Radin, N. Teaching mothers to teach: A home counseling program for low-income parents. Urbana, Ill., 1968. (ERIC Document Reproduction Service No. ED 028 819).

Palmer, E. Can television really teach? *American Education*, 1969, *5*, 2–6.

Palmer, E. Comments delivered at International Reading Association Convention. Atlantic City, 1971. (a)

Palmer, E. Sesame Street: Shaping broadcast television to the needs of the preschooler. *Educational Technology*, 1971, *11*, 18–22. (b)

Palmer, E. Formative research in the production of television for children. In D. R. Olson (Ed.), *Media and symbols: The forms of expression, communication, and education. The 73 yearbook of the National Society for the Study of Education* (Pt. 1). Chicago: University of Chicago Press, 1974.

Palmer, E., & Connell, D. Sesame Street: A lot of off-beat education. *The National Elementary Principal*, 1971, *50*, 14–25.

Perry preschool project, Ypsilanti, Mich. It works: Preschool program in compensatory education. Urbana, Ill., 1969. (ERIC Document Reproduction Service No. ED 027 975).

Piaget, J. *Play, dreams and imitation in childhood.* New York: W. W. Norton, 1951. (Originally published, 1946.)

Piaget, J. *The origins of intelligence in children.* London: Routledge & Kegan Paul, 1953. (Originally published, 1936).

Piaget, J. *The construction of reality in the child.* New York: Basic Books, 1954. (Originally published, 1937.)

Piaget, J. *The child's conception of physical causality.* Totowa, N.J.: Littlefield, Adams, 1966.

Piaget, J. *On the development of memory and identity.* Barre, Mass.: Clark University Press with Barre Publishers, 1968.

Piaget, J. Problems of equilibration. In C. F. Nodine, J. M. Gallagher, & R. H. Humphreys (Eds.), *Piaget and Inhelder: On equilibration*. Philadelphia, Pa.: The Jean Piaget Society, 1971.

Piaget, J. & Inhelder, B. Intellectual operations and their development. In P. Fraisse & J. Piaget (Eds.), *Experimental psychology, Its scope and method* (Intelligence, Vol. VII). New York: Basic Books, 1969, 144–205. (a)

Piaget, J., & Inhelder, B. *The psychology of the child*. New York: Basic Books, 1969. (b)

Piaget, J., & Inhelder, B. *Mental Imagery in the Child*. New York: Basic Books, 1971. (Originally published, 1966.)

Piaget, J., & Inhelder, B. *Memory and intelligence*. New York: Basic Books, 1973.

Pick, A. D. Improvement of visual and tactual form discrimination. *Journal of Experimental Psychology*, 1965, *69*, 331–339.

Pick, H. L., & Pick, A. D. Sensory and perceptual development. In P. Mussen (Ed.), *Carmichael's manual of child psychology* (Vol. 1) (3d ed.). New York: Wiley, 1970.

Pines, M. Why some three-year-olds get A's—And some get C's. *New York Times Magazine*, July 6, 1969.

Podd'yakov, N. N. The development of elementary forms of thinking in preschool children. *Soviet Psychology*, 1974, *13*(1), 40–101.

Potter, M. C. On perceptual recognition. In J. S. Bruner, R. R. Olver, & P. M. Greenfield (Eds.), *Studies in cognitive growth*. New York: Wiley, 1966.

Pulaski, M. A. Toys and imaginative play. New York: Academic Press, 1973.

Rayder, N. *et al*. An assessment of cognitive growth in children who have participated in the toy-lending component of the parent–child program. Urbana, Ill., 1970. (ERIC Document Reproduction Service No. ED 045 204).

Reeves, B. F. *The first year of Sesame Street: The formative research*. New York: Children's Television Workshop, 1970.

Reeves, B. F. *The responses of children in six small viewing groups to Sesame Street shows Nos. 261–274*. New York: Children's Television Workshop, 1971.

Ritter, K., Kaprove, B. H., Fitch, J. P., & Flavell, J. H. The development of retrieval strategies in young children. *Cognitive Psychology*, 1973, *5*, 310–321.

Rogers, J. M. A summary of the literature on "Sesame Street." *The Journal of Special Education*, 1972, *6*(1), 43–50.

Rohrer, W. D., Jr. Learning, race and school success. *Review of Educational Research*, 1971, *41* (3), 197–209.

Rosenthal, A. The Sesame Street generation arrives. *Today's Health*, 1970, *48*, 42–45.

Schaefer, E. S., & Aaronson, M. Infant education research project: Implementation and implications of a home tutoring program. Urbana, Ill., 1970. (ERIC Document Reproduction Service No. ED 054 865).

Schramm, W., Lyle, J., & Parker, E. B. *Television in the lives of our children*. Stanford, Calif.: Stanford University Press, 1961.

Scott, B. Turning on tots with educational T.V. *Today's Health*, 1969, *47*, 28–32.

Sedulus. *Sesame Street. The New Republic*, June 6, 1970.

Sesame at one. *Newsweek*, November 16, 1970.

Sesame Street evaluation breaks new grounds. *ETS Developments*, 1971, *18*.

Sesame Street lights shine for all. *Report on Preschool Education*. (Biweekly news service on federal programs for early childhood development.) January 27, 1971.

Sesame under attack. *Newsweek*, May 24, 1971.

Sesame Street—What next? *Library Journal*, 1970, *95*, 3958–3961.

Shayon, R. L. Cutting Oedipus ties. *Saturday Review*, February 14, 1970.

Sinclair-de-Zwart, H. Developmental psycholinguistics. In D. Elkind & J. H. Flavell (Eds.), *Studies in cognitive development: Essays in honor of Jean Piaget.* New York: Oxford University Press, 1969.

Sinclair-de-Zwart, H. Piaget's theory of language acquisition. In M. F. Rosskopf, L. P. Steffe, & S. Taback (Eds.), *Piagetian cognitive-development research and mathematical education.* Washington, D.C.: National Council of Teachers of Mathematics, 1971. (a)

Sinclair-de-Zwart, H. Representation and memory. In M. F. Rosskopf, L. P. Steffe, & S. Taback (Eds.), *Piagetian cognitive development research and mathematical education.* Washington, D.C.: National Council of Teachers of Mathematics, 1971. (b)

Singer, J. L. The influence of violence portrayed in television or movies upon overt aggressive behavior. In J. L. Singer (Ed.), *The control of aggression and violence.* New York: Academic Press, 1971.

Smilansky, S. *The effects of sociodramatic play on disadvantaged preschool children.* New York: Wiley, 1968.

Smith, M. B. School and home: Focus on achievement. In Passow, H. A. (Ed.), *Developing programs for the educationally disadvantaged.* New York: Teachers College Press, 1968.

Sprigle, H. Can poverty children live on "Sesame Street"? *Young Children,* 1971, *26,* 202–217.

Sprigle, H. Who wants to live on *Sesame Street? Young Children,* 1972, *27,* 91–108.

Stein, A. H., & Friedrich, L. K. Television content and young children's behavior. In J. P. Murray, E. A. Rubinstein, & G. A. Comstock (Eds.), *Television and social behavior* (Vol. 2). Washington, D.C.: U.S. Government Printing Office, 1972.

Steuer, F. B., Applefield, J. M., & Smith, R. Televised aggression and the interpersonal aggression of preschool children. *Journal of Experimental Child Psychology,* 1971, *11,* 442–447.

Stevenson, H. W. *Children's learning.* New York: Appleton-Century-Crofts, 1972. (a)

Stevenson, H. W. Television and the behavior of preschool children. In G. A. Comstock, E. A. Rubenstein, & J. P. Murray, (Eds.), *Television and social behavior* (Vol. 2). Washington, D.C.: U.S. Government Printing Office, 1972.

Surgeon General's Scientific Advisory Committee on Television and Social Behavior. *Television and growing up: The impact of televised violence.* Washington, D.C.: U.S. Government Printing Office, 1972.

Trout, R. B. Sesame Street: It's changing the school program in this direction—And probably will in yours too. *American School Board Journal,* 1971, *158,* 19–20.

Vurpillot, E. The development of scanning strategies and their relation to visual differentiation. *Journal of Experimental Child Psychology,* 1968, *6,* 632–650.

Walters, R. H., & Brown, M. Studies of reinforcement of aggression. III. Transfer of responses for an interpersonal situation. *Child Development,* 1963, *34,* 563–571.

Webb, R. A., Oliveri, M. A., & O'Keefe, L. Investigations of the meaning of "different" in the language of young children. *Child Development,* 1974, *45,* 984–991.

Weikart, P. P. *et al.,* Longitudinal results of the Ypsilanti Perry Preschool Project. Final report. (Vol. 2 of 2 vols). Urbana, Ill., 1970. (ERIC Document Reproduction Service No. ED 044 536).

Wells, W. D. Television and aggression: Replication of an experimental field study. Unpublished manuscript, University of Chicago, 1971.

White, B. L., Watts, J. C., & Barnett, I. T. *Major influences on the development of the young child.* Englewood Cliffs, N.J.: Prentice-Hall, 1972.

White, S. H. The national impact of Head Start. In J. Hellmuth (Ed.), *Disadvantaged child.* New York: Brunner/Mazel, 1970.

Wilson, J. Q. Violence, pornography, and social science. *The Public Interest,* Winter, 1971, No. 22, 45–61.

Woodring, P. Sesame Street and its critics. *Saturday Review,* 1970, *53,* 49.

Wylie, E. M. At last: A T.V. show good for children. *PTA Magazine,* 1970, *64,* 13–14.

Yendovitskaya, T. V. Development of attention. In A. V. Zaporozhets & D. B. Elkonin (Eds.), *The psychology of preschool children.* Cambridge, Mass.: The MIT Press, 1971. (Originally published, 1964.) (a)

Yendovitskaya, T. V. Development of memory. In A. V. Zaphorozhets & D. B. Elkonin (Eds.), *The psychology of preschool children.* Cambridge, Mass.: M.I.T. Press, 1971. (Originally published, 1964.) (b)

Yendovitskaya, T. V., Zinchenko, V. P., & Ruzskaya, A. G. Development of sensation and perception. In A. V. Zaphorozhets & D. B. Elkonin (Eds.), *The psychology of preschool children,* Cambridge, Mass.: M.I.T. Press, 1971. (Originally published, 1964.)

Zaphorozhets, A. V., Zinchenko, V. P., & Elkonin, D. B. Development of thinking. In A. V. Zaphorozhets & D. B. Elkonin (Eds.), *The psychology of preschool children.* Cambridge, Mass.: M.I.T. Press, 1971. (Originally published, 1964.)

Zazzo, R. L'influence du cinema sur le developpement de la pensée de l'enfant. *L'Ecole des Parents,* Paris, 1956.

APPALACHIA EDUCATIONAL LABORATORY—TECHNICAL REPORTS

Evaluation report: Early Childhood Education Program, 1969 field test, Appalachia Educational Laboratory, Inc., Charleston, W. Va., ED 041 626.

Demographic and socio-economic data of the Beckley, W. Va., area and 1968–1970 developmental costs of the Early Childhood Education Field Study. Technical Report No. 1, ED 052 832.

Attainment of cognitive objectives. Technical Report No. 3, ED 052 833.

Detailed analysis of language development of preschool children in Early Childhood Education Program. Technical Report No. 4, ED 052 834.

Social skills development in the Early Childhood Education project. Technical Report No. 7, ED 052 835.

Results of parent and student reaction questionnaire. Technical Report No. 8, ED 052 836.

Evaluation report: Early Childhood Education Program, 1969–1970 field test. Summary Report, ED 052 837.

Analysis of intelligence scores. Technical Report No. 2 ED 052 838.

Analysis of visual perception of children in the Early Childhood Education Program (Results of the Marianne Frostig Developmental Test of Visual Perception). Technical Report No. 5, ED 052 839.

Factor analysis of the Early Childhood Education test data. Technical Report No. 6, ED 052 840.

Analysis of children's reactions to AEL's preschool television program. Technical Report No. 9, ED 052 841.

A comparison of parents' attitudes toward AEL's *Around the Bend* and other children's television programs. Technical Report No. 10, ED 052 842.

Detailed analysis of the language development of children in AEL's Preschool Education Program. Technical Report No. 15, ED 062 018.

Analysis of visual perception of children in the Appalachia Preschool Education Program. Technical Report No. 16, ED 062 019.

Factor analysis of the Appalachia Preschool Education Program test data. Technical Report No. 17, ED 062 021.

Analysis of social skills development in the Appalachia Preschool Education Program. Technical Report No. 18, ED 062 021.

Measuring children's curiosity. Technical Report No. 22 ED 062 022.

A comparison of AEL's Preschool Education Program with standard kindergarten programs. Technical Report No. 23 ED 062 023.

Evaluation report: Early Childhood Education Program, 1969–1970 field test. Appalachia. Educational Laboratory, Inc., Charleston, W.Va., 1971.

Summative evaluation of the Appalachia Preschool Education Program, Appalachia Educational Laboratory, Inc., Charleston, W. Va., December, 1971.

Index

DATE DUE